i-Ready Classroom
Mathematics

Grade 5 • Volume 2

Curriculum Associates

NOT FOR RESALE

978-1-4957-8041-7
©2020–Curriculum Associates, LLC
North Billerica, MA 01862
No part of this book may be reproduced
by any means without written permission
from the publisher.
All Rights Reserved. Printed in USA.
8 9 10 11 12 13 14 15   21

BTS21

800939

Contents

UNIT 2

Decimals and Fractions
Place Value, Addition, and Subtraction

More Decimals and Fractions
Multiplication and Division

Contents (continued)

Algebraic Thinking and the Coordinate Plane
Expressions, Graphing Points, Patterns and Relationships

More Decimals and Fractions
Multiplication and Division

☑ SELF CHECK

Before starting this unit, check off the skills you know below. As you complete each lesson, see how many more skills you can check off!

I can . . .	Before	After
Multiply decimals, for example: $7.25 \times 9.4 = 68.15$.	☐	☐
Divide decimals, for example: $1.2 \div 6 = 2$.	☐	☐
Understand fractions as division, for example: $\frac{3}{4} = 3 \div 4$.	☐	☐
Multiply fractions, for example: $\frac{2}{3} \times \frac{5}{6} = \frac{10}{18}$ or $\frac{5}{9}$.	☐	☐
Find the area of a rectangle with fractional side lengths by tiling and by multiplying.	☐	☐
Understand multiplication as scaling, for example: will $\frac{2}{3} \times \frac{1}{3}$ be greater than or less than $\frac{1}{3}$?	☐	☐
Multiply fractions and divide with unit fractions in word problems.	☐	☐
Divide with unit fractions, for example: $4 \div \frac{1}{7} = 28$.	☐	☐

Build Your Vocabulary

REVIEW

estimate   fraction

decimal   round

Math Vocabulary

Compare and contrast each set of words. Provide examples or a representation. Then work with your partner to compare your answers.

Review Words	How are they similar?	How are they different?	Example
round estimate			
fraction decimal			

Academic Vocabulary

Place a check next to the academic words you know. Then use the words to complete the sentences.

☐ explanation ☐ restate ☐ interpret ☐ evident

1 You need to .... information to make sense of a word problem.

2 An .... usually helps you better understand information.

3 The problem was not very challenging; the answer was .... and I had to do little work to find it.

4 You can .... what you say if others do not understand it the first time.

Multiply a Decimal by a Whole Number

Dear Family,

This week your child is learning to multiply a decimal by a whole number.

One way your child is learning to show multiplying a decimal by a whole number is with a decimal model called a hundredths grid.

The hundredths grids below show 7×0.15.

Each grid represents one whole (1.0), and each square represents one hundredth (0.01). Each group of fifteen shaded squares shows 15 hundredths (0.15). The decimal model above shows 7 groups of 15 hundredths, or 7×0.15. The total of 105 shaded squares represents 105 hundredths, or $\frac{105}{100}$.

$$\frac{105}{100} = 1.05$$

So, $7 \times 0.15 = 1.05$.

Your child is also learning how to record the steps of multiplying a decimal by a whole number in a vertical format.

$$
\begin{array}{r}
0.15 \\
\times \quad 7 \\
\hline
35 \\
+ \ 70 \\
\hline
105 \\
\end{array}
$$

35 ← 7 ones × 5 hundredths = 35 hundredths
+ 70 ← 7 ones × 1 tenth = 7 tenths = 70 hundredths
105 hundredths = 1.05

Invite your child to share what he or she knows about multiplying decimals by whole numbers by doing the following activity together.

ACTIVITY MULTIPLY WHOLE NUMBERS AND DECIMALS

Do this activity with your child to multiply a decimal by a whole number.

Materials calculator, eight index cards, paper, pencil

Work with your child to solve problems that involve multiplying a decimal by a whole number.

- Write one whole number on four of the index cards. (Each number should be between 2 and 9.) Place in one stack.

- Write one decimal (in tenths or hundredths) on the other four index cards. Place in a second stack.

- Give your child the paper and pencil.

- Select one card from the stack of whole numbers and one card from the stack of decimal numbers. Ask your child to multiply the whole number by the decimal.

- Have your child use any method to find the product.

- Use the calculator to check his or her answer.

- Repeat until all four whole numbers have been used.

Look for real-world examples of multiplying decimals by whole numbers with your child. For instance, you may buy 3 pounds of potatoes at a cost of $0.73 per pound. Work together with your child to multiply to find the total cost of the potatoes. Repeat with other items that you may purchase.

Explore **Multiplying a Decimal by a Whole Number**

You know how to multiply two whole numbers. Now you will learn how to multiply a decimal by a whole number. Use what you know to try to solve the problem below.

> **Margo has 6 square tiles of equal size. Each side of each tile is 0.8 inch long. Margo places all the tiles in a row with sides touching as shown. How long is the row of tiles?**

Learning Target

- Add, subtract, **multiply**, and divide decimals to hundredths, using concrete models or drawings and strategies based on place value, properties of operations, and/or the relationship between addition and subtraction; relate the strategy to a written method and explain the reasoning used.

SMP 1, 2, 3, 4, 5, 6, 7

TRY IT

🧰 Math Toolkit

- base-ten blocks
- tenths grids
- number lines
- grid paper
- sticky notes
- multiplication models

DISCUSS IT

Ask your partner: How did you get started?

Tell your partner: I started by . . .

CONNECT IT

 LOOK BACK

Explain how you found the length of the row of tiles.

 LOOK AHEAD

You can find the length of the row of tiles through repeated addition or multiplication of a decimal by a whole number. Look for patterns in the factors and products when multiplying with the whole numbers and decimals shown below. Use the models to write the products.

a. $2 \times 3 =$ ....   **b.** $2 \times 0.3 =$ ....   **c.** $2 \times 0.03 =$ ....

 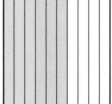

3 **REFLECT**

What patterns do you see in the factors and products in the equations? How are these patterns reflected in the models?

....

....

....

....

Prepare for Multiplying a Decimal by a Whole Number

1 Think about what you know about multiplication. Fill in each box.
   Use words, numbers, and pictures. Show as many ideas as you can.

Word	In My Own Words	Example
partial product		
product		
factor		

2 Look at the multiplication below. What are the factors, partial
   products, and product?

```
   215
 ×   3
─────────
    15   (3 × 5 ones)
    30   (3 × 1 ten)
 + 600   (3 × 2 hundreds)
─────────
   645
```

factors: ....

partial products: ....

product: ....

③ Solve the problem. Show your work.

Kasim has 7 square platters of equal size. Each side of each platter is 0.4 meters long. Kasim places all the platters in a row with no gaps between the sides. How long is the row of platters?

Solution

④ Check your answer. Show your work.

Develop Multiplying a Decimal by a Whole Number

Read and try to solve the problem below.

> **Padma bought 3 pounds of grapes. Each pound of grapes costs $2.75. How much money did Padma spend on grapes?**

TRY IT

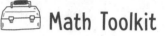

Math Toolkit
- base-ten blocks
- play money
- base-ten grid paper
- decimal grids
- thousandths decimal place-value charts
- multiplication models

DISCUSS IT

Ask your partner: Why did you choose that strategy?

Tell your partner: The strategy I used to find the answer was . . .

Explore different ways to understand multiplying a decimal by a whole number.

> **Padma bought 3 pounds of grapes. Each pound of grapes costs $2.75.**
> **How much money did Padma spend on grapes?**

PICTURE IT

You can use decimal grids to picture multiplying a decimal by a whole number.

Think of 3 × $2.75 as 3 groups of 2.75.

MODEL IT

You can use partial products to multiply a decimal by a whole number.

$$
\begin{array}{r}
2.75 \\
\times \quad 3 \\
\hline
15 \\
210 \\
+ \ 600 \\
\hline
825 \ \text{hundredths}
\end{array}
$$

15 ←— 3 ones × 5 hundredths = 15 hundredths

210 ←— 3 ones × 7 tenths = 21 tenths = 210 hundredths

+ 600 ←— 3 ones × 2 ones = 6 ones = 600 hundredths

CONNECT IT

Now you will use the problem from the previous page to help you understand how to multiply a decimal by a whole number.

1 To solve the problem, you need to find 3 × $2.75. Estimate the total cost of the grapes. Explain your thinking.

2 Look at **Picture It**. How many full grids can you make? ....

How many squares would be shaded in the partially filled grid? ....

3 Look at **Model It**. How is multiplying with a decimal like multiplying with a whole number?

4 825 hundredths = ... ones

5 Both **Picture It** and **Model It** show that 3 × $2.75 = ...

Is the product reasonable? Explain.

6 Explain how to multiply a decimal in the hundredths by a whole number.

7 REFLECT

Look back at your **Try It**, strategies by classmates, and **Picture It** and **Model It**. Which models or strategies do you like best for multiplying a decimal by a whole number? Explain.

....

....

....

APPLY IT

Use what you just learned to solve these problems.

8 Onions cost $0.65 per pound. Sasha bought 4 pounds of onions. How much did she pay for the onions? Show your work.

Solution ....

9 Brian makes a row of 11 paper clips lined up end to end. Each paper clip is 2.48 centimeters long. How long is the row of paper clips? Show your work.

Solution ....

10 What is the product of 14 and 5.3?

Ⓐ 7.42

Ⓑ 0.742

Ⓒ 74.2

Ⓓ 742

Practice Multiplying a Decimal by a Whole Number

Study the Example showing multiplying a decimal by a whole number using partial products. Then solve problems 1–7.

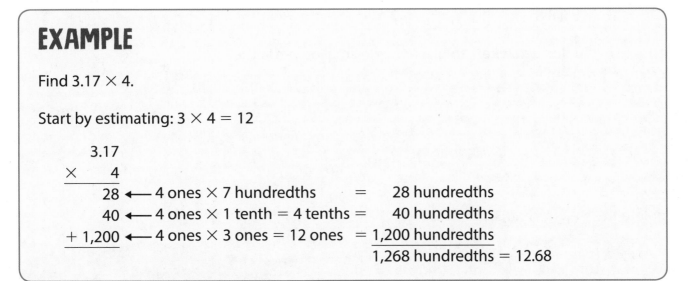

EXAMPLE

Find 3.17 × 4.

Start by estimating: 3 × 4 = 12

$$\begin{array}{r} 3.17 \\ \times \quad 4 \\ \hline 28 \\ 40 \\ + 1{,}200 \\ \hline \end{array}$$

28 ◄─── 4 ones × 7 hundredths   =   28 hundredths
40 ◄─── 4 ones × 1 tenth = 4 tenths =   40 hundredths
+ 1,200 ◄─── 4 ones × 3 ones = 12 ones = 1,200 hundredths
1,268 hundredths = 12.68

1 Look at the Example. Compare the product with the estimate. Is it reasonable that the product is greater than the estimate? Explain.

2 Complete the steps to find the product. Use decimal grids to help, if needed.

$$\begin{array}{r} 0.35 \\ \times \quad 3 \\ \hline \end{array}$$

.... ◄─── 3 ones × .... hundredths = ... hundredths

+ .... ◄─── 3 ones × .... tenths = ... tenths = ... hundredths

.... hundredths = ...

3 Look at problem 2. Why is no partial product shown for the zero in the ones place?

4 Write the decimal point in each product so that the equation is correct.

a. 6 × 8.29 = 4 9 7 4

b. 0.53 × 5 = 2 6 5

c. 9.72 × 7 = 6 8 0 4

d. 3.18 × 16 = 5 0 8 8

5 Explain how you decided where to place the decimal points in the products in problem 4.

6 Complete the steps to find 3.18 × 16.

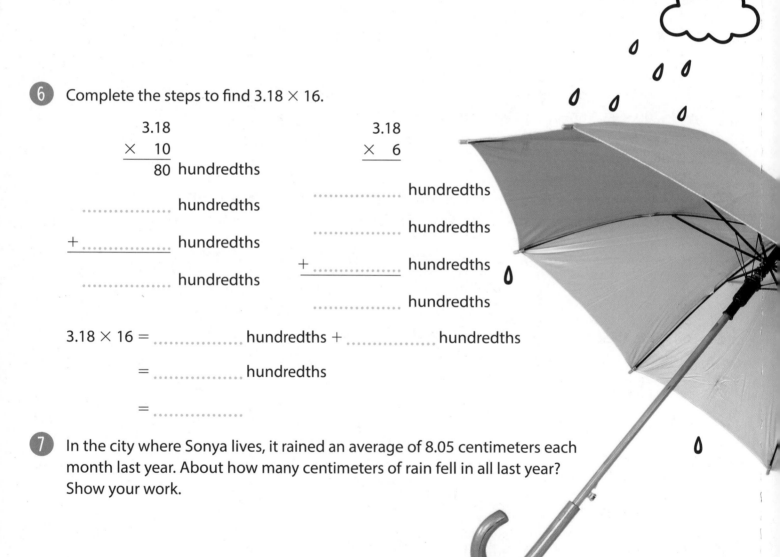

| 3.18 |
| × 10 |
| 80 hundredths |

.... hundredths

+ .... hundredths

.... hundredths

| 3.18 |
| × 6 |

.... hundredths

.... hundredths

+ .... hundredths

.... hundredths

3.18 × 16 = ... hundredths + ... hundredths

= .... hundredths

= ....

7 In the city where Sonya lives, it rained an average of 8.05 centimeters each month last year. About how many centimeters of rain fell in all last year? Show your work.

Solution ....

Refine Multiplying a Decimal by a Whole Number

Complete the Example below. Then solve problems 1–9.

EXAMPLE

Ben swims 2.3 hours each day at practice. He practices once per day. How long will Ben swim in 5 days?

Look at how you could show your work using an area model.

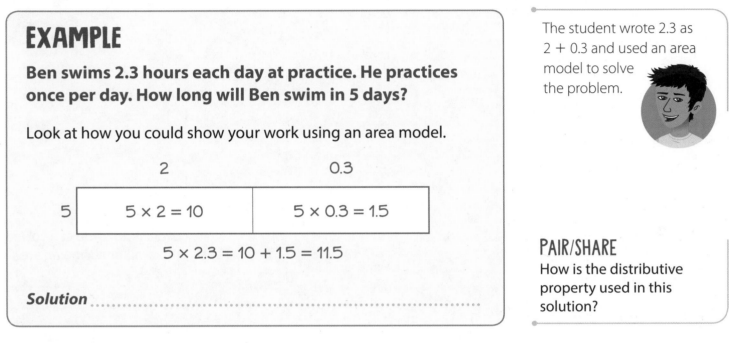

	2	0.3
5	5 × 2 = 10	5 × 0.3 = 1.5

$$5 \times 2.3 = 10 + 1.5 = 11.5$$

Solution ....

The student wrote 2.3 as 2 + 0.3 and used an area model to solve the problem.

PAIR/SHARE
How is the distributive property used in this solution?

APPLY IT

1 Gale sells 16 bags of cherries at the farmers market. Each bag weighs 1.8 pounds. How many pounds of cherries does Gale sell in all? Show your work.

You can use partial products to solve this problem.

PAIR/SHARE
Explain how to check if your answer is reasonable.

Solution ....

2 A person's hair grows 1.2 centimeters in 1 month. How much would the person's hair grow in 9 months? Show your work.

Solution ....

3 What is the product of 2 and 0.73?

Ⓐ 146

Ⓑ 14.6

Ⓒ 1.46

Ⓓ 0.146

Kendall chose Ⓑ as the correct answer. How did she get that answer?

4 Which product has a value of 16.68?

Ⓐ 278 × 6

Ⓑ 27.8 × 60

Ⓒ 27.8 × 6

Ⓓ 2.78 × 6

5 Willa downloads 5 songs. Three of the song files are each 2.75 megabytes. Two song files are each 3.8 megabytes. How many megabytes does Willa download in all?

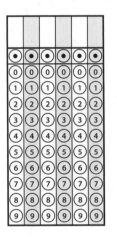

6 Which expressions have the same value as the product of 4.6 and 5?

Ⓐ 460 × 0.5

Ⓑ 460 × 0.05

Ⓒ 46 × 5.0

Ⓓ 46 × 0.5

Ⓔ 0.46 × 50

Lesson 15 Multiply a Decimal by a Whole Number   **321**

7 The area model below can be used to find the product of 3 and 2.17. Complete the area model and find the product.

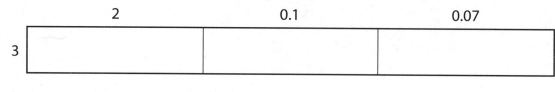

$3 \times 2.17 =$ ....

8 Tyrone said that 2.35 × 5 equals 1.175 because there is only one digit before the decimal point in 2.35, so there must be one digit before the decimal point in the product. Use pictures, numbers, or words to explain whether or not Tyrone is correct.

Solution ....

9 MATH JOURNAL

Myles said that 5 × 0.13 is 6.5. Do you agree? Explain.

☑ SELF CHECK Go back to the Unit 3 Opener and see what you can check off.

Multiply Decimals

Dear Family,

This week your child is learning to multiply decimals.

One way your child is learning to show decimal multiplication is with an area model.

The model at right shows **1.2 × 1.3**.

The width of the model represents 1.2.
The length of the model represents 1.3.

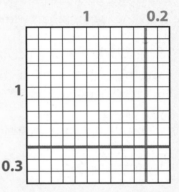

Multiply to find the area of each section in the model.
Then add the partial products.
$1 + 0.2 + 0.3 + 0.06 = 1.56$
$1.2 \times 1.3 = 1.56$

1 × 1 = 1 ← **1 × 0.2 = 0.2**

0.3 × 1 = 0.3 ← **0.3 × 0.2 = 0.06**

To decide whether the product is reasonable, your child is learning to estimate the product of a decimal multiplication such as 1.2 × 1.3.

• Round each factor to the nearest whole number. (Round 1.2 to 1. Round 1.3 to 1.)

• Multiply the rounded numbers to estimate the product. ($1 \times 1 = 1$)

• The product should be about 1.

The product 1.56 is close to the estimated product, 1.

Invite your child to share what he or she knows about multiplying decimals by doing the following activity together.

ACTIVITY MULTIPLYING DECIMALS

Do this activity with your child to multiply decimals.

Materials calculator, pencil, paper

Work with your child to do an activity that involves decimal multiplication.

- On a sheet of paper, one person writes down two decimal numbers. With a calculator, multiply the two numbers without the decimal points.

- The other person estimates the product of the two numbers written on the sheet of paper. He or she then explains where the decimal point should be placed in the product shown on the calculator.

- Check the answer by multiplying the decimals with the calculator.

- Take turns and repeat the activity.

Look for real-world examples of multiplying decimals. For example, you might buy 12.5 gallons of gas at a price of $3.62 a gallon or 2.5 pounds of apples at a price of $0.99 per pound. Work together with your child to estimate the product and then check your estimates with the receipt.

ecimals

l a whole number. Now you
Use what you know to try to

Learning Target

- Add, subtract, **multiply**, and divide decimals to hundredths, using concrete models or drawings and strategies based on place value, properties of operations, and/or the relationship between addition and subtraction; relate the strategy to a written method and explain the reasoning used.

SMP 1, 2, 3, 4, 5, 6, 7

ain.

🧰 Math Toolkit

- play money
- base-ten blocks
- decimal grids
- thousandths decimal place-value charts
- multiplication models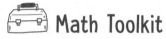

1

DISCUSS IT

Ask your partner: How did you get started?

Tell your partner: I started by . . .

CONNECT IT

1 **LOOK BACK**

Do both Sara and Jon have more money than Martin? Explain.

2 **LOOK AHEAD**

You have seen that finding 1 tenth of a number is the same as multiplying the number by 0.1.

a. Explain how the unit square area model shows that 0.1 of 1 is the same as 0.1×1.

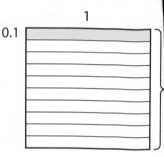

b. In the area model, one column is now shaded blue. What is the area of the purple square in the model? Explain how the area model shows 0.1 of 0.1 is the same as the product 0.1×0.1.

3 **REFLECT**

How would you change the model to show that 0.2 of 0.1 is the same as the product 0.2×0.1? Explain.

Prepare for Multiplying Decimals

1   Think about what you know about place value. Fill in each box. Use words, numbers, and pictures. Show as many ideas as you can.

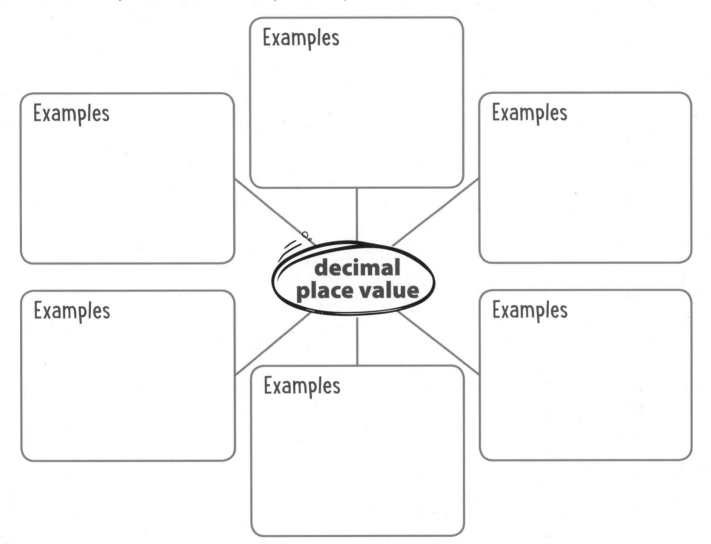

Examples

Examples

Examples

Examples

Examples

Examples

decimal place value

2   Show how to write each phrase as a multiplication expression.

a. 1 tenth of 3: ....

b. 1 tenth of 0.3: ....

3 Solve the problem. Show your work.

Elena has $0.90. Kia has 10 times as much money as Elena. Troy has one tenth as much money as Elena. Does Kia have more money than Elena? Does Troy have more money than Elena? Explain.

Solution ....

....

4 Check your answer. Show your work.

©Curriculum Associates, LLC   Copying is not permitted.

Develop Multiplying Decimals Less Than 1

Read and try to solve the problem below.

> **Harry has 0.5 of a bottle of water in his gym bag. The bottle holds 0.9 liter of water. How many liters of water does Harry have?**

TRY IT

 **Math Toolkit**

- decimal grids
- number lines
- thousandths decimal place-value charts
- multiplication models

DISCUSS IT

Ask your partner: Why did you choose that strategy?

Tell your partner: The strategy I used to find the answer was . . .

Explore different ways to understand multiplying decimals less than 1.

> Harry has 0.5 of a bottle of water in his gym bag. The bottle holds 0.9 liter of water. How many liters of water does Harry have?

PICTURE IT

You can use an area model drawn on a hundredths grid to picture finding 5 tenths of 9 tenths.

The hundredths grid represents 1 whole liter of water.

Each small square is 1 hundredth of the whole.

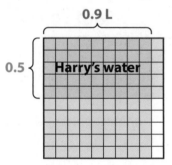

Harry's water is 0.5 of the 0.9 liter of water.

The area of the purple rectangle is the product 0.5 × 0.9.

MODEL IT

You can use equations and properties of operations to multiply decimals.

0.5 × 0.9 = ?

You can break apart each decimal into a whole number factor times 1 tenth.

0.5 × 0.9 = (5 × 0.1) × (9 × 0.1)

= (5 × 9) × (0.1 × 0.1)

= 45 × 0.01

evious page to help you understand how

n an area model, first show each factor on
ow one tenth.

....

ow? ....

hat do the purple squares represent?

mmutative property, or changing the order
0.9?

....

0.5 × 0.9 liter = ...

is less than 0.9?

assmates, and **Picture It** and **Model It**.
best for multiplying decimals less than

....

....

....

APPLY IT

Use what you just learned to solve these problems.

8 What is the value of the expression 0.6 × 0.8? Show your work using an area model on the hundredths grid below.

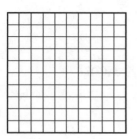

Solution ....

9 A rectangular painting is 0.6 meter long and 0.57 meter wide. How many square meters is the painting? Show your work using equations. Remember that 0.57 = 57 × 0.01 and 0.01 = 0.1 × 0.1.

Solution ....

10 What is the product 0.6 and 0.4?

Ⓐ 24

Ⓑ 2.4

Ⓒ 0.24

Ⓓ 0.024

CONNECT IT

Now you will use the problem from the previous page to help you understand how to multiply decimals less than 1.

1 Look at **Picture It**. To find 0.5 × 0.9 with an area model, first show each factor on the grid. Each row and each column show one tenth.

What factor do the shaded rows show? ....

What factor do the shaded columns show? ....

2 How many purple squares are there? What do the purple squares represent?

3 Look at **Model It**. How can using the commutative property, or changing the order of factors, help you to multiply 0.5 and 0.9?

4 Complete the following equation.

(5 × 9) × (0.1 × 0.1) = 45 × 0.01 = ...

5 Both **Picture It** and **Model It** show that 0.5 × 0.9 liter = ...

6 Why do you think the product 0.5 × 0.9 is less than 0.9?

7 REFLECT

Look back at your **Try It**, strategies by classmates, and **Picture It** and **Model It**. Which models or strategies do you like best for multiplying decimals less than one? Explain.

....

....

....

APPLY IT

Use what you just learned to solve these problems.

8 What is the value of the expression 0.6 × 0.8? Show your work using an area model on the hundredths grid below.

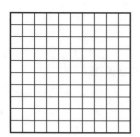

Solution ....

9 A rectangular painting is 0.6 meter long and 0.57 meter wide. How many square meters is the painting? Show your work using equations. Remember that 0.57 = 57 × 0.01 and 0.01 = 0.1 × 0.1.

Solution ....

10 What is the product 0.6 and 0.4?

Ⓐ 24

Ⓑ 2.4

Ⓒ 0.24

Ⓓ 0.024

Practice Multiplying Decimals Less Than 1

Study the Example showing how to multiply decimals less than one using an area model. Then solve problems 1–5.

EXAMPLE

Find 0.5×0.3.

Represent the product as the area of a rectangle on a hundredths grid.

Shade **5 rows** to represent a length of 0.5 units.

Shade **3 columns** to represent a width of 0.3 units.

The area of the rectangle that is shaded twice is the product 0.5×0.3.

Because 15 hundredths, or 0.15, is shaded twice, $0.5 \times 0.3 = 0.15$.

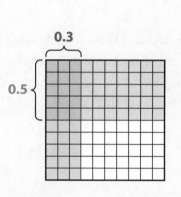

1 Use the area model to find the product 0.9×0.2.

$0.9 \times 0.2 =$ ....

2 Find the product 0.7×0.8. Show your work using an area model on the hundredths grid at the right.

$0.7 \times 0.8 =$ ....

3 Use numbers from the box to complete the equations.

a. $0.5 \times 0.4 =$ ....

b. $0.5 \times 4 =$ ....

c. $0.2 \times 0.5 =$ ....

d. $2 \times 0.5 =$ ....

0.01	0.1	1
0.02	0.2	2

4 Manuel painted 0.75 of a rectangular banner green. After the paint dried, he painted 0.6 of the green area orange. What part of the banner is painted orange? Show your work with equations. (*Hint:* $0.75 = 75 \times 0.01$).

.... of the banner is painted orange.

5 Halen wrote the product 0.4 for the problem at the right. Don says that is not correct because when you multiply tenths by tenths, the product will be in the hundredths. Is Don right? Explain.

$0.5 \times 0.8 = ?$

Develop Multiplying with Decimals Greater Than 1

Read and try to solve the problem below.

> Jaden made a rectangular sign that is 1.4 meters long and 1.2 meters wide to post on the wall of his store. How many square meters of wall does the sign cover?

TRY IT

 **Math Toolkit**
- base-ten blocks
- base-ten grid paper
- thousandths decimal place-value charts
- multiplication models

DISCUSS IT

Ask your partner: Do you agree with me? Why or why not?

Tell your partner: I agree with you about . . . because . . .

Explore different ways to understand multiplying with decimals greater than 1.

> **Jaden made a rectangular sign that is 1.4 meters long and 1.2 meters wide to post on the wall of his store. How many square meters of wall does the sign cover?**

PICTURE IT

You can use an area model to multiply decimals greater than 1.

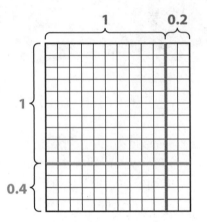

The rectangle measures **1.4 meters** by **1.2 meters**.

Each small square is 1 tenth of a meter by 1 tenth of a meter, or 0.1 meter by 0.1 meter.

The area of each small square is 0.1 meter $\times$ 0.1 meter = 0.01 square meter.

MODEL IT

You can also use partial products to multiply decimals greater than 1.

$$
\begin{array}{r}
1.2 \\
\times\ 1.4 \\
\hline
8 \\
40 \\
20 \\
+\ 100 \\
\hline
168
\end{array}
$$

    8 ⟵ 4 tenths $\times$ 2 tenths   =   8 hundredths

  40 ⟵ 4 tenths $\times$ 1 one = 4 tenths =   40 hundredths

  20 ⟵ 1 one $\times$ 2 tenths = 2 tenths =   20 hundredths

+ 100 ⟵ 1 one $\times$ 1 one = 1 one   = 100 hundredths

168 hundredths

CONNECT IT

Now you will use the problem from the previous page to help you understand how to multiply with decimals greater than 1.

1 To solve the problem, you need to find 1.4 × 1.2. Estimate the area of wall that the sign will cover. Explain your thinking.

2 Look at **Picture It**. Complete the area model below to find the area of each of the four sections of the rectangle.

	1	0.2
1	1 × 1 =	1 × 0.2 =
0.4	0.4 × 1 =	0.4 × 0.2 =

3 Look at **Model It**. How do the partial products relate to the area model above?

4 Both **Picture It** and **Model It** show that 1.4 × 1.2 = ... hundredths.

What is the area of the sign written as a decimal? .... square meters

5 Explain what you know about the product when you multiply tenths by tenths.

6 Is the product of 1.4 × 1.2 greater than or less than 1.2? Why?

7 REFLECT

Look back at your **Try It**, strategies by classmates, and **Picture It** and **Model It**. Which models or strategies do you like best for multiplying decimals greater than 1? Explain.

....

....

APPLY IT

Use what you just learned to solve these problems.

8 What is the value of the expression 0.4 × 1.8?
Show your work using an area model on the base-ten grids below.

Solution ....

9 Rosa filled her car's tank with 9.8 gallons of gas. Each gallon costs $3.85. How much did Rosa spend on gas? Show your work.

Solution ....

10 What is the product 2.8 × 9.5?

Ⓐ 0.26

Ⓑ 0.266

Ⓒ 2.66

Ⓓ 26.6

4 Which of the following has a product of 0.195?

Ⓐ 0.3 × 650

Ⓑ 0.3 × 65

Ⓒ 0.3 × 6.5

Ⓓ 0.3 × 0.65

5 Choose all the expressions that have the same value as the product of 0.11 and 4.5.

Ⓐ 0.45 × 1.1

Ⓑ 4.95 × 1.1

Ⓒ 49.5 × 0.01

Ⓓ 495 × 0.1

Ⓔ 495 × 0.01

6 The area model below represents the product of 2.8 and 1.3. Complete the model by writing each partial product in the correct part of the model. Then find the product.

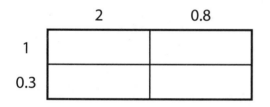

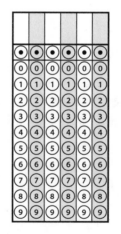

7 Peter earns $12.40 each week for completing his chores. Ria earns 1.2 times as much money per week as Peter. How much does Ria earn each week? Show your work.

Solution ....

8 MATH JOURNAL

Each product below is missing a decimal point.

Part A Place the decimal point in each product so that the equation is correct.

$$12.53 \times 5 = 6\,2\,6\,5$$

$$4.28 \times 3.6 = 1\,5\,4\,0\,8$$

$$1.3 \times 0.89 = 1\,1\,5\,7$$

$$7 \times 6.12 = 4\,2\,8\,4$$

Part B Circle one of the equations. Explain how you decided where to place the decimal point in that equation.

☑ SELF CHECK Go back to the Unit 3 Opener and see what you can check off.

Divide Decimals

Dear Family,

This week your child is learning to divide with decimals.

Your child might see a problem like this:

Marty is running in a 3.2-kilometer race. Water stations are set up at 8 equal sections of the race. How far apart are the water stations?

One way to understand the relationship of the quantities in the problem is to use a bar model.

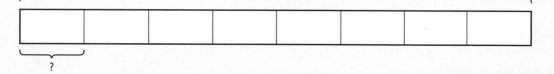

3.2 kilometers

?

The whole bar represents the length of the race, 3.2 kilometers. The bar has 8 equal sections. Find the length of each section to find how far apart the water stations are.

Divide 3.2 by 8 to find the length of each shorter section.

One way your child is learning to divide decimals is to think about multiplying decimals. Division and multiplication are related operations.

To find 3.2 ÷ 8, think 8 × ? = 3.2.
   3.2 = 32 tenths
   8 × ? = 32 tenths
   8 × 4 tenths = 32 tenths

The answer, 4 tenths, is the length represented by each section of the bar model. The water stations are 0.4 kilometer apart.

Invite your child to share what he or she knows about dividing decimals by doing the following activity together.

ACTIVITY DIVIDING DECIMALS

Do this activity with your child to divide decimals.

Work with your child to solve a real-world problem involving dividing decimals.

- Think of something you spend money on for the whole family, such as the grocery bill, tickets to the movies, or a new board game.

- Divide the cost by the number of people in your family. This will describe the cost for each family member.

    For example: A book of puzzles costs $11.76. There are 4 people in the family. To find the cost for each person, divide 11.76 by 4.

- Check that the answer is reasonable. In the example above, is 29.4 a reasonable answer for 11.76 ÷ 4?

Be on the lookout for other real-world examples of dividing decimals that you can share with your child.

Answer: no

Explore Dividing Decimals

Now that you know how to multiply with decimals, you will learn how to divide with decimals. Use what you know to try to solve the problem below.

> **Mr. Kovich is preparing materials for a craft project. He needs to cut 2 meters of string into pieces that are 0.2 meter long. How many 0.2-meter pieces can he cut from 2 meters of string?**

Learning Target

- Add, subtract, multiply, and divide decimals to hundredths, using concrete models or drawings and strategies based on place value, properties of operations, and/or the relationship between addition and subtraction; relate the strategy to a written method and explain the reasoning used.

SMP 1, 2, 3, 4, 5, 6, 8

TRY IT

Math Toolkit
- base-ten blocks
- decimal grids
- number lines
- fraction bars
- fraction models
- thousandths decimal place-value charts

DISCUSS IT

Ask your partner: Why did you choose that strategy?

Tell your partner: The strategy I used to find the answer was . . .

CONNECT IT

 LOOK BACK

Explain how you found how many 0.2-meter pieces are in 2 meters of string.

 LOOK AHEAD

You can look for patterns in division to see how dividing with whole numbers and dividing with decimals is alike and different.

a. Complete the quotients in the table below to see patterns in division.

Expression	Expression in Words	Quotient
2 ÷ 2	How many groups of 2 are in 2?	
2 ÷ 0.2	How many groups of 0.2 are in 2?	
2 ÷ 0.02	How many groups of 0.02 are in 2?	

b. Use the division patterns in the table to complete the equations.

Dividend		Divisor		Quotient
2	÷	2	=	
2	÷	0.2	=	
2	÷	0.02	=	

c. How does the quotient compare to the dividend when the divisor is greater than 1? When the divisor is less than 1?

 REFLECT

Think about 2 meters ÷ 0.2 meter. Why is the quotient greater than the dividend when dividing by a decimal less than 1?

Prepare for Dividing Decimals

1 Think about what you know about multiplication and division. Fill in each box. Use words, numbers, and pictures. Show as many ideas as you can.

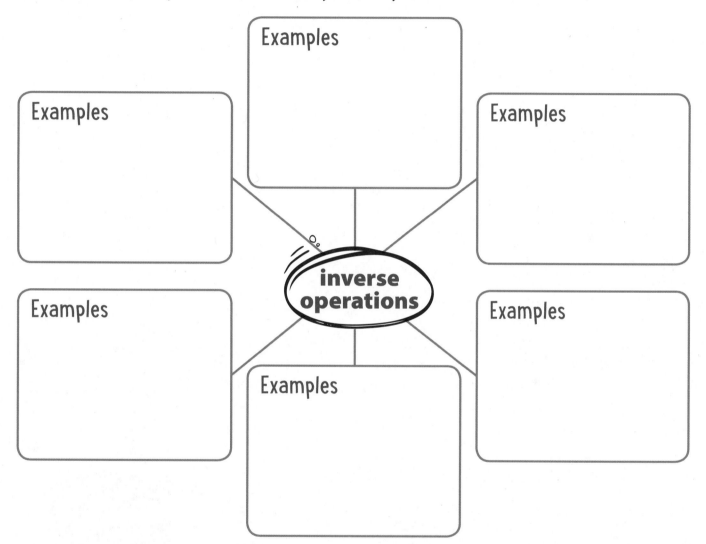

2 Write a related multiplication equation for the division equation $5 \div 0.2 = n$.

3 Solve the problem. Show your work.

Mrs. Carter is preparing materials for a craft project. She needs to cut 5 meters of ribbon into pieces that are 0.5 meter long. How many 0.5-meter pieces can she cut from 5 meters of ribbon?

Solution ....

4 Check your answer. Show your work.

Develop Dividing a Decimal by a Whole Number

Read and try to solve the problem below.

> Coach Ann is setting up a 2.7-kilometer race. She uses flags to mark off 9 equal sections of the race. How far apart should she space the flags to mark off the sections?

TRY IT

 **Math Toolkit**
- base-ten blocks
- counters
- base-ten grid paper
- number lines
- fraction bars
- fraction models

DISCUSS IT

Ask your partner: Do you agree with me? Why or why not?

Tell your partner: I agree with you about . . . because . . .

Explore different ways to understand dividing a decimal by a whole number.

> **Coach Ann is setting up a 2.7-kilometer race. She uses flags to mark off 9 equal sections of the race. How far apart should she space the flags to mark off the sections?**

PICTURE IT

You can draw a bar model to represent the problem.

You know the **number of kilometers to be divided** into equal groups.

You know the **number of equal groups**.

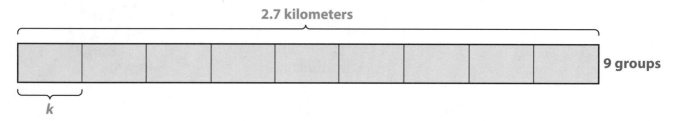

You do not know the **number of kilometers in each group**.

MODEL IT

You can use the relationship between multiplication and division to understand the problem.

To solve **2.7 ÷ 9 = k**, think **9 × k = 2.7**.

Use place-value understanding to find the missing factor.

2.7 = 27 tenths

9 × ? tenths = 27 tenths

CONNECT IT

Now you will use the problem from the previous page to help you understand how to divide a decimal by a whole number.

 Look at **Picture It**. Why is the bar divided into 9 equal parts?

What do you need to find? ....

 Look at **Model It**. How does the division expression 2.7 ÷ 9 relate to the bar model?

3 Explain how you know that 2.7 = 27 tenths.

4 How far apart should Coach Ann space the flags? .... tenths kilometer

Write the distance as a decimal. .... kilometer

5 Explain how you could divide a decimal by a whole number.

6 **REFLECT**

Look back at your **Try It**, strategies by classmates, and **Picture It** and **Model It**. Which models or strategies do you like best for dividing a decimal by a whole number? Explain.

....

....

....

....

APPLY IT

Use what you just learned to solve these problems.

7 How much will each person receive if $20.35 is split equally among 5 people? Show your work.

Solution ....

8 What is 0.99 ÷ 11? Show your work.

Solution ....

9 What is 51.2 ÷ 4?

Ⓐ 1.28

Ⓑ 12.08

Ⓒ 12.8

Ⓓ 120.8

Practice Dividing a Decimal by a Whole Number

Study the Example showing one way to divide a decimal by a whole number. Then solve problems 1–5.

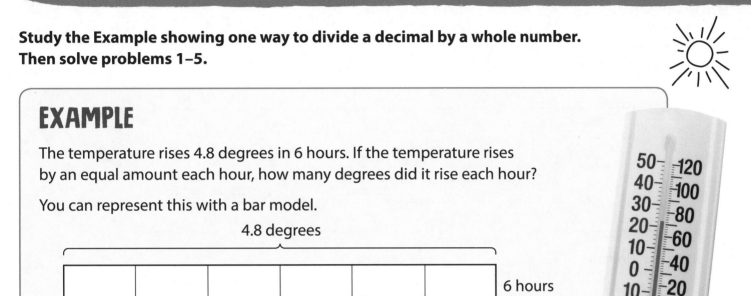

EXAMPLE

The temperature rises 4.8 degrees in 6 hours. If the temperature rises by an equal amount each hour, how many degrees did it rise each hour?

You can represent this with a bar model.

4.8 degrees

6 hours

?

To find 4.8 ÷ 6, think 6 × ? = 4.8.

4.8 = 48 tenths   6 × 8 tenths = 48 tenths
                     6 × 0.8 = 4.8
                     4.8 ÷ 6 = 0.8

The temperature rose 0.8 degree each hour.

1 Look at the Example. Suppose the temperature rises 5.4 degrees in 6 hours. Complete the steps to find 5.4 ÷ 6.

a. 5.4 ÷ 6   Think: .... × ? = ...

b. 5.4 = ... tenths   .... × ? = ... tenths

c. 6 × .... tenths = ... tenths

d. 5.4 ÷ 6 = ...

2 Use numbers from the box. Write the number of tenths and hundredths in each decimal.

3.5	0.79	0.35
350		35
7.9	79	790

3.5 = ... tenths   3.5 = ... hundredths

0.79 = ... tenths   0.79 = ... hundredths

3 Complete the steps for using an area model to solve 1.56 ÷ 12.

1.56 ÷ 12 is the same as .... × ? = ...

1.56 = ... hundredths

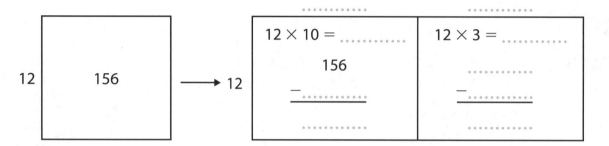

156 hundredths ÷ 12 = ... hundredths

1.56 ÷ 12 = ...

4 Conor earns $9 an hour for yard work. He raked leaves one afternoon and earned $29.25. How many hours did he rake leaves? Show your work.

Solution ....

5 Look at problem 4. How much does Conor earn for each minute he does yard work? (1 hour = 60 minutes) Show your work.

Solution ....

Develop Dividing by Tenths

Read and try solve the problem below.

> Grant has 3.6 pounds of pretzels.
> He puts the pretzels into bags that
> each hold 0.3 pound. How many bags
> does Grant use to hold the pretzels?

TRY IT

Math Toolkit
- base-ten blocks
- counters
- base-ten grid paper
- number lines
- fraction bars
- fraction models

DISCUSS IT

Ask your partner: How did
you get started?

Tell your partner: I started
by . . .

Explore different ways to understand how to divide with tenths.

> Grant has 3.6 pounds of pretzels. He puts the pretzels into bags that each hold 0.3 pound. How many bags does Grant use to hold the pretzels?

PICTURE IT

You can picture dividing by tenths with decimal grids.

Each large square represents 1 pound of pretzels.

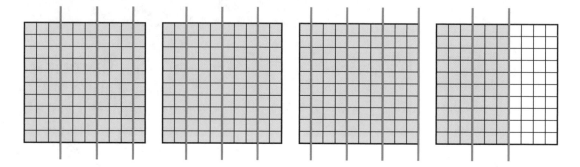

You know the amount to be shared in equal groups and the size of each group.

MODEL IT

You can use the relationship between multiplication and division to understand the problem.

To solve $3.6 \div 0.3 = n$, think $n \times 0.3 = 3.6$.

Use place-value understanding to find the missing factor.

$3.6 = 36$ tenths
$0.3 = 3$ tenths

$n \times 3$ tenths $= 36$ tenths

CONNECT IT

Now you will use the problem from the previous page to help you understand how to divide with tenths.

 Look at **Picture It**. How do you decide what to shade?

 Why are the grids separated into groups of 3 columns?

3 Look at **Model It**. How do you know this is a division problem?

4 Explain why 3.6 = 36 tenths.

5 Both **Picture It** and **Model It** tell you that Grant uses .... bags of pretzels.

6 Explain how to divide tenths by tenths.

7 REFLECT

Look back at your **Try It**, strategies by classmates, and **Picture It** and **Model It** on the previous page. Which models or strategies do you like best for dividing tenths by tenths? Explain.

....

....

....

....

APPLY IT

Use what you just learned to solve these problems.

8 How many dimes are there in a jar of dimes worth $2.70? Show your work.

Solution

9 A fence is 52.5 meters in length. Posts divide the fence into sections that are each 3.5 meters in length. How many sections are in the fence? Show your work.

Solution

10 What is 42 ÷ 0.7?

Ⓐ 0.06

Ⓑ 0.6

Ⓒ 6

Ⓓ 60

Practice Dividing by Tenths

Study the Example showing one way to divide a decimal by a decimal. Then solve problems 1–7.

EXAMPLE

What is 2.1 ÷ 0.7?

You can represent this problem with decimal grids.

Each large square represents 1 whole.

To find 2.1 ÷ 0.7, think 0.7 × ? = 2.1.

The lines separate groups of 0.7.

2.1 = 21 tenths
0.7 = 7 tenths

7 tenths × ? = 21 tenths
7 tenths × 3 = 21 tenths

2.1 ÷ 0.7 = 3

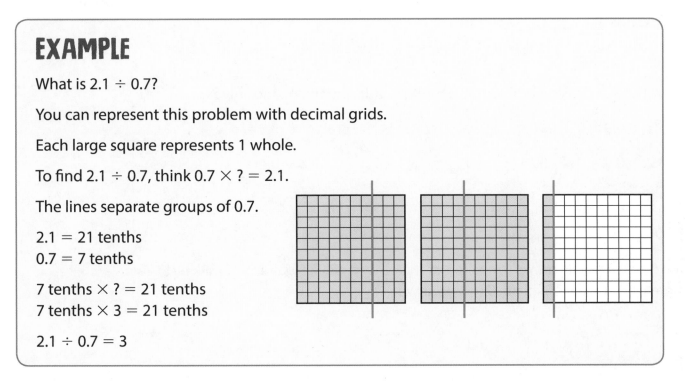

1 Look at the Example. How is the quotient, 3, represented by the grids?

2 Which of these expressions are represented by the decimal grids in the Example?

Ⓐ 0.7 × 3   Ⓑ 3 × 0.7

Ⓒ 0.7 ÷ 3   Ⓓ 2.1 ÷ 3

Ⓔ 21 ÷ 0.7   Ⓕ 0.7 ÷ 2.1

3 How many grids would you need to represent the problem 4.5 ÷ 0.5? Explain.

4 Complete the steps to solve $4.5 \div 0.5$.

   a. $4.5 \div 0.5$ Think: _____ × ? = _____

   b. $4.5 =$ _____ tenths   and $0.5 =$ _____ tenths

   c. 5 tenths × _____ = 45 tenths

   d. $4.5 \div 0.5 =$ _____

5 Rewrite each division problem as a multiplication problem and solve.

   a. $6.3 \div 0.9 = ?$ _____ × ? = _____ $6.3 \div 0.9 =$ _____

   b. $3.2 \div 0.4 = ?$ _____ × ? = _____ $3.2 \div 0.4 =$ _____

   c. $1.8 \div 0.3 = ?$ _____ × ? = _____ $1.8 \div 0.3 =$ _____

   d. $2.4 \div 1.2 = ?$ _____ × ? = _____ $2.4 \div 1.2 =$ _____

6 The Razdan family drinks 0.5 gallon of milk a day. Will 2.5 gallons of milk last them more than 1 week? Explain. Show your work.

   Solution _____

7 Mrs. Lang is hanging pictures for the school art show across a wall that is 2.8 meters wide. She determines that each picture, along with the space needed on the sides of the picture, will take up 0.4 meter across the wall. How many pictures can she hang in one row across the wall? Show your work.

   Solution _____

Develop Dividing by Hundredths

Read and try to solve the problem below.

> **Fiona has $1.20 with which to buy some ribbon. The ribbon is on sale for $0.08 per foot. How many feet of ribbon can Fiona buy?**

TRY IT

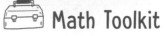 **Math Toolkit**
- base-ten blocks
- play money
- base-ten grid paper
- number lines 🔘
- fraction bars
- fraction models 🔘

DISCUSS IT

Ask your partner: Can you explain that again?

Tell your partner: A model I used was . . . It helped me . . .

Explore different ways to understand how to divide by hundredths.

> Fiona has **$1.20 with which to buy some ribbon. The ribbon is on sale for $0.08 per foot. How many feet of ribbon can Fiona buy?**

PICTURE IT

You can picture the division problem using a bar model.

You know the total amount of money and the size of one group.

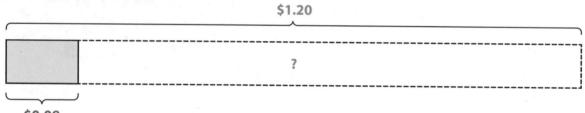

$1.20

?

$0.08

You do not know the **number of groups**.

MODEL IT

You can use place-value reasoning to relate dividing with decimals to dividing with whole numbers.

   1.20   ÷   0.08   = ? ← **How many** groups of size **0.08** are in **1.20**?

120 hundredths ÷ 8 hundredths = ?

   120   ÷   8   = ? ← **How many** groups of size **8** are in **120**?

Then you can divide the hundredths as you might divide with whole numbers, such as using partial quotients.

```
         ?
      ─────
         5
        10
    8)120
     − 80
      ─────
        40
     − 40
      ─────
         0
```

CONNECT IT
Now you will use the problem from the previous page to help you understand how to divide by hundredths.

 Look at **Picture It**. What are you trying to find in this problem?

2 What operation will solve this problem? How do you know?

3 Look at **Model It**. Explain why 1.20 = 120 hundredths.

4 How many feet of ribbon can Fiona buy? Explain how you know.

5 Check your answer using the decimals in a multiplication equation.

.... feet of ribbon × $ .... = $ ....

 Explain how to divide by a decimal in the hundredths.

7 REFLECT

Look back at your **Try It**, strategies by classmates, and **Picture It** and **Model It** on the previous page. Which models or strategies do you like best for dividing by hundredths? Explain.

....

....

....

APPLY IT

Use what you just learned to solve these problems.

8 How many quarters are in a jar of quarters worth $9.75? Show your work.

Solution ....

9 What is $16 \div 0.16$? Show your work.

Solution ....

10 Which division expression can be used to find the quotient $17.6 \div 0.04$?

Ⓐ $1.76 \div 4$

Ⓑ $176 \div 4$

Ⓒ $176 \div 40$

Ⓓ $1760 \div 4$

Practice Dividing by Hundredths

**Study the Example showing one way to divide by hundredths.
Then solve problems 1–6.**

EXAMPLE

Find 1.8 ÷ 0.04.

Find the least place. Write each decimal to the least place.

0.04 = 4 hundredths
1.8 = 180 hundredths

Divide as you would with whole numbers, using
partial quotients or another method.

180 hundredths ÷ 4 hundredths = 45

1.8 ÷ 0.04 = 45

$$
\begin{array}{r}
45 \\
\overline{5} \\
40 \\
4\overline{)180} \\
-160 \\
\overline{20} \\
-20 \\
\overline{0}
\end{array}
$$

1 Complete the steps to solve 1.02 ÷ 0.06.

a. 1.02 = ... hundredths

0.06 = ... hundredths

b. 102 ÷ 6 = ...

c. 1.02 ÷ 0.06 = ...

2 Did you use partial quotients or another method to divide 102 by 6 in problem 1? Explain.

3 Check your answer to problem 1 by writing the decimals in a multiplication equation.

.... × .... = ...

4   Is each equation *True* or *False*?

	True	False
1.23 = 123 hundredths	Ⓐ	Ⓑ
0.5 = 50 hundredths	Ⓒ	Ⓓ
74 hundredths = 7.4	Ⓔ	Ⓕ
1,088 hundredths = 10.88	Ⓖ	Ⓗ

5   Jaden buys 1.15 pounds of cheese at the deli counter. If each slice is 0.05 pound, how many slices of cheese does she buy? Show your work.

Solution ....

6   Alejandro feeds his dog 0.12 kilogram of dry dog food each day. He wants to buy the smallest bag that has enough food to feed his dog for one month. Should he buy the bag that has 1.8 kilograms, 2.4 kilograms, or 4.2 kilograms of dog food? Show your work.

Solution ....

Refine Dividing Decimals

Complete the Example below. Then solve problems 1–8.

EXAMPLE

Nancy ran a total of 35 miles to train for a race. She ran 2.5 miles each day. How many days did Nancy run to train for the race?

Look at how you could show your work using equations.

Let d = number of days.

$2.5 \times d = 35$

$2.5 = 25$ tenths, $35 = 350$ tenths

$25 \times d = 350$

$350 \div 25 = 14$

Solution ....

The student wrote a related multiplication equation to solve the problem.

PAIR/SHARE
Can you solve the problem in another way?

APPLY IT

1 What number multiplied by 8 will give a product of 9.6? Write an equation and solve. Show your work.

What is a good estimate for your answer?

PAIR/SHARE
How could you model this problem with a number line?

Solution ....

2 The length of a screw is 0.75 centimeter. How many screws can be placed end to end to make a row that is 18 centimeters long? Show your work.

Will the answer be greater than or less than 18?

Solution ....

PAIR/SHARE
Explain how you decided what operation to use to solve the problem.

3 What is 6.5 ÷ 0.5?

Ⓐ 3.25

Ⓑ 6

Ⓒ 7

Ⓓ 13

Gwen chose Ⓐ as the correct answer. How did she get that answer?

I could draw a model to represent this problem.

PAIR/SHARE
Does Gwen's answer make sense?

4 Jordan has $3.80 to spend at the used book store. Each book costs $0.95. What is the greatest number of books Jordan can buy?

Ⓐ 3

Ⓑ 4

Ⓒ 5

Ⓓ 6

5 Keith bought 3.4 pounds of peanuts on Monday, 2.5 pounds on Tuesday, and 4 pounds on Wednesday. He is going to divide the peanuts equally between himself and two friends. How many pounds of peanuts will each friend get?

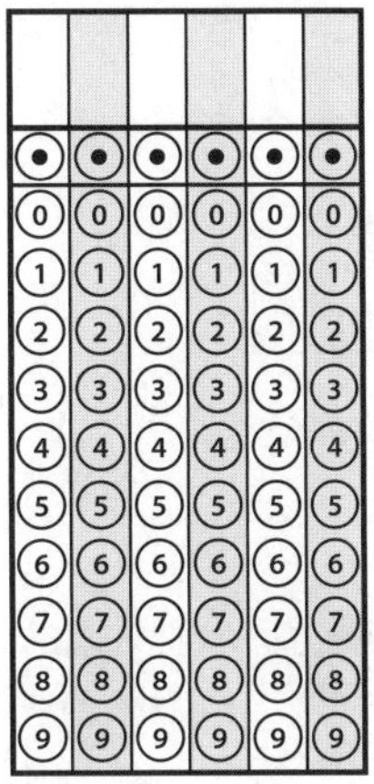

6 If you put 0.7 in the box for each equation, is the equation true?

	Yes	No
$\square \times 5.2 = 36.4$	Ⓐ	Ⓑ
$49 \div \square = 70$	Ⓒ	Ⓓ
$\square \div 3.5 = 0.02$	Ⓔ	Ⓕ
$9.1 \times \square = 6.37$	Ⓖ	Ⓗ

7 Jamie has 5 jars to fill with beads for a carnival game. She has 7.5 bags of multi-colored beads. Jamie wants to put an equal amount of beads in each jar. How many bags of beads can she put into each jar?

Part A Use decimal grids to solve the problem. Explain your solution.

Part B Use multiplication to check your answer.

8 MATH JOURNAL

A sticker is 1.2 centimeters wide. How many stickers will fit edge to edge on a strip of paper that is 108 centimeters long? Explain your thinking.

☑ SELF CHECK Go back to the Unit 3 Opener and see what you can check off.

Fractions as Division

Dear Family,

This week your child is learning how fractions and division are related.

He or she might see a problem like the one below.

Three family members equally share 4 granola bars. How much does each family member receive?

This word problem can be represented as a division problem. The family equally shares 4 granola bars among 3 people, so the division problem to solve is 4 ÷ 3.

A model is a useful way to show the problem.
The model below shows 4 wholes. Each whole is divided into 3 parts.

Each family member receives $\frac{1}{3}$ of each of 4 whole bars. So, the answer to the division problem 4 ÷ 3 is $\frac{4}{3}$. You can say that the fraction $\frac{4}{3}$ represents the division problem 4 ÷ 3.

This shows how fractions and division are related. You can think of fractions as the division of two numbers.

Another way to write the fraction $\frac{4}{3}$ is to show it as a mixed number. So, each family member receives $\frac{4}{3}$, or $1\frac{1}{3}$, granola bars.

Invite your child to share what he or she knows about how fractions and division are related by doing the following activity together.

ACTIVITY FRACTIONS AS DIVISION

Do this activity with your child to explore fractions as division.

Work with your child to find opportunities to practice modeling a division situation as a fraction.

- Together with your child, think of things that can be shared equally among family members, such as boxes of crackers or bags of grapes.

- Choose one idea. Work together with your child to show how to equally divide a number of the items among the people in your family.

  Example: 4 family members equally share 7 bags of trail mix.

- Have your child write the idea as a division problem.

  Example: $7 \div 4 = \frac{7}{4}$

- Have your child explain how much of the item each family member will get.

  Example: Each person will get $\frac{7}{4}$, or $1\frac{3}{4}$, bags of trail mix.

Explore Fractions as Division

You know that division is used for equal sharing and that fractions represent a number of equal parts of a whole. In this lesson, you will learn how division and fractions are related. Use what you know to try to solve the problem below.

> **Mrs. Tatum needs to share 4 fluid ounces of red paint equally among 5 art students. How many ounces of red paint will each student get?**

Learning Target

- Interpret a fraction as division of the numerator by the denominator $\left(\frac{a}{b} = a \div b\right)$. Solve word problems involving division of whole numbers leading to answers in the form of fractions or mixed numbers, e.g., by using visual fraction models or equations to represent the problem.

SMP 1, 2, 3, 4, 5, 6, 7

TRY IT

Math Toolkit

- fraction circles or tiles
- fraction bars
- fraction models
- tenths grids
- number lines
- index cards

DISCUSS IT

Ask your partner: Why did you choose that strategy?

Tell your partner: At first, I thought . . .

CONNECT IT

❶ LOOK BACK

Explain how to find the amount of paint each student gets.

❷ LOOK AHEAD

Suppose Mrs. Tatum wants to share 8 fluid ounces of paint equally among the 5 students. You can think about this quotient in two ways.

a. Think of each student getting $\frac{1}{5}$ of each ounce. Shade $\frac{1}{5}$ of each whole in the model below to show one student's share.

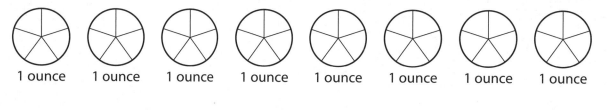

1 ounce   1 ounce   1 ounce   1 ounce   1 ounce   1 ounce   1 ounce   1 ounce

8 ounces ÷ 5 = 8 × .... = ... ounces

b. Think of 8 ounces as 5 ounces + 3 ounces. Explain how the shaded part of the model below shows one student's share.

5 ounces   3 ounces

c. Write the quotient 8 ÷ 5 as a fraction and as a mixed number. ....

❸ REFLECT

How would you write the fraction $\frac{2}{5}$ as a division expression? Write a word problem that can be represented by your expression and by the fraction $\frac{2}{5}$.

....

....

Prepare for Fractions as Division

1 Think about what you know about division. Fill in each box. Use words, numbers, and pictures. Show as many ideas as you can.

Word	In My Own Words	Example
fraction		
division expression		
quotient		
remainder		

2 Write the fraction $\frac{3}{4}$ as a division expression. ....

How could you use multiplication to check your answer?

3 Solve the problem. Show your work.

Mrs. Tatum needs to share 3 grams of glitter equally among 8 art students. How many grams of glitter will each student get?

Solution ....

4 Check your answer. Show your work.

Develop Fractions as Division

Read and try to solve the problem below.

> **Jared, Monica, and Heather have 5 hallways to decorate for the student council. If they share the work equally, how much will each student decorate?**

TRY IT

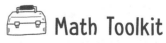 **Math Toolkit**
- fraction circles or tiles
- fraction bars
- fraction models
- tenths grids
- number lines
- index cards

DISCUSS IT

Ask your partner: Do you agree with me? Why or why not?

Tell your partner: I disagree with this part because . . .

Explore different ways to understand fractions as quotients.

> Jared, Monica, and Heather have 5 hallways to decorate for the student council. If they share the work equally, how much will each student decorate?

PICTURE IT

You can use a fraction model to picture how the students divide up the work.

There are 5 hallways for 3 students to decorate, which is 5 ÷ 3.

If they share the work equally, each student can decorate $\frac{1}{3}$ of each hallway.

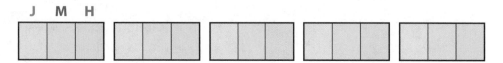

MODEL IT

You can use a number line to model each student's share of the work.

The number line is numbered from 0 to 5 because there are 5 hallways. It is divided into thirds because each student can decorate one third of each hallway.

The thirds can be rearranged to show each student's share of the work.

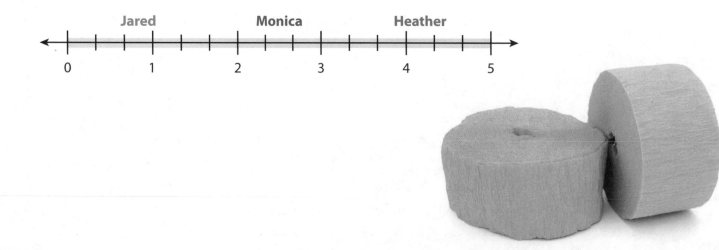

©Curriculum Associates, LLC   Copying is not permitted.

CONNECT IT

Now you will use the problem from the previous page to help you understand fractions as quotients.

1 How many thirds of a hallway are there to decorate in 5 hallways? .... thirds

2 How many thirds of a hallway will each student decorate? .... thirds

Write this as a fraction. .... of a hallway

3 Write a division equation that shows the quotient as a fraction. ....

Write a multiplication equation to check this equation. ....

4 How many whole hallways can each student decorate? ....

How many hallways remain after those are done? ....

How much of the 2 remaining hallways will each student decorate? ....

Write a mixed number to show how many hallways each student will decorate.

.... hallways

5 Calculate using remainder notation: $5 \div 3 =$ .... R ....

Compare this answer to the mixed number. How are they alike?

6 How does the bar in a fraction represent division?

7 REFLECT

Look back at your **Try It**, strategies by classmates, and **Picture It** and **Model It**. Which models or strategies do you like best for finding fraction quotients? Explain.

....

....

....

APPLY IT

Use what you just learned to solve these problems.

8 Five friends are equally sharing 3 packs of football cards. How many packs of cards will each friend get? Use a visual model to support your answer.

Solution ....

9 Elena made 10 ounces of apple chips. She puts the same amount of apple chips into each of 4 containers. How many ounces of apple chips are in 1 container? Write a division expression to represent the problem and solve. Write the solution in remainder form and as a mixed number. Use a visual model to support your answer.

Solution ....

Does the remainder form or the mixed number form best answer the question? Explain.

10 Which expression is equivalent to $\frac{12}{7}$?

   Ⓐ 12 − 7   Ⓑ 7 − 12

   Ⓒ 12 ÷ 7   Ⓓ 7 ÷ 12

Practice Fractions as Division

Study the Example showing whole-number division with a fraction quotient. Then solve problems 1–5.

EXAMPLE

There are 4 packages of printer paper to be divided equally among 6 classrooms. How much paper will each classroom get?

There are 4 packages for 6 classrooms to share, which is $4 \div 6$.

If you divide each package into sixths, each classroom would get one sixth of each package. So, $\frac{1}{6}$ of each package from 4 packages is the same as $\frac{4}{6}$ of a package.

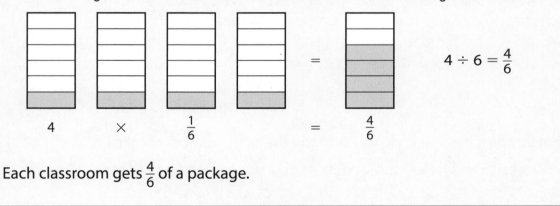

Each classroom gets $\frac{4}{6}$ of a package.

1. Circle the number line you would use to solve the problem in the Example.

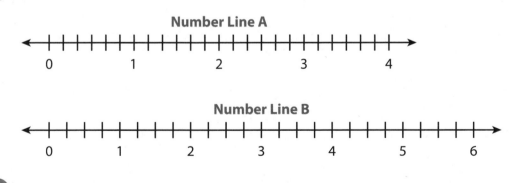

2. Look at the Example. Suppose only 5 classrooms share 4 packages. How would the model in the Example change? How would the answer change?

3 Trish is taking care of the Han family's dogs. The Hans leave 7 cans of dog food for the 3 days they will be away. How much food will the dogs get each day if Trish feeds them an equal amount each day? Show your work. Write the answer in remainder form and as a mixed number.

Solution

Which best answers the question, the remainder form or the mixed number? Explain.

4 Raul plans to run 30 miles this week. He wants to run the same number of miles each day of the week. He says he will run $\frac{7}{30}$ mile each day. Is he correct? Explain.

5 Gus makes 48 fluid ounces of spiced cider. If he serves an equal amount to each of 7 people, will each person get more than 1 cup of cider or less than 1 cup? (1 cup = 8 fluid ounces) Show your work.

Solution

Refine Fractions as Division

Complete the Example below. Then solve problems 1–9.

EXAMPLE

Luke, Carter, and Ava have 2 quarts of juice. They want to share it equally. How many quarts of juice will each of them get?

Look at how you could show your work using a model and equations.

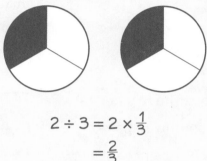

$$2 \div 3 = 2 \times \frac{1}{3}$$
$$= \frac{2}{3}$$

Solution ....

2 quarts are shared equally by 3 friends, so I know that each friend will have less than 1 quart of juice. That means the quotient is a fraction.

APPLY IT

1 Erica has 7 square feet of space in her rectangular garden to plant carrots, beans, peppers, and lettuce. Suppose she gives each vegetable an equal amount of space. How much space will each vegetable get?
Show your work.

Each vegetable will get at least 1 square foot of garden space. How will the rest of the space be divided up?

Solution ....

2 Deon needs to make 36 pizza crusts. He has 120 ounces of dough and wants to use the same amount of dough for each crust. He weighs a portion of dough for 1 crust on a scale. The weight, in ounces, should fall between what two whole numbers? Show your work.

How many whole ounces of dough will each crust get? What will happen with the remaining ounces?

Solution ....

PAIR/SHARE
Create a different division story to represent $\frac{120}{36}$.

3 Jonas is doing a science experiment with his class. The teacher has 21 fluid ounces of pond water to share equally among 10 pairs of students. How much pond water will Jonas and his science partner receive?

Ⓐ $\frac{10}{21}$ fluid ounce

Ⓑ $1\frac{1}{10}$ fluid ounces

Ⓒ 2 fluid ounces

Ⓓ $\frac{21}{10}$ fluid ounces

Olivia chose Ⓐ as the correct answer. How did she get that answer?

About how much water will each pair of students receive? Will it be more or less than 2 fluid ounces?

PAIR/SHARE
Does Olivia's answer make sense?

4 Teddy makes 32 fluid ounces of hot cocoa. He pours equal amounts of cocoa into 5 cups. The amount of hot cocoa in each cup will fall between which two amounts?

Ⓐ 3 and 4 fluid ounces

Ⓑ 4 and 5 fluid ounces

Ⓒ 5 and 6 fluid ounces

Ⓓ 6 and 7 fluid ounces

5 Pierce swims 10 laps in a pool in 8 minutes. He spends the same amount of time on each lap. How much time does each lap take him?

Ⓐ $\frac{2}{10}$ minute

Ⓑ $\frac{8}{10}$ minute

Ⓒ $\frac{10}{8}$ minutes

Ⓓ $1\frac{2}{8}$ minutes

6 Dani needs 8 equal sections from a board that is 13 feet long. Does the expression represent the largest possible length of 1 section of the board, in feet?

	Yes	No
$1\frac{5}{8}$	Ⓐ	Ⓑ
$\frac{8}{13}$	Ⓒ	Ⓓ
$\frac{13}{8}$	Ⓔ	Ⓕ
$8 \div 13$	Ⓖ	Ⓗ
$13 \times \frac{1}{8}$	Ⓘ	Ⓙ

7　Which situations can be represented by $\frac{25}{9}$?

　　Ⓐ Melanie equally shares 25 yards of paper to make 9 banners.

　　Ⓑ Quill gives away 9 baseball cards from a pack of 25 cards.

　　Ⓒ George invites 25 kids and 9 adults to his birthday party.

　　Ⓓ Becca makes 9 rows with 25 buttons each.

　　Ⓔ Joe makes 9 equal servings from a 25-ounce bag of peanuts.

8　Paco is trying to explain to his friend that $7 \div 2 = \frac{7}{2}$.

Part A Draw a model or number line showing $7 \div 2 = \frac{7}{2}$.

Part B Explain the equivalence of $7 \div 2$ and $\frac{7}{2}$ using words.

9　MATH JOURNAL

Write a division word problem that can be represented by the expression $12 \div 5$.
Then explain how to solve your problem.

 SELF CHECK Go back to the Unit 3 Opener and see what you can check off.

Understand Multiplication by a Fraction

Dear Family,

This week your child is exploring multiplying fractions.

An area model can help you visualize finding a fraction of a fraction.

The model shows $\frac{1}{4}$ and $\frac{1}{3}$ of the same whole.

Each row shows $\frac{1}{4}$ of the whole.

Each column shows $\frac{1}{3}$ of the whole.

The part shaded purple shows $\frac{1}{4}$ of $\frac{1}{3}$ of the whole, or $\frac{1}{12}$.

Your child is learning that finding a fraction of a fraction is the same as finding the product of the fractions. Your child might see a problem like the one below.

> If $\frac{2}{3}$ of the gym floor has been cleaned and students can play on $\frac{3}{4}$ of the cleaned floor, what part of the whole gym floor can the students play on?

To solve the problem, you find $\frac{3}{4}$ of $\frac{2}{3}$, or $\frac{3}{4} \times \frac{2}{3}$.

The model shows $\frac{3}{4}$ and $\frac{2}{3}$ of the same whole.

3 rows show $\frac{3}{4}$ of the whole.

2 columns show $\frac{2}{3}$ of the whole.

The part shaded purple shows $\frac{3}{4}$ of $\frac{2}{3}$ of the whole.

The model is divided into 12 equal parts, **6** of which are shaded purple.

You can see that $\frac{6}{12}$ of the whole is shaded purple. So, $\frac{3}{4} \times \frac{2}{3} = \frac{6}{12}$.

Students can play on $\frac{6}{12}$, or $\frac{1}{2}$, of the gym floor.

Invite your child to share what he or she knows about multiplying fractions by doing the following activity together.

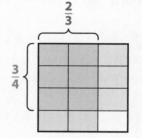

ACTIVITY MULTIPLY BY A FRACTION

Do this activity with your child to understand multiplication by a fraction.

Materials 2 different colors of crayons or colored pencils, number cube

- Together with your child, draw a blank rectangle at the bottom of the page to show the product of two fractions.

- One person rolls the number cube. This number tells how many equal parts to show in the rectangle. Draw vertical lines to show the equal parts.

    Example: Roll a 6 and draw vertical lines to show 6 equal parts in the rectangle.

- The same person shades a fraction of the rectangle and names that fraction.

    Example: Shade $\frac{5}{6}$.

- The other person rolls the number cube. This number tells how many equal parts to show in the same rectangle. Draw horizontal lines to show the equal parts.

    Example: Roll a 2 and draw a horizontal line to show 2 equal parts (top and bottom) of the rectangle.

- The same person shades a fraction of the rectangle and names that fraction.

    Example: Shade $\frac{1}{2}$.

- The part where the shading overlaps shows the product. Together, write the fraction multiplication equation that the picture shows.

    Example: $\frac{1}{2} \times \frac{5}{6} = \frac{5}{12}$

Explore Multiplication by a Fraction

What does it mean to multiply by a fraction?

Learning Targets

- Apply and extend previous understandings of multiplication to multiply a fraction or whole number by a fraction.
  - Interpret the product $\frac{a}{b} \times q$ as a parts of a partition of q into b equal parts; equivalently, as the result of a sequence of operations $a \times q \div b$.

SMP 1, 2, 3, 4, 5, 6, 8

MODEL IT

Complete the models below.

1 Shade and label three $\frac{1}{2}$-inch sections of the ruler. Then complete the sentence and the multiplication equation that represents the total length you shaded.

3 sections of $\frac{1}{2}$ inch are .... inches.

$3 \times \frac{1}{2} =$ ....

2 Shade and label $\frac{1}{2}$ of a 3-inch section of the ruler. Then complete the sentence and the multiplication equation that represents the total length you shaded.

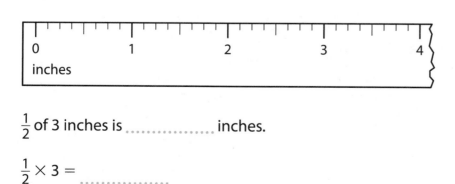

$\frac{1}{2}$ of 3 inches is .... inches.

$\frac{1}{2} \times 3 =$ ....

DISCUSS IT

- How does the length of three $\frac{1}{2}$-inch segments compare to the length of half of a 3-inch segment?

- I think $\frac{1}{2}$ of 3 is equal to both $3 \div 2$ and $3 \times \frac{1}{2}$ because ...

MODEL IT

Complete the models below.

3 Shade and label the ruler to find the length of $\frac{1}{4}$ of $\frac{1}{2}$ inch.
Complete the sentence and the multiplication equation that
represents the total length you shaded.

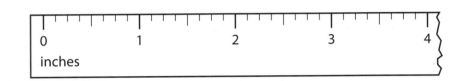

0   1   2   3   4

inches

$\frac{1}{4}$ of $\frac{1}{2}$ inch is .... of an inch.

$\frac{1}{4} \times \frac{1}{2} =$ ....

4 Shade and label the ruler to show $\frac{3}{4}$ of $\frac{1}{2}$ inch. Write a multiplication
equation that represents the total length you shaded.

0   1   2   3   4

inches

Equation ....

5 REFLECT

Based on the two problems above, explain how to find $\frac{2}{4}$ of $\frac{1}{2}$, or $\frac{2}{4} \times \frac{1}{2}$.

....

....

....

DISCUSS IT

- How many parts did you divide the whole inch into when you found $\frac{1}{4}$ of $\frac{1}{2}$ inch?
- I think finding $\frac{1}{4}$ of a number or multiplying a number by $\frac{1}{4}$ is like dividing by 4 because . . .

Prepare for Multiplication by a Fraction

1   Think about what you know about fractions. Fill in each box. Use words, numbers, and pictures. Show as many ideas as you can.

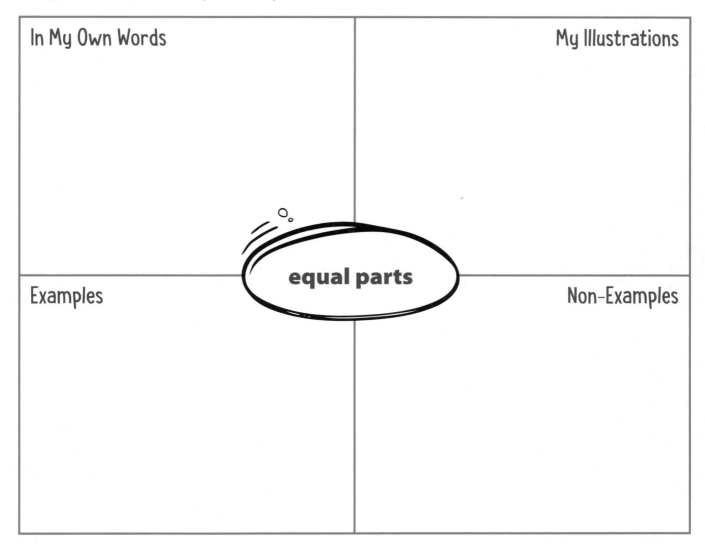

In My Own Words	My Illustrations
Examples	Non-Examples

equal parts

2   Shade and label three $\frac{1}{4}$-inch sections of the ruler. Complete the sentence and the multiplication equation that represents the total length you shaded.

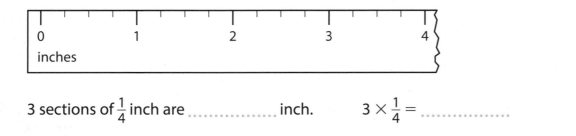

3 sections of $\frac{1}{4}$ inch are .... inch. $3 \times \frac{1}{4} =$ ....

Solve.

3 Shade and label the ruler to find the length of $\frac{1}{2}$ of $\frac{1}{2}$ inch. Complete the sentence and the multiplication equation that represents the total length you shaded.

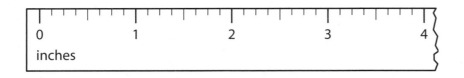

$\frac{1}{2}$ of $\frac{1}{2}$ inch is .... inch.

$\frac{1}{2} \times \frac{1}{2} =$ ....

4 Shade and label the ruler to show $\frac{1}{2}$ of $\frac{3}{4}$ inch. Write a multiplication equation that represents the total length you shaded.

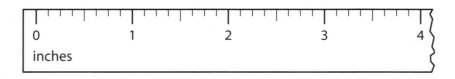

Equation ....

Develop Understanding of Multiplying by a Fraction

MODEL IT: NUMBER LINES

Try these two problems.

1 Mark and shade the number line to show $\frac{2}{5}$ of $\frac{1}{2}$.

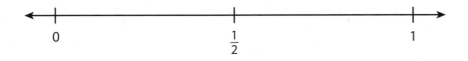

What fraction of the whole did you shade? ....

Complete the multiplication equation.

$\frac{2}{5} \times \frac{1}{2} =$ ....

2 Mark and shade the number line to show $\frac{3}{4}$ of $\frac{1}{3}$.
Then write a multiplication equation for the model.

Equation ....

DISCUSS IT

• How did you know how many of the parts to shade for each problem?

• I think the number line in problem 1 shows $\frac{2}{5} \times \frac{1}{2}$ because . . .

MODEL IT: AREA MODELS

Use the area models to show multiplying fractions.

3 Explain why the purple rectangle, where the shading overlaps, represents $\frac{1}{2}$ of $\frac{1}{3}$. Then complete the product.

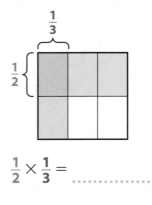

$\frac{1}{2} \times \frac{1}{3} =$ ....

4 Shade the area model to show $\frac{2}{5}$ of $\frac{2}{3}$. Then complete the product.

$\frac{2}{5} \times \frac{2}{3} =$ ....

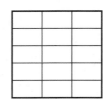

CONNECT IT

Complete the problems below.

5 How are the number line and area models for fraction multiplication alike? How are they different?

6 Choose any model you like to show $\frac{1}{3} \times \frac{3}{4}$.

$\frac{1}{3} \times \frac{3}{4} =$ ....

Practice Multiplying by a Fraction

**Study how the Example shows multiplying a fraction by a fraction.
Then solve problems 1–6.**

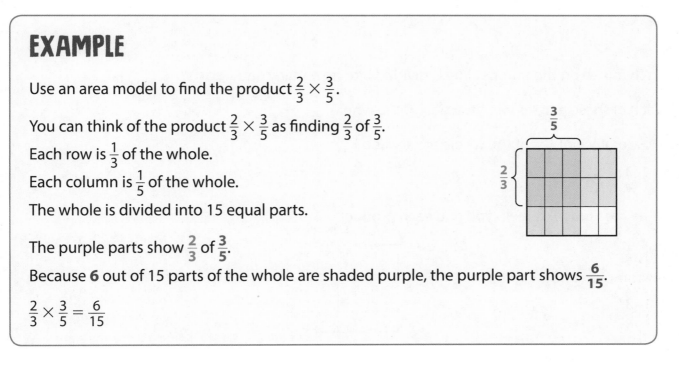

EXAMPLE

Use an area model to find the product $\frac{2}{3} \times \frac{3}{5}$.

You can think of the product $\frac{2}{3} \times \frac{3}{5}$ as finding $\frac{2}{3}$ of $\frac{3}{5}$.

Each row is $\frac{1}{3}$ of the whole.

Each column is $\frac{1}{5}$ of the whole.

The whole is divided into 15 equal parts.

The purple parts show $\frac{2}{3}$ of $\frac{3}{5}$.

Because **6** out of 15 parts of the whole are shaded purple, the purple part shows $\frac{6}{15}$.

$\frac{2}{3} \times \frac{3}{5} = \frac{6}{15}$

1 Why are fifteenths shown in the Example model?

2 Use the area model in the Example to write each product.

$\frac{1}{3} \times \frac{3}{5} =$ .... $\frac{2}{3} \times \frac{4}{5} =$ .... $\frac{3}{3} \times \frac{2}{5} =$ ....

3 Choose *Yes* or *No* to tell whether the denominator of each product is 12.

	Yes	No
$\frac{1}{2} \times \frac{1}{6}$	Ⓐ	Ⓑ
$\frac{3}{4} \times \frac{2}{5}$	Ⓒ	Ⓓ
$\frac{1}{4} \times \frac{2}{3}$	Ⓔ	Ⓕ
$\frac{5}{6} \times \frac{2}{2}$	Ⓖ	Ⓗ

4 The number line shows $\frac{1}{2} \times \frac{3}{4}$.

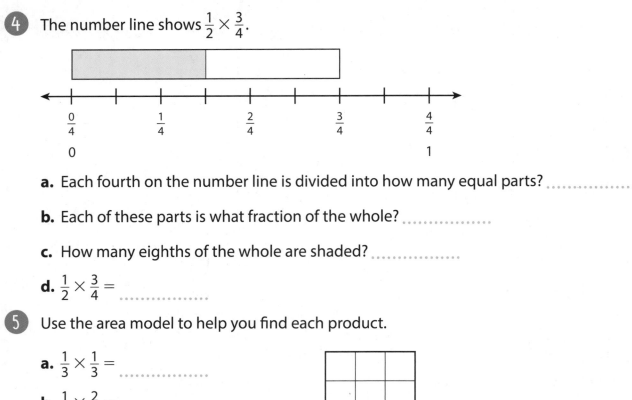

a. Each fourth on the number line is divided into how many equal parts? ....

b. Each of these parts is what fraction of the whole? ....

c. How many eighths of the whole are shaded? ....

d. $\frac{1}{2} \times \frac{3}{4} =$ ....

5 Use the area model to help you find each product.

a. $\frac{1}{3} \times \frac{1}{3} =$ ....

b. $\frac{1}{3} \times \frac{2}{3} =$ ....

c. $\frac{2}{3} \times \frac{2}{3} =$ ....

d. $\frac{3}{3} \times \frac{2}{3} =$ ....

e. $\frac{3}{3} \times \frac{3}{3} =$ ....

6 Tell whether each statement is *True* or *False* for the product $\frac{2}{4} \times \frac{3}{5}$.

	True	False
The denominator of the product is 20.	Ⓐ	Ⓑ
The denominator of the product is 9.	Ⓒ	Ⓓ
The product is less than each factor.	Ⓔ	Ⓕ
The product is greater than each factor.	Ⓖ	Ⓗ

Refine Ideas About Multiplying by a Fraction

APPLY IT
Complete these problems on your own.

1 DESCRIBE

Tell what multiplication problem the model shows. Explain why.

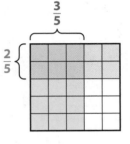

2 EXPLAIN

Landon said that $\frac{2}{3} \times \frac{1}{6} = \frac{5}{6}$. Tell how Landon found his product and then explain how to find the correct product.

3 ANALYZE

Fill in the products in the table. Look for patterns as you work.

$\frac{1}{4} \times \frac{1}{3} =$	$\frac{2}{4} \times \frac{1}{3} =$	$\frac{3}{4} \times \frac{1}{3} =$	$\frac{4}{4} \times \frac{1}{3} =$
$\frac{1}{4} \times \frac{2}{3} =$	$\frac{2}{4} \times \frac{2}{3} =$	$\frac{3}{4} \times \frac{2}{3} =$	$\frac{4}{4} \times \frac{2}{3} =$

How do the numerators and denominators of two fractions relate to the numerator and denominator of their product?

PAIR/SHARE
Discuss your solutions for these three problems with a partner.

Use what you have learned to complete problem 4.

4 **Part A** Start with a sheet of paper. Fold it in half and then fold it in half again. Continue folding the paper in half. After each fold, fill in the blanks to tell what fraction of the whole each equal part is.

$\frac{1}{2} \times 1 =$ ....

$\frac{1}{2} \times \frac{1}{2} =$ ....

$\frac{1}{2} \times$ .... $=$ ....

$\frac{1}{2} \times$ .... $=$ ....

Part B Look at the denominators of the products you found in Part A.

Each time you multiply by $\frac{1}{2}$, what happens to the denominator?

Without folding the paper, what do you think the next product in the pattern will be? Why?

Part C Now look at the sizes of the equal parts of the folded paper. Each time you fold the paper in half, what happens to the size of the parts?

5 MATH JOURNAL

Genet says that $\frac{3}{8}$ of $\frac{1}{2}$ is $\frac{3}{16}$ because $\frac{1}{8}$ of $\frac{1}{2}$ is $\frac{1}{16}$. Is Genet correct? Explain.

Multiply Fractions to Find Area

Dear Family,

This week your child is learning to multiply fractions to find the area of rectangles.

He or she might see a problem like this:

Mark has a square placemat that measures 1 foot on each side. He divides it in half vertically and in thirds horizontally. He wants to decorate each part with a different pattern. What is the area of each part of the placemat?

To understand the problem, your child could draw and label a picture.

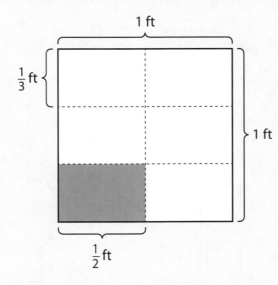

The dashed lines show 6 equal parts.

Each part is $\frac{1}{2}$ foot wide and $\frac{1}{3}$ foot long. Each part is $\frac{1}{6}$ of the whole.
Multiply to find the area of each part.

$$\frac{1}{2} \text{ foot} \times \frac{1}{3} \text{ foot} = \frac{1}{6} \text{ square foot}$$

The area of each part of the placemat is $\frac{1}{6}$ square foot.

Invite your child to share what he or she knows about multiplying fractions to find the area of rectangles by doing the following activity together.

Do this activity with your child to find the area of a rectangle by multiplying fractions.

- Look at the rectangle below.

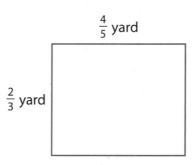

$\frac{4}{5}$ yard

$\frac{2}{3}$ yard

- Remind your child that you can find the area of a rectangle by multiplying the length by the width. (area = length × width)

- Together with your child, find the area of the rectangle shown above by multiplying the length by the width.

- Check your answer by using an area model. The square below has an area of 1 square yard. Ask your child to shade parts of the square below to show the same area as the rectangle above.

1 yard

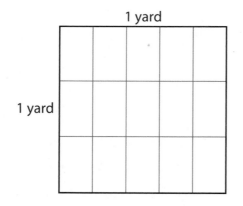

1 yard

- Together with your child, find the area of the shaded part of the square by finding the fraction of the square that is shaded. Ask your child: *Does this match your answer from above?*

Answer: Area = $\frac{4}{5}$ yard × $\frac{2}{3}$ yard = $\frac{8}{15}$ square yard

Explore Multiplying Fractions to Find Area

Previously, you learned about multiplying fractions. Now you will use area models to multiply fractions and find areas of rectangles. Use what you know to try to solve the problem below.

> **Mr. Thompson designs a 1-mile square park. He makes a square with $\frac{5}{10}$-mile sides on his design for a dog play space. How many square miles of the park does he use for the dog play space?**

Learning Target

- Find the area of a rectangle with fractional side lengths by tiling it with unit squares of the appropriate unit fraction side lengths, and show that the area is the same as would be found by multiplying the side lengths. Multiply fractional side lengths to find areas of rectangles, and represent fraction products as rectangular areas.

SMP 1, 2, 3, 4, 5, 6, 7

TRY IT

Math Toolkit
- fraction models
- multiplication models
- geoboard
- rubber bands
- base-ten blocks
- grid paper
- index cards

DISCUSS IT

Ask your partner: How did you get started?

Tell your partner: I am not sure how to find the answer because . . .

CONNECT IT

 LOOK BACK

Explain how you found the area of the park used for the dog play space.

 LOOK AHEAD

Suppose you want to find the area of a rectangular section of the park that is $\frac{3}{10}$ mile by $\frac{3}{10}$ mile. You can find the area in different ways.

a. Tile the section with unit squares. The 1-mile square park is divided up into 10 columns and 10 rows so that one tile is $\frac{1}{10}$ mile by $\frac{1}{10}$ mile.

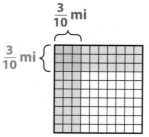

What is the area of one tile? .... square mile

How many tiles are in the $\frac{3}{10}$ mile-by-$\frac{3}{10}$ mile section? ....

What is the area of the $\frac{3}{10}$ mile-by-$\frac{3}{10}$ mile section? .... square mile

b. You can find the area by multiplying the side lengths of the section, $\frac{3}{10} \times \frac{3}{10}$.

Multiply the fractions to find the area.

$\frac{3}{10} \times \frac{3}{10} =$ .... The area of the section is .... square mile.

 REFLECT

Look at the area model and equation for $\frac{3}{10} \times \frac{3}{10}$. Explain how the numerators and denominators in the equation are related to the squares in the area model.

....

....

....

©Curriculum Associates, LLC   Copying is not permitted.

Prepare for Multiplying Fractions to Find Area

1   Think about what you know about the area of a rectangle. Fill in each box. Use
     words, numbers, and pictures. Show as many ideas as you can.

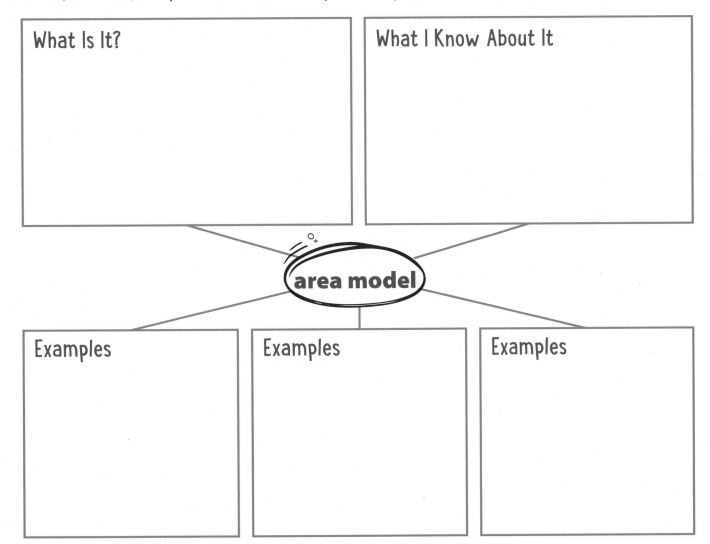

What Is It?	What I Know About It

area model

Examples	Examples	Examples

2   The area of the whole square at the right is 1 square mile.
     What is the area of the shaded part of the square?

Solution ....

③ Solve the problem. Show your work.

Mrs. Beaker designs a 1-mile square park. She makes a square with $\frac{6}{10}$-mile sides in her park for sports fields. How many square miles of the park does she use for sports fields?

Solution ....

④ Check your answer. Show your work.

Develop Multiplying Unit Fractions to Find Area

Read and try to solve the problem below.

> **Titus is making flashcards to use for vocabulary review. He cuts out rectangular cards that are $\frac{1}{2}$ foot long and $\frac{1}{4}$ foot wide. What is the area of one card in square feet?**

TRY IT

🧰 Math Toolkit
- fraction models 🔖
- multiplication models 🔖
- grid paper
- index cards
- cardstock
- rulers
- scissors

DISCUSS IT

Ask your partner: Why did you choose that strategy?

Tell your partner: A model I used was . . . It helped me . . .

Explore different ways to understand multiplying two unit fractions to find area.

> Titus is making flashcards to use for vocabulary review. He cuts out rectangular cards that are $\frac{1}{2}$ foot long and $\frac{1}{4}$ foot wide. What is the area of one card in square feet?

PICTURE IT

You can understand the problem by picturing how the cards could fill a square.

You can arrange 8 cards, each $\frac{1}{2}$ foot by $\frac{1}{4}$ foot, to form a square. When rectangles fill a square without gaps or overlaps, they are said to *tile* the square.

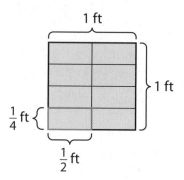

MODEL IT

You can model the problem with an equation.

Each rectangular flashcard has a length of $\frac{1}{2}$ foot and a width of $\frac{1}{4}$ foot.

    area = length × width

    area = $\frac{1}{2}$ foot × $\frac{1}{4}$ foot

$\frac{1}{2}$ foot × $\frac{1}{4}$ foot = $\left(\frac{1}{2} \times \frac{1}{4}\right)$ square foot

CONNECT IT

Now you will use the problem from the previous page to help you understand how to multiply two unit fractions to find area.

1 Why can a sheet of paper that is 1 square foot be tiled by 4 rows of 2 flashcards?

2 What portion of the 1-square-foot sheet of paper is represented by each flashcard?

.... of the sheet of paper, or .... of 1 square foot

3 Look at the equations in **Model It**. What product of unit fractions can you use

to find the area of one flashcard? ....

4 Multiply the denominators of the unit fractions. How does the product relate to the size of the units compared to the size of the whole model?

5 Multiply the numerators of the unit fractions. How does the product relate to the number of outlined parts of the model?

6 Explain how to find the area of one flashcard.

7 **REFLECT**

Look back at your **Try It**, strategies by classmates, and **Picture It** and **Model It**. Which models or strategies do you like best for finding the area of a rectangle with fractional side lengths? Explain.

....

....

....

APPLY IT

Use what you just learned to solve these problems.

8 What is the area of a rectangular paper strip with a length of $\frac{1}{3}$ yard and width of $\frac{1}{6}$ yard? Use an area model and an equation to show your work.

Solution ....

9 Marnie has a square picture with an area of 1 square foot. Draw lines in the model below to show one way to tile a 1-foot square with rectangular tiles that each have an area of $\frac{1}{12}$ square foot. What are the length and width of your tile?

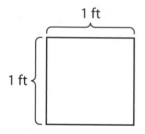

1 ft

1 ft

Solution ....

10 What is the area of a rectangle that has a length of $\frac{1}{4}$ inch and a width of $\frac{1}{8}$ inch?

Ⓐ $\frac{1}{12}$ square inch

Ⓑ $\frac{2}{12}$ square inch

Ⓒ $\frac{1}{32}$ square inch

Ⓓ $\frac{2}{32}$ square inch

Practice Multiplying Unit Fractions to Find Area

**Study the Example that shows multiplying unit fractions to find area.
Then solve problems 1–5.**

EXAMPLE

A sheet of cardboard that measures 1 yard on each side is cut into rectangular cards that are $\frac{1}{8}$ yard wide and $\frac{1}{2}$ yard long. What is the area of each card?

You can model the problem with a picture as shown.

You also can model the problem with an equation.

$$\text{area} = \frac{1}{2} \times \frac{1}{8}$$
$$= \frac{1 \times 1}{2 \times 8}$$
$$= \frac{1}{16}$$

The area of each card is $\frac{1}{16}$ square yard.

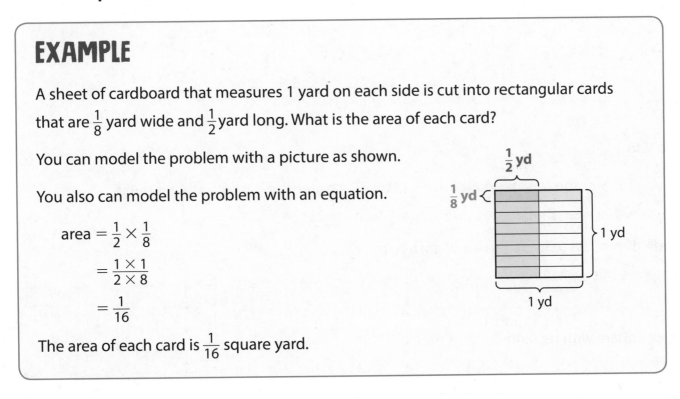

1. Suppose the length of each card in the Example is shortened to $\frac{1}{4}$ yard. Will the area of each card now be greater than or less than $\frac{1}{16}$ square yard? Explain.

2. Which expression represents the area of a rectangular card described in problem 1?

Ⓐ $\frac{1}{2} \times \frac{1}{4}$

Ⓑ $\frac{1}{2} \times \frac{1}{8}$

Ⓒ $\frac{1}{4} \times \frac{1}{8}$

Ⓓ $\frac{1}{4} \times \frac{1}{16}$

3 What is the area of a rectangular card that is $\frac{1}{8}$ yard wide and $\frac{1}{4}$ yard long? Show your work.

Solution ....

4 Mr. Von's 5th-grade class is going on a field trip. Each student is given a rectangular name card to wear that is $\frac{1}{4}$ foot wide and $\frac{1}{3}$ foot long.

Shade the model to find the area of each name card.
Complete the equation.

$\frac{1}{4}$ foot $\times$ $\frac{1}{3}$ foot $=$ $\dfrac{\Box}{\Box}$ square foot

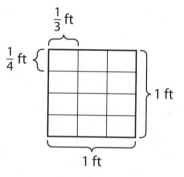

5 Signs for project displays are cut from pieces of poster board that measure 1 yard on each side. Each rectangular sign is $\frac{1}{3}$ yard long and $\frac{1}{9}$ yard wide. How many signs can be cut from one piece of poster board? What is the area of each sign? Show your work.

Solution ....

Develop Tiling a Rectangle to Find Area

Read and try to solve the problem below.

A rectangular postage stamp has a length of $\frac{3}{2}$ inches and a width of $\frac{3}{4}$ inch. What is the area of the stamp in square inches?

TRY IT

Math Toolkit
- fraction models
- multiplication models
- half-inch grid paper
- index cards
- rulers

DISCUSS IT

Ask your partner: Can you explain that again?

Tell your partner: I started by . . .

Explore different ways to understand modeling the area of a rectangle through tiling and equations.

> A rectangular postage stamp has a length of $\frac{3}{2}$ inches and a width of $\frac{3}{4}$ inch. What is the area of the stamp in square inches?

PICTURE IT

You can picture tiling the rectangular stamp with smaller rectangles that have unit fractions as side lengths.

You can tile a unit square with rectangles that have unit fractions as side lengths. Each rectangular tile is $\frac{1}{2}$ inch by $\frac{1}{4}$ inch.

You can also use $\frac{1}{2}$ inch-by-$\frac{1}{4}$ inch tiles to tile a rectangular stamp with length $\frac{3}{2}$ inches and width $\frac{3}{4}$ inch.

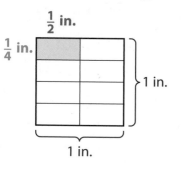

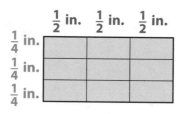

MODEL IT

You can model the area of the rectangular stamp with an equation.

Think of the stamp as part of two whole square inches. Use the area formula to multiply the side lengths.

area = length × width

area = $\frac{3}{2}$ **inches** × $\frac{3}{4}$ **inch**

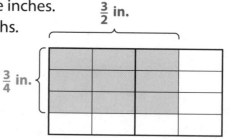

$\frac{3}{2}$ inches × $\frac{3}{4}$ inch = $\left(\frac{3}{2} \times \frac{3}{4} \right)$ square inches

CONNECT IT

Now you will use the problem from the previous page to help you understand how to use tiling or equations to find area.

1 Use the unit square in **Picture It** to explain how to find the area of one tile.

2 Look at the model of the stamp in **Picture It**. Explain why nine $\frac{1}{2}$ inch-by-$\frac{1}{4}$ inch rectangles tile the $\frac{3}{2}$ inches-by-$\frac{3}{4}$ inch stamp.

3 Write an equation that uses the area of one tile to find the area of the stamp.

.... square inches = ... square inches

4 Now look at the area formula equation in **Model It**. Complete the equation to find the area of the stamp as shown in this model.

$\frac{3}{2} \times \frac{3}{4} = \dfrac{\boxed{} \times \boxed{}}{\boxed{} \times \boxed{}} = $ .... The area is .... square inches.

5 Does using the area formula equation result in the same area as you found by tiling the rectangle? Why?

6 REFLECT

Look back at your **Try It**, strategies by classmates, and **Picture It** and **Model It**. Which models or strategies do you like best for finding the area of a rectangle with fractional side lengths? Explain.

....

....

....

APPLY IT

Use what you just learned to solve these problems.

7 Bernice's rectangular math workbook is $\frac{2}{3}$ foot wide and $\frac{5}{6}$ foot long. What is the area of a page in her workbook? Show your work.

Solution ....

8 Show one way to use tiles to find the area of the rectangle below. What are the length and width of one of your tiles? What is the area of the rectangle?

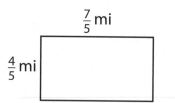

$\frac{7}{5}$ mi

$\frac{4}{5}$ mi

Solution ....

9 John's rectangular poster is $\frac{7}{4}$ yards in length and $\frac{2}{3}$ yard in width. What is the area of John's poster?

Ⓐ $\frac{2}{3}$ square yards

Ⓑ $\frac{14}{12}$ square yards

Ⓒ $\frac{9}{7}$ square yards

Ⓓ $\frac{7}{4}$ square yards

Practice Tiling a Rectangle to Find Area

**Study the Example that shows tiling a rectangle to find its area.
Then solve problems 1–6.**

EXAMPLE

What is the area of a rectangle that is $\frac{1}{2}$ yard wide and $\frac{4}{3}$ yards long?

The top area model shows that
$\frac{1}{2}$ yard $\times \frac{1}{3}$ yard $= \frac{1}{6}$ square yard.

$\frac{1}{3}$ yd

$\frac{1}{2}$ yd

$\frac{1}{2} \times \frac{1}{3}$

The bottom model uses the same $\frac{1}{6}$-square-yard
parts to show an area that is $\frac{1}{2}$ yard $\times \frac{4}{3}$ yards.

Four $\frac{1}{6}$-square-yard parts are shaded purple.

$\frac{1}{2}$ yard $\times \frac{4}{3}$ yards $= \frac{4}{6}$ square yard

$\frac{4}{3}$ yd

$\frac{1}{2}$ yd

$\frac{1}{2} \times \frac{4}{3}$

1 How many $\frac{1}{2}$-yard lengths are in 1 yard? ....

2 How many $\frac{1}{3}$-yard lengths are in 1 yard? ....

3 Draw a line around the part of the model from the
Example that represents 1 square yard.

Does $\frac{4}{6}$ square yard cover more area or less area than
1 square yard? Explain.

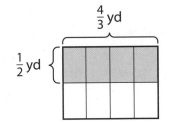

$\frac{4}{3}$ yd

$\frac{1}{2}$ yd

4 Danah has a rectangular strawberry patch in her garden. Its border is $\frac{7}{8}$ yard wide and $\frac{3}{2}$ yards long. Use a visual model to find the area of Danah's strawberry patch. Then write an equation to describe your model. Show your work.

Solution ....

5 Danah is planting a second rectangular strawberry patch and wants it to have an area of exactly 1 square yard. Which of the following could be the width and length of its borders? Select all that apply.

Ⓐ $\frac{1}{2}$ yard wide and $\frac{3}{2}$ yards long

Ⓑ $\frac{2}{3}$ yard wide and $\frac{3}{2}$ yards long

Ⓒ $\frac{4}{5}$ yard wide and $\frac{5}{4}$ yards long

Ⓓ $\frac{2}{3}$ yard wide and $\frac{6}{4}$ yards long

Ⓔ $\frac{3}{4}$ yard wide and $\frac{12}{8}$ yards long

6 Look at problem 5. If Danah wants the area of her rectangular strawberry patch to be exactly 1 square yard, can the length of the strawberry patch be greater than 1 yard? Explain.

Refine Multiplying Fractions to Find Area

Complete the Example below. Then solve problems 1–9.

EXAMPLE

Rachel is designing a newspaper ad. The ad will include a rectangular piece of art whose dimensions are $\frac{5}{8}$ inch long and $\frac{1}{2}$ inch wide. How many square inches of space will the art cover?

Look at how you could show your work using a unit square area model and an equation.

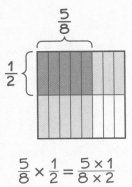

$$\frac{5}{8} \times \frac{1}{2} = \frac{5 \times 1}{8 \times 2}$$

Solution ....

$\frac{1}{8}$ inch $\times \frac{1}{2}$ inch is $\frac{1}{16}$ square inch. How many one-sixteenth square inches are shown in the model?

PAIR/SHARE
How can you write $\frac{5}{8} \times \frac{1}{2}$ as a product of unit fractions and whole numbers?

APPLY IT

1 What is the area of a rectangle with a length of $\frac{1}{2}$ yard and a width of $\frac{11}{6}$ yards? Write an equation to represent your solution. Show your work.

How can you represent a fractional side length with an area model?

PAIR/SHARE
Find the area of a rectangle with side lengths of $\frac{3}{4}$ yard and $\frac{6}{5}$ yards. How is the model different?

Solution ....

2 Kwame is designing a poster that has an area of 1 square foot. He is going to paste a photo collage on a rectangular section of the poster that is $\frac{1}{3}$ foot wide and $\frac{3}{4}$ foot long. What part of a square foot will the photo collage cover? Show your work.

> If I draw a square to represent a square foot, how can I represent thirds and fifths on the square?

Solution . . . .

PAIR/SHARE
Write an equation to represent your model. Explain the meaning of the numerators.

3 What is the area of the square?

Ⓐ $\frac{36}{64}$ square yard

Ⓑ $\frac{12}{16}$ square yard

Ⓒ $\frac{64}{36}$ square yards

Ⓓ $\frac{12}{8}$ square yards

$\frac{6}{8}$ yd

$\frac{6}{8}$ yd

> Think about the size of the two fractions. Will the product of the fractions be greater than 1 or less than 1?

Ollie chose Ⓓ as the correct answer. How did he get that answer?

PAIR/SHARE
Does Ollie's answer make sense?

4 The square at the right represents 1 square unit.

Which expression represents the area of the purple section?

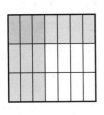

Ⓐ $\frac{7}{3} \times \frac{3}{1}$ square units

Ⓑ $\frac{3}{7} \times \frac{1}{3}$ square units

Ⓒ $\frac{1}{7} \times \frac{1}{3}$ square units

Ⓓ $\frac{7}{3} \times \frac{1}{3}$ square units

5 Fill in the missing numbers to make the equation true. Then complete the area model to check your answer.

$$\frac{1}{6} \times \frac{\square}{\square} = \frac{1}{24}$$

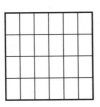

6 Which products could you find by shading the model below?

Ⓐ $\frac{3}{4} \times \frac{1}{3}$

Ⓑ $\frac{1}{3} \times \frac{1}{6}$

Ⓒ $\frac{2}{3} \times \frac{1}{4}$

Ⓓ $\frac{5}{3} \times \frac{1}{4}$

Ⓔ $\frac{3}{4} \times \frac{3}{4}$

7 Draw an area model to represent the expression $\frac{5}{4}$ miles $\times \frac{4}{5}$ mile.

What are the dimensions of one of the rectangular tiles in your model?

8 Explain how to find the area of the model you drew in problem 7. Then find the area.

9 MATH JOURNAL

Find the area of a rectangle $\frac{5}{3}$ units in length and $\frac{3}{4}$ units in width. Show and explain how to find the area.

 SELF CHECK Go back to the Unit 3 Opener and see what you can check off.

Understand Multiplication as Scaling

Dear Family,

This week your child is exploring multiplication as scaling.

Scaling is resizing a quantity through multiplication. You can think of scaling as stretching or shrinking.

You can *stretch*, or increase, a quantity by multiplying the quantity by a factor greater than 1. You can *shrink*, or decrease, a quantity by multiplying the quantity by a factor less than 1.

Look at the length of the bar below. It has a length of 4 units.

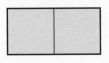

If you multiply the length by 2, you double the length of the bar.

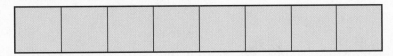

If you multiply the original length by $\frac{1}{2}$, you shrink the bar to half its original length.

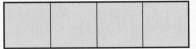

Your child is learning to generalize about multiplication and scaling. Multiplying by a number . . .

- greater than 1 increases the quantity.

- less than 1 decreases the quantity.

- equal to 1, such as $\frac{4}{4}$, means that the quantity stays the same.

Invite your child to share what he or she knows about multiplication as scaling by doing the following activity together.

ACTIVITY MULTIPLICATION AS SCALING

Do this activity with your child to understand multiplication as scaling.

Use the examples below to talk with your child about multiplication as scaling.

- This is the actual size of a pencil that is 4 centimeters long.

- Ask your child the following questions.

  1. *What if the pencil were twice as long? How long would it be? How do you know?*

  2. *What if the pencil were half as long as the original pencil? How long would it be? How do you know?*

  3. *What if the pencil were 3 times as long? Would it be shorter or longer than the original pencil? How do you know?*

  4. *What if the pencil were $\frac{3}{4}$ as long? Would it be shorter or longer than the original pencil? How do you know?*

  5. *What if the pencil were $\frac{4}{4}$ as long? How would the length of the pencil compare to the length of the original pencil?*

  6. *What would it mean to multiply the length of the pencil by $\frac{7}{4}$? How would the length of the pencil change?*

Answers:
1. It would be two times the length of the original pencil, or 8 centimeters. It would be longer than the original pencil because we multiplied by a number greater than 1.
2. It would be half the length of the original pencil, or 2 centimeters. It would be shorter than the original pencil because we multiplied by a number less than 1.
3. It would be longer because we are multiplying by a number greater than 1.
4. It would be shorter because we are multiplying by a number less than 1.
5. It would be the same length as the original pencil because we are multiplying by a number equal to 1.
6. It would be longer because we are multiplying by a number greater than 1.

Explore Multiplication as Scaling

What does scaling mean?

Learning Target
• Interpret multiplication as scaling (resizing), by:
  ○ Comparing the size of a product to the size of one factor on the basis of the size of the other factor, without performing the indicated multiplication.
SMP 1, 2, 3, 4, 5, 6, 7, 8

MODEL IT

Complete the problems below.

1 Changing the size of a quantity by multiplication is called **scaling**. *Stretching* and *shrinking* are two different ways to scale a quantity.

This bar has a length of 6 units.

Use the bars at the bottom of the page to complete parts a and b.

a. Circle the bar that shows the length of 6 units being doubled, or stretched. Underline the bar that shows the length of 6 units being halved, or shrunk.

b. Write a multiplication equation for each bar. Circle the factor that describes how the length of 6 units has been stretched or shrunk.

Equation ....

Equation ....

DISCUSS IT

• Did you and your partner agree on which bar shows shrinking and which shows stretching?

• I think you can double the value of a quantity by multiplying by . . .
I think you can halve the value of a quantity by multiplying by . . .

MODEL IT

Complete the problems below.

2 Use the table to make generalizations about scaling the whole number 6 through multiplication by various factors.

Factor	$\frac{1}{10}$	$\frac{1}{3}$	$\frac{1}{2}$	1	$\frac{4}{4}$	$\frac{3}{2}$	$2\frac{1}{2}$	3
Factor	6	6	6	6	6	6	6	6
Product	$\frac{6}{10}$	2	3	6	6	9	15	18

a. Underline the products less than 6. What do the factors for these products have in common?

b. Circle the products greater than 6. What do the factors for these products have in common?

c. Put a box around the products equal to 6. What do the factors for these products have in common?

3 REFLECT

Describe the products you get if you multiply 8 by factors less than 1. Describe the products you get if you multiply 8 by factors greater than 1. Give some examples that justify your answers.

....

....

....

....

....

DISCUSS IT

- How did you and your partner describe what the products less than, greater than, and equal to 6 have in common?

- I think when you multiply by a fraction less than 1, the product will be . . .

  I think when you multiply by a fraction greater than 1, the product will be . . .

  I think when you multiply by a fraction equal to 1, the product will be . . .

Prepare for Multiplication as Scaling

1 Think about what you know about multiplying by numbers greater than or less than 1. Fill in each box. Use words, numbers, and pictures. Show as many ideas as you can.

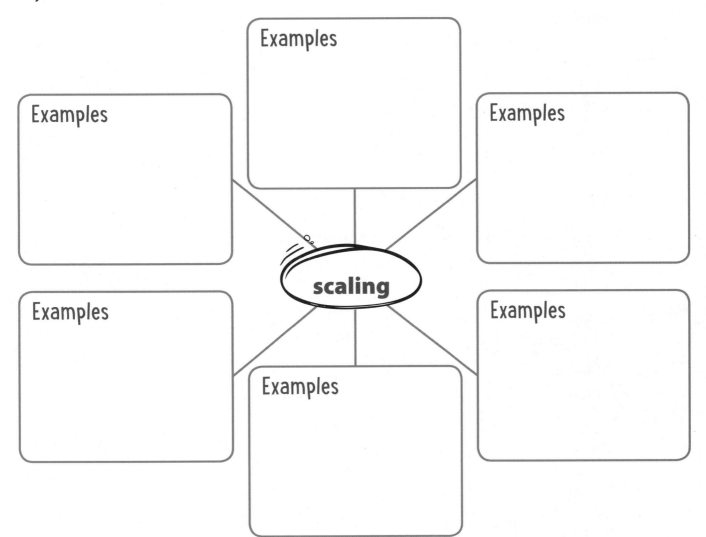

Examples

Examples

Examples

Examples

Examples

Examples

scaling

2 Complete the sentences to describe two kinds of scaling.

Shrinking: When I multiply the whole number 6 by a fraction less than 1, the

product will be ....

Stretching: When I multiply the whole number 6 by a fraction greater than 1,

the product will be ....

Solve.

This bar has a length of 8 units.

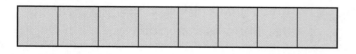

3 This bar shows the length of the 8 units scaled.

a. Use words to describe how the length of 8 units is scaled.

b. Write a multiplication equation to show how the length is scaled.

4 This bar shows the length of 8 units scaled in a different way.

a. Use words to describe how the length of 8 units is scaled.

b. Write a multiplication equation to show how the length is scaled.

Develop Understanding of Multiplication as Scaling

MODEL IT: NUMBER LINES

Try these three problems.

1 The first number line shows $\frac{3}{4}$. Show $\frac{1}{3} \times \frac{3}{4}$ on the second number line.

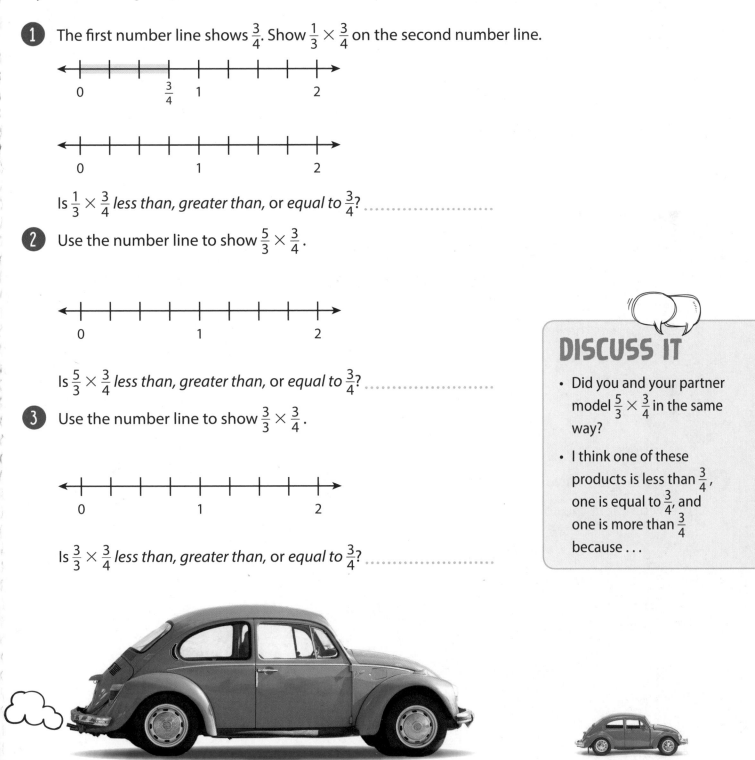

Is $\frac{1}{3} \times \frac{3}{4}$ *less than, greater than,* or *equal to* $\frac{3}{4}$? ....

2 Use the number line to show $\frac{5}{3} \times \frac{3}{4}$.

Is $\frac{5}{3} \times \frac{3}{4}$ *less than, greater than,* or *equal to* $\frac{3}{4}$? ....

3 Use the number line to show $\frac{3}{3} \times \frac{3}{4}$.

Is $\frac{3}{3} \times \frac{3}{4}$ *less than, greater than,* or *equal to* $\frac{3}{4}$? ....

DISCUSS IT

- Did you and your partner model $\frac{5}{3} \times \frac{3}{4}$ in the same way?

- I think one of these products is less than $\frac{3}{4}$, one is equal to $\frac{3}{4}$, and one is more than $\frac{3}{4}$ because . . .

MODEL IT: AREA MODELS

Use an area model to show scaling.

4 Shade the area model to show $\frac{1}{3} \times \frac{3}{4}$.

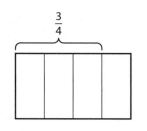

$$\frac{3}{4}$$

Is $\frac{1}{3} \times \frac{3}{4}$ *less than*, *greater than*, or *equal to* $\frac{3}{4}$? ....

DISCUSS IT

- Did you and your partner model $\frac{1}{3} \times \frac{3}{4}$ in the same way?

- I think $\frac{7}{5} \times \frac{3}{4}$ is greater than $\frac{3}{4}$ because . . .

CONNECT IT

Complete the problems below.

5 In problem 1, you modeled $\frac{1}{3} \times \frac{3}{4}$ on a number line, and in problem 4 you used an area model to show the same product. Do both models show the same comparison between $\frac{1}{3} \times \frac{3}{4}$ and $\frac{3}{4}$? Explain.

6 Choose any model you like to show how the product $\frac{3}{2} \times \frac{4}{3}$ compares to $\frac{4}{3}$. Then complete the comparison.

$\frac{3}{2} \times \frac{4}{3}$ is .... $\frac{4}{3}$.

Practice Multiplication as Scaling

Study the Example showing how to use a number line to multiply by fractions less than 1 and greater than 1. Then solve problems 1–6.

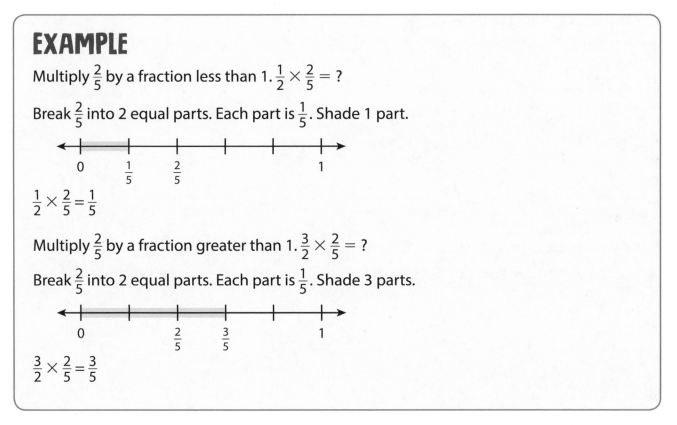

EXAMPLE

Multiply $\frac{2}{5}$ by a fraction less than 1. $\frac{1}{2} \times \frac{2}{5} = ?$

Break $\frac{2}{5}$ into 2 equal parts. Each part is $\frac{1}{5}$. Shade 1 part.

$\frac{1}{2} \times \frac{2}{5} = \frac{1}{5}$

Multiply $\frac{2}{5}$ by a fraction greater than 1. $\frac{3}{2} \times \frac{2}{5} = ?$

Break $\frac{2}{5}$ into 2 equal parts. Each part is $\frac{1}{5}$. Shade 3 parts.

$\frac{3}{2} \times \frac{2}{5} = \frac{3}{5}$

1. When you multiply a whole number by a fraction less than 1, the product is less than the whole number. Does the Example showing $\frac{1}{2} \times \frac{2}{5}$ support a similar rule when multiplying a fraction by a fraction less than 1? Explain.

2. Use the Example showing $\frac{3}{2} \times \frac{2}{5}$. Which statements correctly describe how the product compares to one of its factors?

   Ⓐ $\frac{3}{2} \times \frac{2}{5}$ is one and one-half times $\frac{2}{5}$.

   Ⓑ $\frac{3}{2} \times \frac{2}{5}$ is equal to $\frac{3}{2}$.

   Ⓒ $\frac{3}{2} \times \frac{2}{5}$ is less than $\frac{2}{5}$.

   Ⓓ $\frac{3}{2} \times \frac{2}{5}$ is greater than $\frac{3}{2}$.

   Ⓔ $\frac{3}{2} \times \frac{2}{5}$ is greater than $\frac{2}{5}$.

3 Shade the number line to show $\frac{3}{5} \times \frac{5}{8}$.

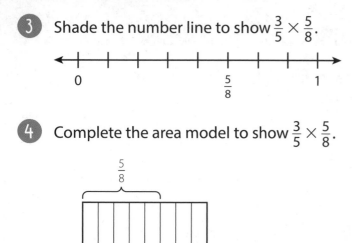

0                    $\frac{5}{8}$ 1

4 Complete the area model to show $\frac{3}{5} \times \frac{5}{8}$.

$\frac{5}{8}$

5 Look at your models in problems 3 and 4. Is $\frac{3}{5} \times \frac{5}{8}$ greater than or less than $\frac{5}{8}$? Is it easier to compare the product to $\frac{5}{8}$ using the number-line model or the area model? Explain.

6 Choose the correct word to fill in each blank below.

a. When you multiply a given fraction by a fraction equal to 1, the product will ____ be equal to the original fraction.

   Ⓐ never   Ⓑ sometimes   Ⓒ always

b. When you multiply a given fraction by a factor less than 1, the product will ____ be greater than the given fraction.

   Ⓐ never   Ⓑ sometimes   Ⓒ always

c. When you multiply a given fraction by a factor greater than 1, the product will ____ be less than 1.

   Ⓐ never   Ⓑ sometimes   Ⓒ always

Refine Ideas About Multiplication as Scaling

APPLY IT

Complete these problems on your own.

1 ANALYZE

Use reasoning to order the following expressions from least to greatest. Do not calculate any of the products. Explain your reasoning.

$\frac{7}{9} \times 348{,}980$ $\frac{12}{11} \times 348{,}980$ $\frac{50}{50} \times 348{,}980$

2 INTERPRET

Two towns are comparing populations. Town A has 285,310 residents, and Town B has $\frac{9}{10} \times 285{,}310$ residents.

To compare the populations of the two towns, Jonah said the population of Town A is nine tenths of the population of Town B. Is he correct? Explain your answer.

3 EXPLAIN

Gillian said that the product of a given number and a fraction is always less than the given number. Is Gillian correct? Explain and give an example.

PAIR/SHARE
Discuss your solutions for these three problems with a partner.

Use what you have learned to complete problem 4.

4 You can compare the size of a product to the size of the factors in a multiplication equation if you know whether the factors are greater than, less than, or equal to 1.

Part A Write a multiplication equation (different than any in this lesson) in which the product is greater than both of its factors. At least one factor should be a fraction. Draw a model to support your answer.

Solution ....

Part B Write a multiplication equation (different from any in this lesson) in which both factors are fractions and the product is less than both of its factors. Draw a model to support your answer.

Solution ....

5 MATH JOURNAL

How does $\frac{4}{4} \times \frac{8}{5}$ compare to $\frac{8}{5}$? Explain your reasoning.

Multiply Fractions in Word Problems

Dear Family,

This week your child is learning about multiplying fractions in word problems.

He or she might see a problem like this:

Michael found $\frac{3}{8}$ of a pizza in the refrigerator. He ate $\frac{2}{3}$ of it. How much of the original whole pizza did Michael eat?

- One way to understand this problem is to draw a picture. Your child could draw $\frac{3}{8}$ of a pizza.

  To show the part of the pizza that Michael ate, your child could shade 2 of the 3 pieces to show $\frac{2}{3}$.

  The shaded parts show how much of the original whole pizza Michael ate. Michael ate $\frac{2}{8}$, or $\frac{1}{4}$, of the original whole pizza.

- Another way your child could solve the problem is to write a multiplication equation.

  $\frac{2}{3}$ of $\frac{3}{8}$ means $\frac{2}{3} \times \frac{3}{8}$.

  $$\frac{2}{3} \times \frac{3}{8} = \frac{2 \times 3}{3 \times 8} = \frac{6}{24}$$

  So, $\frac{6}{24}$ is equivalent to $\frac{2}{8}$, or $\frac{1}{4}$.

The answer is the same using either way to solve the problem. Michael ate $\frac{1}{4}$ of the original whole pizza.

Invite your child to share what he or she knows about multiplying fractions and word problems by doing the following activity together.

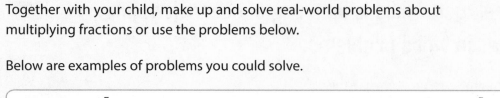

ACTIVITY MULTIPLYING FRACTIONS IN WORD PROBLEMS

Do this activity with your child to multiply fractions in word problems.

Together with your child, make up and solve real-world problems about multiplying fractions or use the problems below.

Below are examples of problems you could solve.

1. Pete found $\frac{5}{6}$ of a party sandwich left in the refrigerator. He took $\frac{1}{2}$ of the $\frac{5}{6}$ of the sandwich to his neighbor. How much of the original sandwich did Pete take to his neighbor?

2. Shawn had $\frac{3}{5}$ of a gallon of paint left in the can. He used $\frac{2}{3}$ of it to paint a cabinet. How much of the gallon of paint did he use?

3. Renee made some money babysitting. She saved $\frac{3}{4}$ of the money. She spent $\frac{2}{5}$ of the money she saved to buy a shirt. What fraction of the money did Renee spend on the shirt?

Answers:
1. $\frac{5}{12}$; **2.** $\frac{6}{15}$ or $\frac{2}{5}$; **3.** $\frac{6}{20}$ or $\frac{3}{10}$

Explore Multiplying Fractions in Word Problems

Now that you have learned how to multiply fractions, you will use what you know in problem situations. Use what you know to try to solve the problem below.

> Grayson lives $\frac{4}{5}$ mile from the park. He has already walked $\frac{3}{4}$ of the way to the park. How far has Grayson walked? Use a visual fraction model to show your thinking.

TRY IT

Math Toolkit
- fraction tiles or circles
- fraction bars
- fraction models
- grid paper
- number lines
- index cards
- multiplication models

DISCUSS IT

Ask your partner: Can you explain that again?

Tell your partner: A model I used was . . . It helped me . . .

CONNECT IT

 LOOK BACK

Explain how you can use a visual model to show how far Grayson has already walked.

 LOOK AHEAD

You can use what you know about multiplying fractions to think through and solve word problems involving fractions. Consider this word problem:

Ehrin spills $\frac{1}{2}$ of a $\frac{3}{4}$-pound box of cereal. How many pounds did she spill?

a. Finding $\frac{1}{2}$ of a quantity is the same as multiplying by $\frac{1}{2}$. What equation could you write for the cereal problem? Use p for the unknown amount in the problem.

b. Estimate the product. Is the amount of cereal Ehrin spills on the floor more than $\frac{3}{4}$ pound or less than $\frac{3}{4}$ pound? Why?

c. Complete the area model to show the problem. How many pounds of cereal did Ehrin spill on

the floor? .... pound

3 REFLECT

How does writing an equation, making an estimate, and drawing a model help you think through the problem?

....

....

....

Prepare for Multiplying Fractions in Word Problems

1 Think about what you know about fractions. Fill in each box. Use words, numbers, and pictures. Show as many ideas as you can.

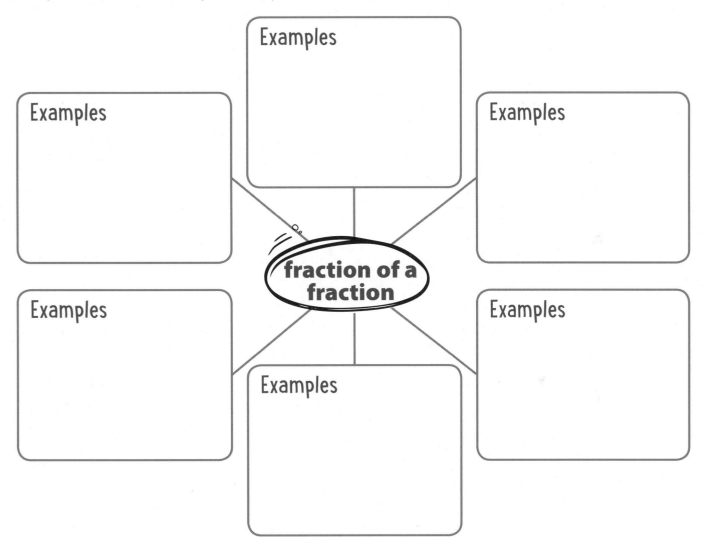

Examples

Examples

Examples

Examples

fraction of a fraction

Examples

Examples

2 Write a multiplication expression that can be used to find $\frac{1}{5}$ of $\frac{3}{8}$.

Why is the product less than $\frac{3}{8}$?

③ Solve the problem. Show your work.

Lola lives $\frac{3}{4}$ mile from the basketball court. She has already walked $\frac{2}{3}$ of the way to the basketball court. How far has Lola walked? Use a visual fraction model to show your thinking.

Solution ....

④ Check your answer. Show your work.

Develop Multiplying Fractions in Word Problems

Read and try to solve the problem below.

> Brandon's mother left $\frac{3}{4}$ of a pizza on the counter. If Brandon eats $\frac{2}{3}$ of the leftover pizza, how much of the whole pizza did Brandon eat?

TRY IT

Math Toolkit
- fraction tiles or circles
- fraction bars
- fraction models
- grid paper
- number lines
- index cards
- multiplication models

DISCUSS IT

Ask your partner: How did you get started?

Tell your partner: I am not sure how to find the answer because . . .

Explore different ways to understand strategies for solving word problems that involve finding a fraction of a fraction.

> Brandon's mother left $\frac{3}{4}$ of a pizza on the counter. If Brandon eats $\frac{2}{3}$ of the leftover pizza, how much of the whole pizza did Brandon eat?

PICTURE IT

You can draw a picture to help you understand the problem.

Show $\frac{3}{4}$ of a pizza.

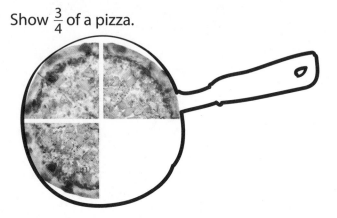

Since Brandon eats $\frac{2}{3}$ of what is left, outline 2 of the 3 pieces that are left. You can see from the outlined parts how much of the whole pizza Brandon ate.

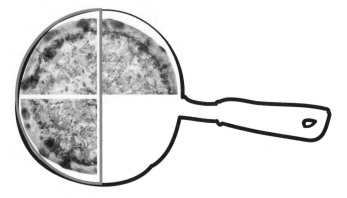

MODEL IT

You can write an equation to help you understand the problem.

You need to find a fraction of a fraction: $\frac{2}{3}$ of $\frac{3}{4}$ of a pizza.

$\frac{2}{3}$ of $\frac{3}{4}$ means $\frac{2}{3} \times \frac{3}{4}$.

$$\frac{2}{3} \times \frac{3}{4} = \frac{2 \times 3}{3 \times 4}$$

CONNECT IT

Now you will use the problem from the previous page to help you understand strategies for solving word problems that involve finding a fraction of a fraction.

 Look at **Picture It**. Why do you outline 2 of the 3 parts of the pizza?

2 How much of the whole pizza did Brandon eat? Explain your reasoning.

3 Look at **Model It**. How do you know that you should multiply $\frac{2}{3} \times \frac{3}{4}$?

4 What is $\frac{2 \times 3}{3 \times 4}$? ....

Is this product the same as your answer to problem 2? Explain.

5 What strategies can you use to solve a word problem that involves finding a fraction of a fraction?

 REFLECT

Look back at your **Try It**, strategies by classmates, and **Picture It** and **Model It**. Which models or strategies do you like best for solving word problems that involve finding a fraction of a fraction? Explain.

....

....

....

APPLY IT

Use what you just learned to solve these problems.

7 Lewis walked $\frac{8}{10}$ of a mile. Todd walked $\frac{3}{4}$ of the way with Lewis. How many miles did Todd walk with Lewis? Show your work.

Solution

8 Stan has a recipe for vegetable lasagna that calls for $\frac{9}{16}$ pound of eggplant. He wants to make a batch of lasagna that is $\frac{2}{3}$ of the amount of the recipe. How much eggplant will Stan need? Show your work.

Solution

9 Jamie worked $\frac{5}{6}$ hour filing papers for her mother. She listened to music for $\frac{4}{5}$ of the time she spent filing. How much time did Jamie spend listening to music? Show your work.

Solution

Practice Multiplying Fractions in Word Problems

Study the Example showing one way to solve a word problem with fractions. Then solve problems 1–5.

EXAMPLE

Vicky's favorite beach towel is green and white and has a fish design. The green part covers $\frac{5}{8}$ of the towel. A fish design is drawn on $\frac{3}{5}$ of that part. What part of the towel has a fish design?

You can draw a picture.

Show a towel with $\frac{5}{8}$ shaded green.

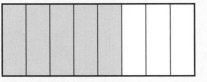

Draw fish on $\frac{3}{5}$ of the green part.

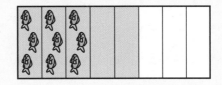

Because 3 of the 8 parts of the towel have fish drawn on them, $\frac{3}{8}$ of the towel has a fish design.

1. You can also write an equation to solve the Example. Write the numbers to complete the equation showing what part of the towel has the fish design.

$\frac{3}{5}$ of $\frac{5}{8}$ means $\frac{3}{5} \times \frac{5}{8}$.

$$\frac{3}{5} \times \frac{\square}{\square} = \frac{\square \times 5}{\square \times 8} = \frac{\square}{\square}$$

2. Is your answer to problem 1 the same as the answer of $\frac{3}{8}$ shown in the Example? Explain.

3 Suppose that the green part of Vicky's towel covers $\frac{4}{5}$ of the towel and the fish design is drawn on $\frac{3}{4}$ of that part. Draw a picture to find the part of the towel that has the fish design. Then write the answer.

Solution

4 Write an equation to show the answer to problem 3.

Solution

5 Write a word problem that can be solved by finding the product $\frac{1}{6} \times \frac{3}{8}$. Then solve your problem.

Problem

Show your work.

Solution

Develop Multiplying with Mixed Numbers in Word Problems

Read and try to solve the problem below.

> Janie has a rectangular garden that is $2\frac{3}{4}$ yards in length and 1 yard in width. She grows roses in $\frac{1}{2}$ of her garden.
>
> How many square yards in Janie's garden has roses?

TRY IT

Math Toolkit
- fraction tiles or circles
- fraction bars
- fraction models
- grid paper
- number lines
- index cards
- multiplication models

DISCUSS IT

Ask your partner: Do you agree with me? Why or why not?

Tell your partner: At first, I thought . . .

Explore different ways to understand multiplying fractions and mixed numbers.

> Janie has a rectangular garden that is $2\frac{3}{4}$ yards in length and 1 yard in width. She grows roses in $\frac{1}{2}$ of her garden. How many square yards in Janie's garden has roses?

PICTURE IT

You can use an area model to help you understand the problem.

The purple shaded region of the area model shows **half** of $2\frac{3}{4}$.

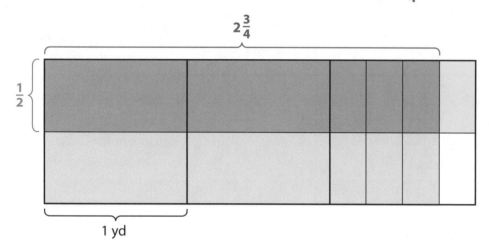

MODEL IT

You can write equations to model the problem.

You can write $2\frac{3}{4}$ as a fraction.

$$2\frac{3}{4} = 2 + \frac{3}{4}$$
$$= \frac{8}{4} + \frac{3}{4}$$
$$= \frac{11}{4}$$

You need to find a fraction of a fraction: $\frac{1}{2}$ of $\frac{11}{4}$ square yards.

$\frac{1}{2}$ of $\frac{11}{4}$ means $\frac{1}{2} \times \frac{11}{4}$.

$$\frac{1}{2} \times \frac{11}{4} = \frac{1 \times 11}{2 \times 4}$$

©Curriculum Associates, LLC   Copying is not permitted.

CONNECT IT

Now you will use the problem from the previous page to understand how to multiply fractions and mixed numbers.

1 Use the last equation in **Model It** to find the area of Janie's garden that has roses.

Janie's garden has .... square yards of roses.

Explain how you can use the area model in **Picture It** to find the area of Janie's garden that has roses.

2 Look at the first equation in **Model It**. Why is the mixed number rewritten as a fraction?

3 How can you multiply $\frac{1}{2} \times 2\frac{3}{4}$ without changing $2\frac{3}{4}$ to a fraction?

What is $\frac{1}{2} \times 2$? ....   What is $\frac{1}{2} \times \frac{3}{4}$? ....

Add the two products. .... + ... = ...

Is this result the same as your answer to problem 1? ....

4 How can you multiply a mixed number by a fraction?

5 REFLECT

Look back at your **Try It**, strategies by classmates, and **Picture It** and **Model It**. Which models or strategies do you like best for multiplying fractions and mixed numbers? Explain.

....

....

....

APPLY IT

Use what you just learned to solve these problems.

6 Izzy has $3\frac{1}{2}$ yards of rope. She uses $\frac{3}{5}$ of the rope to attach a tire swing to a tree in her yard. How many yards of rope does Izzy use for the tire swing? Show your work.

Solution ....

7 Colin has a chain that is $\frac{5}{6}$ foot long. He adds links to his chain so that it is $4\frac{1}{2}$ times as long as the original chain. How many feet long is his chain now? Show your work.

Solution ....

8 George has $1\frac{5}{9}$ yards of fabric. He plans to use $\frac{3}{4}$ of the fabric to make a pillow. How many yards of fabric will George use for the pillow?

Ⓐ $1\frac{6}{36}$

Ⓑ $1\frac{8}{13}$

Ⓒ $1\frac{17}{36}$

Ⓓ $1\frac{5}{12}$

Practice Multiplying with Mixed Numbers

Study the Example showing one way to solve a word problem with a mixed number. Then solve problems 1–5.

EXAMPLE

Mr. Urrego is painting his deck for the summer. He has painted a rectangular area that is $3\frac{1}{4}$ yards long and $\frac{2}{3}$ yard wide. How many square yards of deck are painted?

You can use an area model.

The larger sections of the area model are $\frac{1}{3} \times 1 = \frac{1}{3}$ square yard.

The smaller sections of the area model are $\frac{1}{3} \times \frac{1}{4} = \frac{1}{12}$ square yard.

The model shows the number of square yards painted is:

$$\frac{2}{3} + \frac{2}{3} + \frac{2}{3} + \frac{2}{12} = \frac{6}{3} + \frac{2}{12} = 2 + \frac{2}{12} = 2\frac{2}{12}$$

1 Write the missing numbers to complete the multiplication equation showing how much of the deck is painted.

Multiply the length and width of the painted area:

$$3\frac{1}{4} \times \frac{\square}{\square} = \left(\square \times \frac{2}{3}\right) + \left(\frac{\square}{\square} \times \frac{2}{3}\right) = \frac{\square}{3} + \frac{2}{\square} = \square \frac{2}{12}$$

.... square yards

2 To multiply by a mixed number, you can also write the mixed number as a fraction and then multiply. Use this method to find the product $3\frac{1}{4} \times \frac{2}{3}$ in order to find how many square yards of the deck are painted. Show your work.

Solution ....

3 On Saturday, Kira ran $\frac{3}{4}$ mile. On Sunday, she ran $2\frac{1}{2}$ times as far as on Saturday. Use a multiplication equation to find how far Kira ran on Sunday. Show your work.

Solution ....

4 Use a visual model to show another way to find the distance Kira ran on Sunday.

5 The multipurpose room at the Cortez School is being set up for the annual book sale. Graphic novels will be displayed in a rectangular area $1\frac{1}{4}$ yards long and $\frac{3}{4}$ yard wide. Will the graphic novels be displayed in an area greater than or less than 1 square yard? Show your work.

Solution ....

Refine Multiplying Fractions in Word Problems

Complete the Example below. Then solve problems 1–8.

EXAMPLE

Chris uses $4\frac{1}{4}$ tubes of paint. Nico uses $1\frac{1}{2}$ times as much paint as Chris. How much paint did Nico use?

Look at how you can solve this problem using equations.

$$4\frac{1}{4} \times 1 = 4\frac{1}{4}$$

$$4\frac{1}{4} \times \frac{1}{2} = \left(4 \times \frac{1}{2}\right) + \left(\frac{1}{4} \times \frac{1}{2}\right) = 2 + \frac{1}{8}$$

$$4\frac{1}{4} + 2 + \frac{1}{8} = 6\frac{1}{4} + \frac{1}{8} = 6\frac{2}{8} + \frac{1}{8} = 6\frac{3}{8}$$

Solution ....

Breaking apart a mixed number happens twice in this problem.

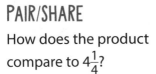

PAIR/SHARE

How does the product compare to $4\frac{1}{4}$?

APPLY IT

1 Josh exercises at the gym $3\frac{3}{4}$ hours a week. He spends $\frac{2}{5}$ of his time at the gym lifting weights. How many hours a week does Josh spend lifting weights at the gym? Show your work.

How do I know what operation to use to solve this problem?

PAIR/SHARE

What is a reasonable estimate for the number of hours Josh lifts weights each week?

Solution ....

2 A field is in the shape of a rectangle $\frac{5}{6}$ mile long and $\frac{3}{4}$ mile wide. What is the area of the field? Show your work.

What model can I use to help understand this problem?

PAIR/SHARE
Can you solve this problem in another way?

Solution ....

3 Ari had $\frac{3}{4}$ of a bag of popcorn. His friends ate $\frac{1}{2}$ of his popcorn. What fraction of the whole bag of popcorn did Ari's friends eat?

What equation can I write to solve this problem?

Ⓐ $\frac{1}{4}$

Ⓑ $\frac{3}{8}$

Ⓒ $\frac{5}{4}$

Ⓓ $\frac{3}{2}$

Kayla chose Ⓐ as the correct answer. How did she get that answer?

PAIR/SHARE
Does Kayla's answer make sense?

4 On Sunday, Kristen bought a carton of 24 bottles of water.

- On Monday, Kristen drank $\frac{1}{6}$ of the bottles in the carton.

- On Tuesday, Kristen drank $\frac{1}{4}$ of the bottles that remained in the carton after Monday.

Which picture represents the number of bottles of water remaining in the carton after Kristen drank her water on Tuesday?

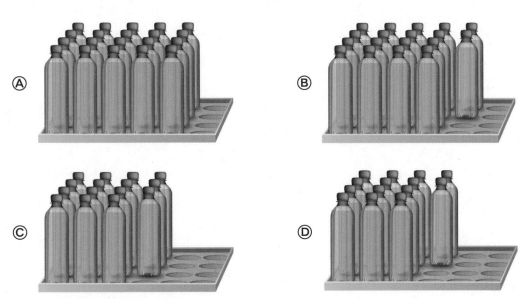

5 Milo's pancake recipe makes 9 servings. It calls for $\frac{3}{4}$ cup milk. Milo wants to make 6 servings. How much milk will he need?

.... cup

6 Jillian draws a rectangle with the dimensions shown below. What is the area of Jillian's rectangle?

$2\frac{2}{5}$ units

$4\frac{1}{8}$ units

Solution ....

7 Lily paints 3 trees for a wall mural. The middle tree is $2\frac{1}{2}$ ft tall. The tree on the left is $\frac{3}{4}$ as tall as the middle tree. The tree on the right is $1\frac{3}{4}$ times as tall as the middle tree. How tall is each tree? Show your work.

Solution ....

....

8 MATH JOURNAL

Write a word problem for the expression $3\frac{1}{2} \times \frac{1}{2}$. Use a visual model or an equation to show how to solve your problem.

 SELF CHECK Go back to the Unit 3 Opener and see what you can check off.

Understand Division with Unit Fractions

LESSON 23

Dear Family,

This week your child is exploring division with unit fractions.

A **unit fraction** is a fraction that has 1 as the numerator. $\frac{1}{6}$ and $\frac{1}{4}$ are examples of unit fractions. To learn about division with unit fractions, your child might see a problem like the one below.

> *A butcher wants to divide 3 pounds of meat into packages that will each contain $\frac{1}{2}$ pound of meat. How many packages can she make?*

This problem can be solved by finding $3 \div \frac{1}{2}$. It can be helpful to use a number line model to understand the problem.

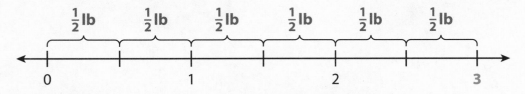

The model shows that $3 \div \frac{1}{2} = 6$. The butcher can make 6 packages that each contain $\frac{1}{2}$ pound of meat.

Another way to say this is that the butcher can make 2 packages of meat per pound. An equation that shows this is $3 \times 2 = 6$.

So, $3 \div \frac{1}{2} = 6$, and $3 \times 2 = 6$. Your child is learning that division and multiplication with fractions are related, just like division and multiplication with whole numbers are related.

Invite your child to share what he or she knows about division with unit fractions by doing the following activity together.

ACTIVITY DIVIDING WITH UNIT FRACTIONS

Do this activity with your child to understand division with unit fractions.

Work together with your child to solve real-life problems involving division with unit fractions.

• Together with your child, use the picture to solve the problem below.

1. Suppose we want to give each person in our family half of a sandwich. The sandwiches are shown below. How many people can we feed with these 4 sandwiches? Do we have enough for our family, too many, or too few?

• Look for similar situations in everyday life that involve dividing with a unit fraction. Below are some examples of problems you could solve.

2. If you divide 2 hours of piano practice into sessions of $\frac{1}{2}$ hour each, how many sessions do you have to practice?

3. One lap around the track is $\frac{1}{4}$ mile. How many laps do you need to do to run 3 miles?

Answers:

1. $4 \div \frac{1}{2} = 8$; You can feed 8 people with the four sandwiches; **2.** $2 \div \frac{1}{2} = 4$ sessions; **3.** $3 \div \frac{1}{4} = 12$ laps

Explore Division with Unit Fractions

How is dividing with fractions related to multiplying with fractions?

MODEL IT

Complete the problems below.

1 Mrs. Cook wants to share $\frac{1}{4}$ pound of fish equally among 3 cats. How much fish will each cat get?

a. Draw on the area model to solve the problem.

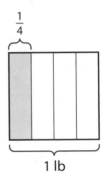

b. Each cat will get .... pound of fish.

c. Complete the division equation to match your area model.

$\frac{1}{4} \div 3 = $ ....

2 Look at the problem about Mrs. Cook again. Complete the statements below to solve the same division problem using multiplication.

a. Each cat will get .... of $\frac{1}{4}$ pound of fish.

b. Write a multiplication equation to tell how much fish each cat will get.

DISCUSS IT

- Compare your model and equations to your partner's model and equations. How are they alike? How are they different?

- I think $\frac{1}{4} \div 3$ is the same as $\frac{1}{3} \times \frac{1}{4}$ because . . .

MODEL IT
Complete the problems below.

3 Mr. Putnam wants to cut a 3-foot rope into $\frac{1}{4}$-foot pieces.
How many $\frac{1}{4}$-foot pieces can he cut?

a. Draw on the bar model to solve the problem.

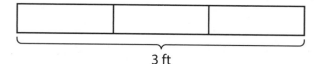

3 ft

b. Mr. Putnam can cut .... pieces of rope that are
each $\frac{1}{4}$ foot long.

c. Complete the division equation to match your model.

$3 \div \frac{1}{4} =$ ....

4 Look at your model again. Complete the statements below to solve
the same division problem using multiplication.

a. There are .... fourths in each whole foot.

b. Write a multiplication equation to find the number of fourths
in 3 feet.

....

c. Mr. Putnam can cut .... $\frac{1}{4}$-foot pieces of rope.

5 REFLECT

Explain what it means to divide 3 by $\frac{1}{4}$. Include a different real-world
example from the problem above in your explanation.

....

....

....

....

DISCUSS IT

• Look at problems 3 and 4.
Why can both a division
equation and a
multiplication equation be
used?

• I think dividing by a unit
fraction is like dividing by a
whole number because . . .
I think it is different
because . . .

Prepare for Division with Unit Fractions

1 Think about what you know about unit fractions. Fill in each box. Use words, numbers, and pictures. Show as many ideas as you can.

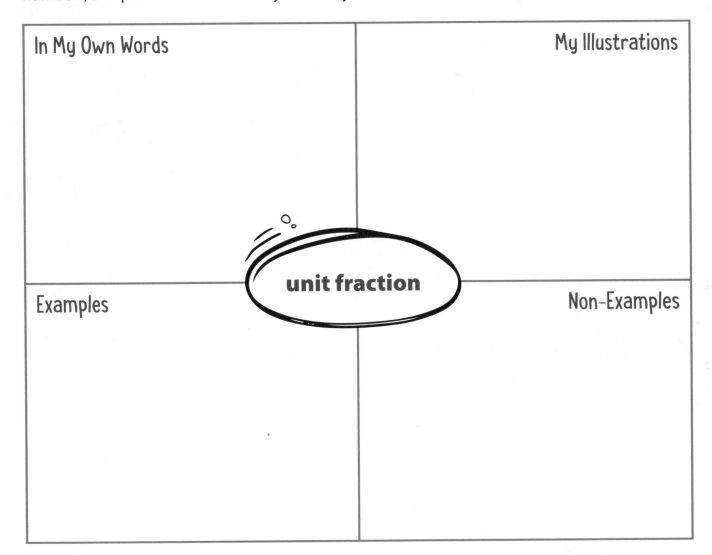

In My Own Words	My Illustrations
Examples	**Non-Examples**

(center: unit fraction)

2 Shade the fraction model to show a unit fraction. Write the unit fraction.

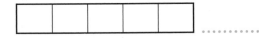

Solve.

3 Mai See wants to share $\frac{1}{3}$ of a cake equally among 3 people. How much of the cake will each person get?

a. Draw on the area model to solve the problem.

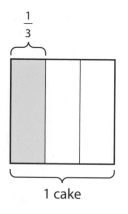

1 cake

b. Complete the division equation to match your area model.

$\frac{1}{3} \div 3 = $ ....

c. Each person will get .... of the cake.

4 Look at your area model again. Complete the statements below to solve the division problem using multiplication.

a. Each person will get .... of $\frac{1}{3}$ of the cake.

b. Write a multiplication equation to tell how much of the cake each person will get.

Develop Understanding of Division with Unit Fractions

MODEL IT: AREA MODELS

Try these two problems.

1 Jemma made 5 cups of pancake batter. She uses a scoop that holds $\frac{1}{3}$ cup to pour batter onto the skillet to make each large pancake. Use the model to show how many large pancakes Jemma can make.

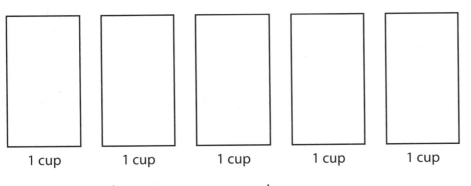

| 1 cup | 1 cup | 1 cup | 1 cup | 1 cup |

Jemma can make .... pancakes.

Explain why your model represents $5 \div \frac{1}{3}$.

2 Suppose Jemma uses $\frac{1}{3}$ cup of pancake batter to make 4 mini pancakes. Use the model to find the fraction of a cup of batter used for each mini pancake.

Each mini pancake uses .... cup of batter.

Explain why your model represents the quotient $\frac{1}{3} \div 4$.

1 cup

DISCUSS IT

• How did you and your partner model the division problems?

• I think $5 \div \frac{1}{3}$ is equal to 5×3 because . . . I think $\frac{1}{3} \div 4$ is equal to $\frac{1}{3} \times \frac{1}{4}$ because . . .

MODEL IT: NUMBER LINES

Use number lines to show dividing with unit fractions.

 Circle the quotient that matches the question. Then model the quotient on the number line. Write the division equation that represents your model.

a. What is $\frac{1}{4}$ divided into 2 equal parts? $2 \div \frac{1}{4}$ OR $\frac{1}{4} \div 2$

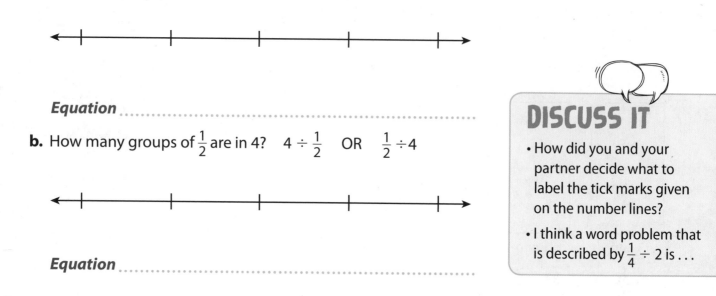

Equation ....

b. How many groups of $\frac{1}{2}$ are in 4? $4 \div \frac{1}{2}$ OR $\frac{1}{2} \div 4$

Equation ....

DISCUSS IT

• How did you and your partner decide what to label the tick marks given on the number lines?

• I think a word problem that is described by $\frac{1}{4} \div 2$ is . . .

CONNECT IT

Complete the problems below.

4 Look at the area models and the number lines. What do they show about how the quotient compares to the dividend when you divide a whole number by a unit fraction and when you divide a unit fraction by a whole number?

 Use any model to find $5 \div \frac{1}{2}$.

$5 \div \frac{1}{2} =$

Practice Division with Unit Fractions

Study how the Example shows dividing a whole number by a unit fraction. Then solve problems 1–6.

EXAMPLE

Teams of students in Mr. Reed's classroom decorate rectangular bulletin boards to show their team name, colors, and mascot. Each team uses $\frac{1}{5}$ of a bulletin board. The team decorations fill 2 bulletin boards. How many teams are there in all?

The 2 large rectangles represent the 2 bulletin boards.

Each team's decorations use $\frac{1}{5}$ of a board, so each rectangle is divided into 5 equal sections.

From the model, you can write the division equation: $2 \div \frac{1}{5} = 10$

You can also write the multiplication equation: $2 \times 5 = 10$

Both equations show 10 teams in all.

1　Explain how the model in the Example shows $2 \div \frac{1}{5} = 10$.

2　Explain how the model in the Example shows $2 \times 5 = 10$.

3　Suppose Mr. Reed's class has 3 full rectangular bulletin boards showing team decorations. How many teams would there be in all? Show your solution by writing both a division equation and a multiplication equation.

> ### Vocabulary
>
> **unit fraction** a fraction with a numerator of 1.
>
> Examples: $\frac{1}{2}, \frac{1}{3}, \frac{1}{4}$

4 Mr. Reed put 3 students on each team. The teams divides its $\frac{1}{5}$-board space equally so each student decorates the same amount of a board. Complete the steps below to see what fraction of a rectangular bulletin board each student decorates.

a. Use the square at the right. Shade $\frac{1}{5}$ of the square to show $\frac{1}{5}$ of the board for one team.

b. Divide the square into 3 equal parts to represent 3 students on each team.

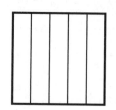

c. Shade $\frac{1}{3}$ of the square so that the overlapping shading represents 1 student.

d. What fraction of the board does each student decorate? ....

e. $\frac{1}{5} \div 3 =$ ....

5 Look at the model in problem 4. Write the multiplication equation you can also use to find $\frac{1}{3}$ of $\frac{1}{5}$.

6 a. Write a word problem that can be represented by the quotient $3 \div \frac{1}{3}$.

b. Use the number line below to solve your problem. Then write a multiplication equation that also solves the problem.

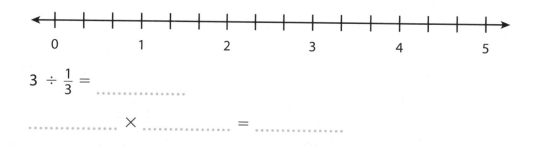

$3 \div \frac{1}{3} =$ ....

.... $\times$ .... $=$ ....

Refine Ideas About Division with Unit Fractions

APPLY IT

Complete these problems on your own.

 COMPARE

Draw a model to represent $\frac{1}{4} \div 4$ and a model to represent $\frac{1}{4} \times \frac{1}{4}$.
Explain the relationship between the two expressions.

 ANALYZE

Mary has 12 boards. She cuts each board into pieces that are
each $\frac{1}{3}$ of a board long. Helena tells Mary that $12 \div \frac{1}{3}$ is 4. Draw a
model and use words to explain why Helena's statement is not
reasonable.

3 **JUSTIFY**

Show that $\frac{1}{2} \div 3 = \frac{1}{6}$ by using a model. Explain why the quotient
is less than the number you started with, $\frac{1}{2}$.

PAIR/SHARE
Discuss your solutions to
these three problems with
a partner.

Use what you have learned to complete problem 4.

4 Choose one of the following problems to solve.
Circle the problem you choose.

Drew wants to run at least 6 miles this month. He plans to run $\frac{1}{4}$ mile each day. How many days will it take Drew to run 6 miles?

Maya made $\frac{1}{2}$ quart of strawberry jam. She plans to share it equally among 4 friends. How much jam will each friend get?

Part A Draw a model to represent the problem.

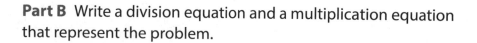

Part B Write a division equation and a multiplication equation that represent the problem.

5 **MATH JOURNAL**

Find $2 \div \frac{1}{3}$. Write a word problem and use a visual model to show the problem.

Divide Unit Fractions in Word Problems

Dear Family,

This week your child is learning about dividing with unit fractions in word problems.

He or she might see a word problem like the one below.

Molly used $\frac{1}{4}$ square yard of fabric to decorate 4 flags. She used an equal amount of fabric for each flag. How much fabric did she use for each flag?

This problem can be solved by finding $\frac{1}{4} \div 4$.
One way to understand this problem is to use a model.

The square shown at the right represents 1 whole square yard of fabric. The shaded rectangle represents the $\frac{1}{4}$ square yard that Molly used to decorate the 4 flags.

You can divide the shaded rectangle into 4 equal parts to represent the 4 flags Molly decorated.

The part shaded dark blue shows the amount used for one flag. 1 out of 16 parts of the whole square yard is used for 1 flag. Molly used $\frac{1}{16}$ square yard of fabric for each flag.

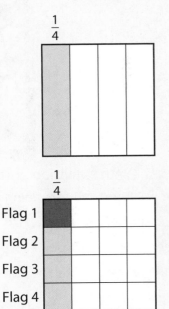

Your child can also write a division equation to solve the problem.

$$\frac{1}{4} \div 4 = \frac{1}{16}$$

Invite your child to share what he or she knows about dividing with unit fractions in word problems by doing the following activity together.

ACTIVITY DIVIDING BY UNIT FRACTIONS

Do this activity with your child to divide by unit fractions in word problems.

Materials yardstick, tape measure, or ruler

- Together with your child, solve the problem below about dividing by a unit fraction.

    How many square tiles are needed to make a border along a wall? Each tile measures $\frac{1}{3}$ foot on each side, and the wall is 6 feet long.

- Now suppose you are going to use the tiles to make a border along a wall in your own house. First, measure to find the length of the wall in feet. Then round your measurement to the nearest foot. Last, divide that number by $\frac{1}{3}$ to find the number of tiles you would need.

Answer: $6 \div \frac{1}{3} = 18$ tiles

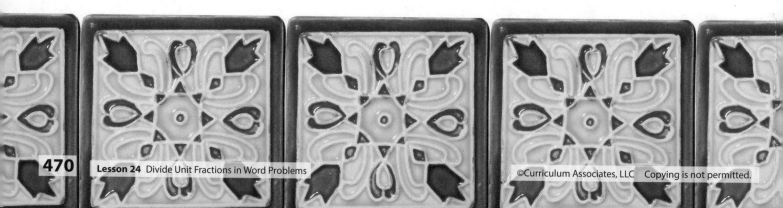

Explore Dividing Unit Fractions in Word Problems

Previously, you learned about what it means to divide with unit fractions. Use what you know to try to solve the problem below.

> Micah is running a 6-mile race.
> There are water stops every $\frac{1}{2}$ mile and at the 6-mile finish line.
> How many water stops are there in all? Use a visual model to show your solution.

TRY IT

Math Toolkit
- fraction bars
- fraction models
- number lines
- grid paper
- index cards
- sticky notes

DISCUSS IT

Ask your partner: Why did you choose that strategy?

Tell your partner: A model I used was . . . It helped me . . .

CONNECT IT

 LOOK BACK

How many water stops are there in all? Explain how you can use a number line to support your answer.

 LOOK AHEAD

On the previous page, you used a visual model to solve a word problem involving dividing a whole number by a unit fraction. You can also use equations to represent and solve these types of problems. Consider this word problem.

Micah now runs in a 5-mile race. There are water stops every $\frac{1}{3}$ mile and at the 5-mile finish line in this new race. How many water stops are there in all?

a. Complete the division equation below.

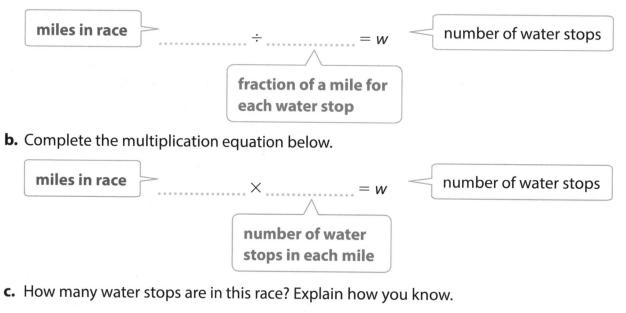

miles in race .... ÷ .... = w number of water stops

fraction of a mile for each water stop

b. Complete the multiplication equation below.

miles in race .... × .... = w number of water stops

number of water stops in each mile

c. How many water stops are in this race? Explain how you know.

 REFLECT

Explain what it means to divide 5 by $\frac{1}{3}$, or $5 \div \frac{1}{3}$.

Prepare for Dividing Unit Fractions in Word Problems

1 Think about what you know about fraction models. Fill in each box. Use words, numbers, and pictures. Show as many ideas as you can.

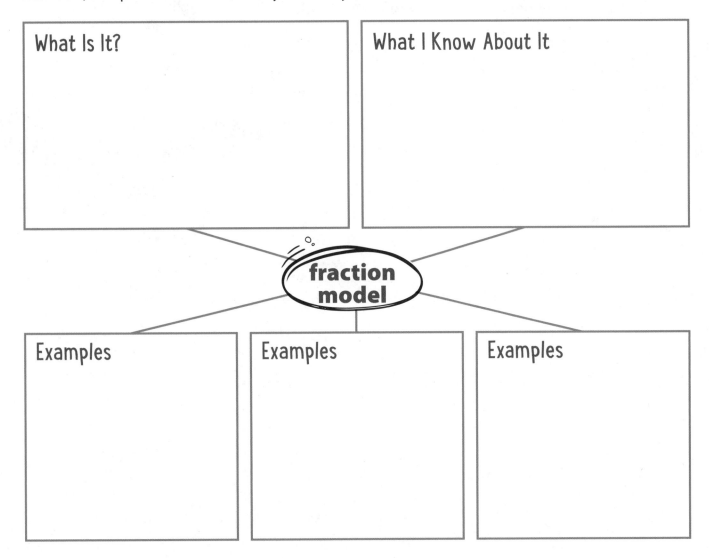

What Is It?

What I Know About It

fraction model

Examples

Examples

Examples

2 Draw a fraction model to show the expression $4 \div \frac{1}{2}$.

Solve the problem. Show your work.

Adela has a ribbon that is 2 yards long. She cuts the ribbon into pieces that are $\frac{1}{4}$ yard long. How many pieces of ribbon are there in all? Use a visual model to show your solution.

Solution ....

4 Check your answer. Show your work.

Develop Dividing a Unit Fraction by a Whole Number

Read and try to solve the problem below.

> Piper uses $\frac{1}{6}$ yard of ribbon to make a border around an equilateral triangle. How long is the piece of ribbon that Piper uses for each side?

TRY IT

Math Toolkit
- fraction bars
- fraction models
- number lines
- grid paper
- ribbon or yarn
- index cards

DISCUSS IT

Ask your partner: How did you get started?

Tell your partner: I knew . . . so I . . .

Explore different ways to understand dividing a unit fraction by a whole number to solve word problems.

> Piper uses $\frac{1}{6}$ yard of ribbon to make a border around an equilateral triangle. How long is the piece of ribbon that Piper uses for each side?

PICTURE IT

You can draw a picture to help understand the problem.

Draw a **1-yard** length of ribbon and then draw and label a $\frac{1}{6}$-yard length.

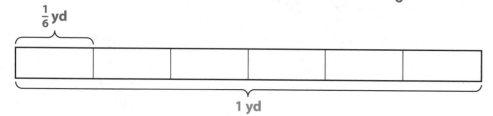

Divide the $\frac{1}{6}$-yard length into **3 equal parts**, one for each side of the equilateral triangle.

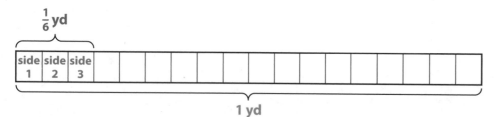

MODEL IT

You can use equations to model the problem.

Write a division equation.

$$\frac{1}{6} \div 3 = s \quad \longleftarrow \text{length of each part}$$

length of ribbon   **number of equal parts**

Write a multiplication equation.

$$\frac{1}{3} \times \frac{1}{6} = s \quad \longleftarrow \text{length of each part}$$

fraction of the ribbon   **length of ribbon**

CONNECT IT

Now you will use the problem from the previous page to help you understand how to divide a unit fraction by a whole number.

1 Look at **Picture It**. What does the first diagram show? What whole is being divided?

Why does the second diagram show each $\frac{1}{6}$-yard section divided into 3 equal parts?

2 Look at **Model It**. How does each equation relate to the second diagram in **Picture It**?

3 How long is the piece of ribbon Piper uses for each side of the triangle?

4 What is $\frac{1}{6} \div 3$? How can you use a multiplication equation different from the one shown in **Model It** to check that your answer is correct?

5 REFLECT

Look back at your **Try It**, strategies by classmates, and **Picture It** and **Model It**. Which models or strategies do you like best for dividing a unit fraction by a whole number to solve word problems? Explain.

....

....

....

Lesson 24 Divide Unit Fractions in Word Problems   **477**

APPLY IT

Use what you just learned to solve these problems.

6 Felipe has $\frac{1}{4}$ of a pizza. He wants to share it equally with a friend. How much of the original whole pizza will each of them get? Show your work.

Solution ....

7 Angela uses $\frac{1}{3}$ of her rectangular flower garden for roses. She plants equal rectangular areas of red, white, pink, and orange roses in this part of the garden. What fraction of the whole garden has red roses? Draw a model and write a division equation to represent and solve the problem.

Solution ....

8 Look at problem 7. Which multiplication expressions can be used to represent the situation or check the division equation?

Ⓐ $\frac{1}{4} \times \frac{1}{3}$

Ⓑ $4 \times \frac{1}{3}$

Ⓒ $\frac{1}{12} \times 4$

Ⓓ 3×4

Ⓔ $3 \times \frac{1}{4}$

Practice Dividing a Unit Fraction by a Whole Number

Study the Example showing one way to solve a word problem involving dividing a fraction by a whole number. Then solve problems 1–5.

EXAMPLE

Felicia makes $\frac{1}{2}$ gallon of fruit punch. She pours an equal amount into 8 glasses. What fraction of a gallon of fruit punch is in each glass?

Find $\frac{1}{2} \div 8$.

The model shows a rectangle divided into halves and then divided into 8 equal parts. There are a total of 16 parts, and one part is the amount of fruit punch in 1 glass.

$$\frac{1}{2} \div 8 = \frac{1}{16}$$

The amount in 1 glass is $\frac{1}{16}$ gallon.

$\frac{1}{2}$

glass 1
glass 2
glass 3
glass 4
glass 5
glass 6
glass 7
glass 8

1 What multiplication equation could you write to solve the Example?

2 Suppose Felicia had made $\frac{1}{4}$ gallon of punch and poured an equal amount into 8 glasses. Would the amount in each glass be more or less than $\frac{1}{16}$ gallon? Explain how the model in the Example would change to show this.

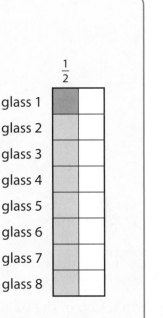

3 Donal buys a $\frac{1}{4}$-pound package of cheese. There are 8 slices of cheese in the package. Each slice has the same weight. What fraction of a pound is each slice? Draw a model and write a division equation to represent and solve the problem.

Solution ....

4 Student volunteers are getting ready to hand out programs at a talent show. Leah and Tomas are each given $\frac{1}{2}$ of a stack of programs to hand out. Leah divides her $\frac{1}{2}$ equally among herself and 2 friends. What fraction of the original stack of programs do Leah and her 2 friends each have? Show your work.

Solution ....

5 Look at problem 4. If Tomas divides his stack of programs between himself and his 3 friends, what fraction of the original stack will each of his friends have? Write a division equation to represent and solve the problem.

Solution ....

Develop Dividing a Whole Number by a Unit Fraction

Read and try to solve the problem below.

> Alex makes 2 pounds of bread dough. He splits the dough into $\frac{1}{4}$-pound loaves before baking them in the oven. How many loaves does he make?

TRY IT

🧰 Math Toolkit
- fraction tiles
- fraction bars
- fraction models
- number lines
- grid paper
- index cards

DISCUSS IT

Ask your partner: Can you explain that again?

Tell your partner: The strategy I used to find the answer was . . .

Explore different ways to understand how to divide a whole number by a unit fraction in order to solve word problems.

> **Alex makes 2 pounds of bread dough. He splits the dough into $\frac{1}{4}$-pound loaves before baking them in the oven. How many loaves does he make?**

MODEL IT
You can use a number line to help understand the problem.

Draw a number line and label it to show the 2 pounds of bread dough.

Mark the number line to divide each whole into fourths.

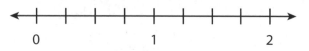

MODEL IT
You can use what you know about equations, equivalent fractions, and common denominators to solve the problem.

The equation $2 \div \frac{1}{4} = n$ models the problem with n being the number of loaves Alex makes.

Write the numbers in the equation with a common denominator.

$$\frac{8}{4} \div \frac{1}{4} = n$$

Now you can divide $\frac{8}{4}$ into equal groups of $\frac{1}{4}$.

CONNECT IT

Now you will use the problem from the previous page to help you understand how to divide a whole number by a unit fraction.

1 In the first **Model It** number line, how are the 2 pounds of bread dough represented?

2 How are the $\frac{1}{4}$-pound loaves represented on the number line?

3 How many fourths are in one whole?................... In two wholes?.................

4 Look at the second **Model It**. How was the equation $2 \div \frac{1}{4} = n$ changed to an equation involving fractions with common denominators?

5 How many groups of $\frac{1}{4}$ are in $\frac{8}{4}$? What is $\frac{8}{4} \div \frac{1}{4}$? Explain.

6 How many loaves does Alex make? How are the first **Model It** and second **Model It** alike in showing how to find the solution?

7 What multiplication equation can you write to check your answer to $2 \div \frac{1}{4}$? Explain.

8 REFLECT

Look back at your **Try It**, strategies by classmates, and **Model Its**. Which models or strategies do you like best for dividing a whole number by a unit fraction? Explain.

....

....

....

APPLY IT

Use what you just learned to solve these problems.

9 Stacy has 4 sheets of paper to make cards. Each card requires $\frac{1}{2}$ sheet of paper. How many cards can Stacy make? Draw a model and write a division equation to represent and solve the problem.

Solution ....

10 Look at problem 9 above. Which multiplication expressions can be used to represent the situation or check the division equation?

Ⓐ 8×2

Ⓑ $4 \times \frac{1}{2}$

Ⓒ $16 \times \frac{1}{2}$

Ⓓ $8 \times \frac{1}{2}$

Ⓔ 4×2

11 Dylan makes 3 submarine sandwiches. He cuts each sandwich into sixths to share. He stacks all the sandwich pieces on a plate. How many sandwich pieces does Dylan stack on the plate? Show your work.

Solution ....

Practice Dividing a Whole Number by a Unit Fraction

Study the Example showing one way to solve a word problem involving dividing a whole number by a fraction. Then solve problems 1–6.

EXAMPLE

Darius walks dogs at an animal shelter. He walks each dog for $\frac{1}{5}$ hour. He walks the dogs one at a time. How many dogs can Darius walk in 2 hours?

Find $2 \div \frac{1}{5}$.

The number line shows two hours. Each hour is divided into fifths.

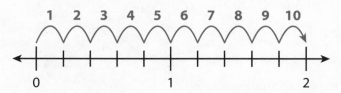

There are 10 fifths in 2.

$$2 \div \frac{1}{5} = 10$$

Darius can walk 10 dogs in 2 hours.

1 What multiplication equation could you write to solve the Example?

2 Use the information from the Example. In one month, Darius spends 9 hours walking dogs. How many times does he walk a dog in one month?

3 Explain how you got your answer to problem 2.

4 Mrs. Wing will tape up posters made by her students on the wall. She cuts tape into $\frac{1}{4}$-foot pieces. How many $\frac{1}{4}$-foot pieces can she cut from 5 feet of tape? Show your work.

Solution

5 Taylor is helping decorate tables with flowers for a graduation celebration. She has 7 bunches of tulips. She will put $\frac{1}{2}$ of each bunch in a vase. How many vases does she need? Draw a model and write a division equation to represent and solve the problem.

Solution

6 Look at how you solved problem 5. Use a different way to solve the problem and show how a multiplication equation can be used to check the answer.

Solution

Refine Dividing Unit Fractions in Word Problems

Complete the Example below. Then solve problems 1–9.

EXAMPLE

Sierra has a photo album with 3 empty pages. Each photo uses $\frac{1}{6}$ of an album page. How many photos can Sierra put on the empty pages?

Look at how you could show your work using rectangles.

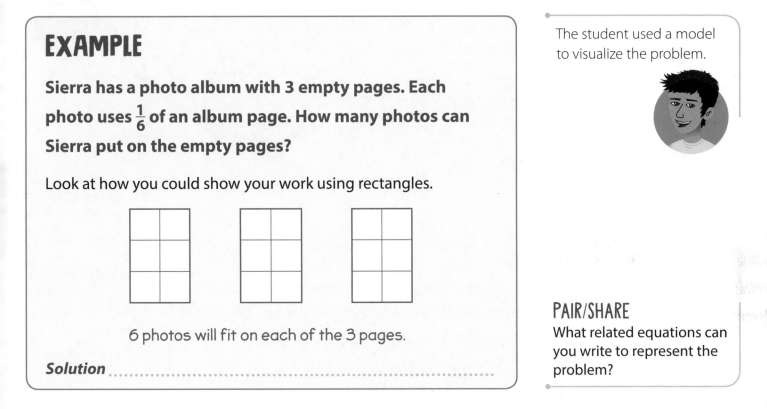

6 photos will fit on each of the 3 pages.

Solution ....

The student used a model to visualize the problem.

PAIR/SHARE
What related equations can you write to represent the problem?

APPLY IT

1 Corrine picked $\frac{1}{4}$ gallon of blackberries. She poured equal amounts of berries into 4 containers. What fraction of a gallon is in each container? Show your work.

Can you draw a model to help understand the problem?

PAIR/SHARE
How will the answer compare to $\frac{1}{4}$ gallon?

Solution ....

2 Cooper's USB drive is $\frac{1}{2}$ full with 5 video files. Each video file is the same size. What fraction of the USB drive does 1 video file use? Show your work.

How could I represent this problem using an equation?

Solution

3 Devonte is studying for a history test. He uses $\frac{1}{8}$ of a side of one sheet of paper to write notes for each historical event. He fills 2 full sides of one sheet of paper. Which expression could be used to find how many events Devonte makes notes for?

Ⓐ $2 \times \frac{1}{8}$

Ⓑ $2 \div \frac{1}{8}$

Ⓒ $\frac{1}{8} \times 2$

Ⓓ $\frac{1}{8} \div 2$

Barry chose Ⓓ as the correct answer. How did he get that answer?

Is this problem like one you have seen before?

④ Elise picks 6 pounds of apples. She uses $\frac{1}{2}$ pound of apples to make 1 container of applesauce. How many containers of applesauce can Elise make with all the apples?

Ⓐ 12 containers

Ⓑ $6\frac{1}{2}$ containers

Ⓒ $5\frac{1}{2}$ containers

Ⓓ 3 containers

⑤ Students are running in a relay race. Each team will run a total of 3 miles. Each member of a team will run $\frac{1}{3}$ mile. How many students will a team need to complete the race? Circle the correct number below.

$\frac{1}{9}$ 3   9   12   36

You may use the number line to help find your answer.

⑥ Tanya has $\frac{1}{3}$ of a cake left over from a party. She cuts the leftover cake into 6 equal pieces to store in the freezer. What fraction of the original cake is each piece? Show your work.

Solution

7 Marina has a pattern to make bows that requires $\frac{1}{4}$ yard of ribbon for each bow. Fill in the table to show how many bows she can make from a given length of ribbon.

Ribbon Length (yards)	Number of Bows
1	
2	
3	
4	

8 **Part A** Ted serves $\frac{1}{6}$ gallon of ice cream. He puts an equal amount of ice cream in each of 4 bowls. How many gallons of ice cream does Ted put in each bowl? Use a visual model to support your answer.

Solution ....

Part B Write a division equation to represent this situation. Then write a multiplication equation you can use to check your answer.

Solution ....

9 MATH JOURNAL

Write a word problem represented by $\frac{1}{5} \div 4$. Explain or show how to find the answer.

☑ SELF CHECK Go back to the Unit 3 Opener and see what you can check off.

In this unit you learned to . . .

Skill	Lesson
Multiply decimals, for example: $7.25 \times 9.4 = 68.15$.	15, 16
Divide decimals, for example: $1.2 \div 6 = 0.2$.	17
Understand fractions as division, for example: $\frac{3}{4} = 3 \div 4$.	18
Multiply fractions, for example: $\frac{2}{3} \times \frac{5}{6} = \frac{10}{18}$ or $\frac{5}{9}$.	19
Find the area of a rectangle with fractional side lengths by tiling and by multiplying.	20
Understand multiplication as scaling, for example: will $\frac{2}{3} \times \frac{1}{3}$ be greater than or less than $\frac{1}{3}$?	21
Multiply fractions and divide with unit fractions in word problems.	22, 24
Divide with unit fractions, for example: $4 \div \frac{1}{7} = 28$.	23, 24

Think about what you have learned.

Use words, numbers, and drawings.

1 I am proud that I can . . .

2 I worked hardest to learn how to . . .

3 One thing I am still confused about is . . .

Use Fractions and Decimals

Study an Example Problem and Solution

SMP 1 Make sense of problems and persevere in solving them.

Read this problem involving fractions. Then look at G.O.'s solution to this problem.

Solar Lights

G.O. and his neighbors are taking steps to save energy and water. G.O.'s street is $1\frac{1}{2}$ miles long. They plan to install solar lights along the sidewalk. Read G.O.'s plan.

Solars Light Plan
- Install the lights at equal intervals.
- Use a fraction of the whole length to choose the interval length.
- Use a fraction greater than $\frac{1}{8}$ but less than $\frac{1}{2}$.

Choose an appropriate fraction. Find the length of the interval. Tell how many solar lights are needed and where along the street the lights should be located.

Read the sample solution on the next page. Then look at the checklist below. Find and mark parts of the solution that match the checklist.

✓ PROBLEM-SOLVING CHECKLIST

☐ Tell what is known.
☐ Tell what the problem is asking.
☐ Show all your work.
☐ Show that the solution works.

a. Circle something that is known.
b. Underline something that you need to find.
c. Draw a box around what you do to solve the problem.
d. Put a checkmark next to the part that shows the solution works.

G.O.'S SOLUTION

Hi, I'm G.O. Here's how I solved this problem.

- **I know the length of the street.** I have to use the length and a fraction between $\frac{1}{8}$ and $\frac{1}{2}$ to find the distance between the lights.

- **I can use $\frac{1}{4}$.** The fractions $\frac{1}{8}$, $\frac{1}{4}$, and $\frac{1}{2}$ all have the same numerator, so I can look at the denominators to compare.

  Since 4 is < 8, $\frac{1}{4} > \frac{1}{8}$.

  Since 4 is > 2, $\frac{1}{4} < \frac{1}{2}$.

- **I know that** the distance is a fraction of the whole length, so I multiply $\frac{1}{4}$ by $1\frac{1}{2}$.

  $1\frac{1}{2} = \frac{3}{2}$ and $\frac{1}{4} \times \frac{3}{2} = \frac{3}{8}$

  The interval length is $\frac{3}{8}$ mile.

  "Fraction of" means multiply by a fraction.

- **Now I can** make a number line to find where the lights will go and how many are needed. It represents the street, so it goes to $1\frac{1}{2}$.

  I divided the number line into eighths so I can count by $\frac{3}{8}$.

- **I put a light at 0**, which is one end of the street. Then I marked each $\frac{3}{8}$ mile along the number line.

- **The number line shows** that there will be 5 lights installed at intervals of $\frac{3}{8}$ mile. The locations are at:

  0 miles, $\frac{3}{8}$ mile, $\frac{6}{8}$ mile, $\frac{9}{8} = 1\frac{1}{8}$ miles, and $\frac{12}{8} = 1\frac{1}{2}$ miles.

- There are 5 lights but only 4 intervals. Each interval is $\frac{3}{8}$ mile long and $4 \times \frac{3}{8} = \frac{12}{8}$. That's the same as $1\frac{1}{2}$ miles.

  My answer makes sense because it fits the information in the problem.

Try Another Approach

There are many ways to solve problems. Think about how you might solve the Solar Lights problem in a different way.

Solar Lights

G.O. and his neighbors are taking steps to save energy and water. G.O.'s street is $1\frac{1}{2}$ miles long. They plan to install solar lights along the sidewalk. Read G.O.'s plan.

Solar Light Plan

- Install the lights at equal intervals.
- Use a fraction of the whole length to choose the interval length.
- Use a fraction greater than $\frac{1}{8}$ but less than $\frac{1}{2}$.

Choose an appropriate fraction. Find the length of the interval. Tell how many solar lights are needed and where along the street the lights should be located.

PLAN IT

Answer these questions to help you start thinking about a plan.

A. What are some other fractions that you can use?

B. What can you do if you want to use more lights? Fewer lights?

SOLVE IT

Find a different solution for the Solar Lights problem. Show all your work on a separate sheet of paper.

You may want to use the Problem-Solving Tips to get started.

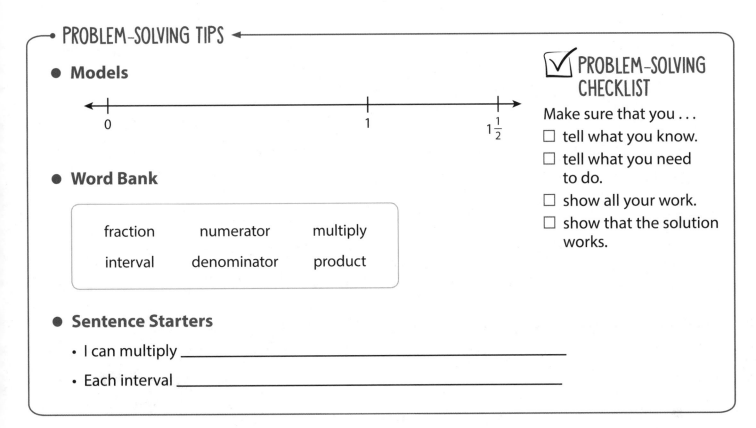

PROBLEM-SOLVING TIPS

- **Models**

- **Word Bank**

fraction	numerator	multiply
interval	denominator	product

- **Sentence Starters**

  • I can multiply _____

  • Each interval _____

☑ PROBLEM-SOLVING CHECKLIST

Make sure that you . . .

☐ tell what you know.

☐ tell what you need to do.

☐ show all your work.

☐ show that the solution works.

REFLECT

Use Mathematical Practices As you work through the problem, discuss these questions with a partner.

- **Persevere** What is your first step? What will you do next?

- **Repeated Reasoning** How can you use what you know about the denominators of unit fractions to find an appropriate fraction?

Discuss Models and Strategies

Read the problem. Write a solution on a separate sheet of paper. Remember, there can be lots of ways to solve a problem!

Plant Shrubs

The neighborhood has a small piece of common land that is now covered with grass. To save water, the neighbors will plant shrubs on part of the common area. Read G.O.'s notes.

Planting Notes

- Plant shrubs on a rectangular area a little more than half of the common land area.

- One side of the shrub section has a length greater than 8 feet and less than 9 feet.

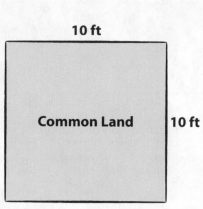

What is the area of the part where G.O. and his neighbors will plant shrubs? Describe the area.

PLAN IT AND SOLVE IT
Find a solution to the Plant Shrubs problem.

Write a detailed plan and support your answer. Be sure to include:

• a diagram.

• the area of the common land.

• the length, width, and area of the rectangle where G.O. and his neighbors will plant shrubs.

You may want to use the Problem-Solving Tips to get started.

PROBLEM-SOLVING TIPS

● **Questions**

• What are some fractions equivalent to $\frac{1}{2}$?

• What are some fractions that are a little more than $\frac{1}{2}$?

● **Word Bank**

area	multiply	numerator
fraction	product	denominator

☑ **PROBLEM-SOLVING CHECKLIST**

Make sure that you . . .
☐ tell what you know.
☐ tell what you need to do.
☐ show all your work.
☐ show that the solution works.

REFLECT

Use Mathematical Practices As you work through the problem, discuss these questions with a partner.

• **Reason Mathematically** How can you compare fractions to find a fraction a little more than $\frac{1}{2}$?

• **Use Models** What models can you use to help you visualize the problem?

Persevere On Your Own

Read the problems. Write a solution on a separate sheet of paper.

Water Shrubs

G.O. and his neighbors clear a rectangular area $8\frac{1}{2}$ feet by $6\frac{1}{4}$ feet to plant the shrubs. Now they have to decide how many shrubs to plant and how much water to use on the shrubs.

Read G.O.'s planting instructions.

Shrub Planting Instructions

- Each shrub needs an area of about 2 square feet.
- Each shrub will need about 1.25 liters of water a week.

How many shrubs should G.O. plant?
How much water will the shrubs need?

SOLVE IT

Help G.O. make a plan for planting shrubs.

- Tell how many shrubs G.O. should plant and why you chose this number.

- Find the amount of water this number of shrubs will need in a week.

REFLECT

Use Mathematical Practices After you complete the task, choose one of these questions to discuss with a partner.

- **Reason Mathematically** How did you decide the number of shrubs that G.O. should plant?

- **Make an Argument** How could you justify the number of shrubs that you suggested?

Use Compost

A local nursery hears about the shrub planting project that G.O. and his neighbors are planning. The nursery gives them 50 pounds of compost to use. G.O. reads about using compost on a website.

USING COMPOST TO PLANT

When you plant a shrub, it can help to mix the soil with some compost. You can use a scoop of compost for each shrub. An average scoop of compost is between $\frac{1}{4}$ and $\frac{1}{2}$ pound.

About how many shrubs can G.O. plant with the compost that the nursery gave him?

SOLVE IT

Help G.O. estimate how many shrubs he can plant with the compost.

• Decide on a fraction of a pound to use as the weight of an average scoop.

• Show how to use this fraction to find the number of shrubs that can be planted. Explain.

REFLECT

Use Mathematical Practices After you complete the task, choose one of these questions to discuss with a partner.

• **Make Sense of Problems** How did you use each of the numbers given in the problem?

• **Persevere** Why might you try using different fractions before giving your final answer? Explain.

Unit 3 Math in Action Use Fractions and Decimals

1 Anna makes a rectangular banner that is 2.2 meters long and 0.9 meter wide. How many square meters does the banner cover? Record your answer on the grid. Then fill in the bubbles.

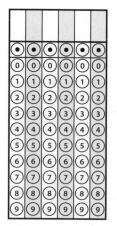

2 Which equations are true? Choose all the correct answers.

Ⓐ $7 \times \frac{1}{4} = \frac{7}{4}$ Ⓑ $6 \times \frac{1}{5} = \frac{5}{6}$

Ⓒ $\frac{2}{3} \times \frac{1}{6} = \frac{2}{18}$ Ⓓ $\frac{1}{8} \times \frac{1}{8} = \frac{2}{8}$

Ⓔ $\frac{1}{3} \times 4 = \frac{4}{3}$

3 Without multiplying, decide whether each expression's value is less than, greater than, or equal to $\frac{3}{7}$.

Choose *Less than* $\frac{3}{7}$, *Greater than* $\frac{3}{7}$, or *Equal to* $\frac{3}{7}$, for each expression.

	Less than $\frac{3}{7}$	Greater than $\frac{3}{7}$	Equal to $\frac{3}{7}$
$\frac{1}{10} \times \frac{3}{7}$	Ⓐ	Ⓑ	Ⓒ
$\frac{2}{3} \times \frac{3}{7}$	Ⓓ	Ⓔ	Ⓕ
$\frac{9}{4} \times \frac{3}{7}$	Ⓖ	Ⓗ	Ⓘ
$\frac{9}{8} \times \frac{3}{7}$	Ⓙ	Ⓚ	Ⓛ
$2 \times \frac{3}{7}$	Ⓜ	Ⓝ	Ⓞ
$\frac{5}{5} \times \frac{3}{7}$	Ⓟ	Ⓠ	Ⓡ

4 James has a rope that is 2 feet long. He cuts the rope into pieces that are $\frac{1}{4}$ foot long. How many pieces does he cut?

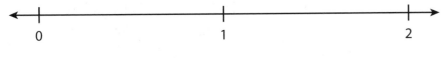

Show your work.

.... pieces

5 Anya and three friends equally share $\frac{1}{2}$ pound of peanuts. How many pounds of peanuts will each person get? Show your work.

Solution .... pound

6 Coach Miller is having a cookout at the park for his baseball team.

Part A Coach Miller bought 5 pounds of ground turkey to make burgers. The cost of ground turkey is $3.25 for each pound. What was the total cost of the ground turkey? Show your work.

Part B Coach Miller has a bag of popcorn that weighs 7.8 ounces. One serving of popcorn is 0.65 ounces. How many servings of popcorn are there in the bag? Show your work.

There are .... servings of popcorn in the bag.

Performance Task

Answer the questions and show all your work on separate paper.

The Drama Club is painting sets for their next play. Blue and red paint is on sale at the hardware store, so the students have sketched the design for a rectangular set that will use only those two paint colors.

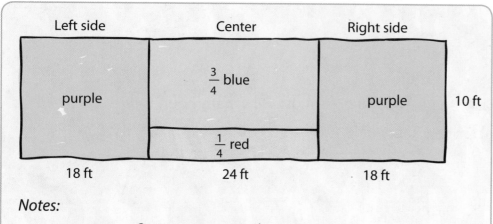

Notes:

- 1 pint purple $= \frac{2}{3}$ pint red and $\frac{1}{3}$ pint blue
- 1 pint of paint covers about 40 square feet.

How much of each color will they need to buy in order to paint the set?

REFLECT

Use Mathematical Practices After you complete the task, choose one of the following questions to answer.

- **Persevere** What was your first step in solving this problem?

- **Model** How did you use fractions to help you solve this problem?

Vocabulary

Draw or write to show examples for each term. Then draw or write to show other math words in the unit.

scaling resizing a quantity by multiplying by a factor.

My Example

My Word: _____

_____

_____

My Example

My Word: _____

_____

_____

My Example

My Word: _____

_____

_____

My Example

My Word: _____

_____

_____

My Example

My Word: _____

_____

_____

My Example

My Word: _____

_____

_____

My Example

My Word: _____

_____

_____

My Example

My Word: _____

_____

_____

My Example

My Word: _____

_____

_____

My Example

My Word: _____

_____

_____

My Example

My Word: _____

_____

_____

My Example

Measurement, Data, and Geometry
Converting Units, Using Data, and Classifying Figures

☑ SELF CHECK

Before starting this unit, check off the skills you know below. As you complete each lesson, see how many more skills you can check off!

I can . . .	Before	After
Convert from one measurement unit to another, for example: 4 feet = 48 inches.	☐	☐
Make a line plot of data represented as fractions of measurements.	☐	☐
Classify two-dimensional figures based on their properties, for example: a square is also a rhombus and a rectangle, but not all rhombuses and rectangles are squares.	☐	☐
Use a Venn diagram and a tree diagram to organize shapes that share the same properties.	☐	☐

Build Your Vocabulary

Math Vocabulary

Describe what you know about the two systems of measurement. Then match the review words to the appropriate system.

	Customary System	Metric System
In Your Own Words		
Units of Measurement		

Academic Vocabulary

Place a check next to the academic words you know. Then use the words to complete the sentences.

☐ classify　　☐ predict　　☐ model　　☐ support

1 I can sometimes .... the answer before working out the problem.

2 You can justify the solution to a problem by providing details that

.... your answer.

3 You can .... shapes by the number of their sides.

4 A number line is a .... we often use in math.

Convert Measurement Units

Dear Family,

This week your child is learning to convert from one measurement unit to another.

Your child is learning to make measurement conversions, such as:

- from one unit of length to another, using kilometers, meters, and centimeters.

- from one unit of weight to another, using pounds and ounces.

- from one unit of capacity to another, using gallons, quarts, and cups.

You can describe the same measurement using different units. For example, 1 kilometer describes the same distance as 1,000 meters. The length is the same. The units used to measure the length are different, so the number of units in the measurement is different, too.

Kilometers are a larger unit of measurement than meters. Since there are 1,000 meters in each kilometer, you can multiply the length, or distance, in kilometers by 1,000 to convert the measurement to meters.

> 4.5 kilometers = ? meters
> 4.5 × 1,000 = 4,500
> 4.5 kilometers = 4,500 meters

Meters are a smaller unit of measurement than kilometers. Since 1 kilometer is equivalent to 1,000 meters, you can divide the length, or distance, in meters by 1,000 to convert the measurement to kilometers.

> 6,700 meters = ? kilometers
> 6,700 ÷ 1,000 = 6.7
> 6,700 meters = 6.7 kilometers

Your child is becoming familiar with the relative sizes of units by identifying which units are larger and which units are smaller. Also, as your child practices converting units, he or she is applying multiplication and division skills.

Invite your child to share what he or she knows about converting measurement units by doing the following activity together.

ACTIVITY CONVERTING MEASUREMENT UNITS

Do this activity with your child to convert measurement units.

Materials ruler or measuring tape, sheet of paper

Play a game with your child to convert measurements in real-life situations.

- Choose a place to mark a starting line. It can be inside your home or outside. Make sure there is enough open space if you choose to play inside.

- Make a paper ball by crumpling a sheet of paper.

- Have your child stand at the starting line and toss the paper ball.

- Together, measure the length of the toss to the nearest foot. Then convert the length of the toss from feet to inches. [1 foot = 12 inches] So, multiply the number of feet by 12 to find the number of inches.

- Take turns tossing the ball, measuring, and converting measurements.

Look out for other real-life opportunities to practice converting measurements with your child. You might convert measurements when you use a recipe, do a craft project together, make a home repair, or plan a trip.

Explore Converting Measurement Units

You have worked with measurement units in earlier grades. Now you will convert between different units in the same measurement system. Use what you know to try to solve the problem below.

Learning Target

- Convert among different-sized standard measurement units within a given measurement system (e.g., convert 5 cm to 0.05 m), and use these conversions in solving multi-step, real world problems.

SMP 1, 2, 3, 4, 5, 6, 7

> **Lira finds an antique dresser that is 4 feet wide. She wants to know if it will fit in her room. She measures the space in inches. How many inches wide is the dresser?**
> **(1 foot = 12 inches)**

TRY IT

🧰 **Math Toolkit**
- ruler
- yardstick
- number lines
- grid paper
- math reference sheet

DISCUSS IT

Ask your partner: Why did you choose that strategy?

Tell your partner: I knew ... So I ...

CONNECT IT

1 LOOK BACK

Look at the problem on the previous page. Is the number of inches in 4 feet greater than or less than the number of feet? Explain.

2 LOOK AHEAD

You solved a problem using the relationship between units to find the equivalent measure. You can use what you know about unit sizes and operations to convert other measurement units.

The table shows equivalent measurements of weight.

a. Is an ounce a smaller unit or larger unit than a pound?

....

A melon weighs about 2 pounds.
How many ounces is 2 pounds? ....

Units of Weight
1 pound = 16 ounces
1 ton = 2,000 pounds

b. Suppose a basket of melons weighs 64 ounces.
Is the weight in pounds greater than or less than 64 pounds? How do you know?

....

....

Complete the table to convert from ounces to pounds.

Ounces	16	32		64
Pounds	1		3	

64 ounces = ... pounds

3 REFLECT

Describe a real-world object that can be measured using two different units and tell which two units you could use. Which unit would you need more of to measure the object?

....

....

Prepare for Converting Measurement Units

1 Think about what you know about equivalent measurements. Fill in each box.
Use words, numbers, and pictures. Show as many ideas as you can.

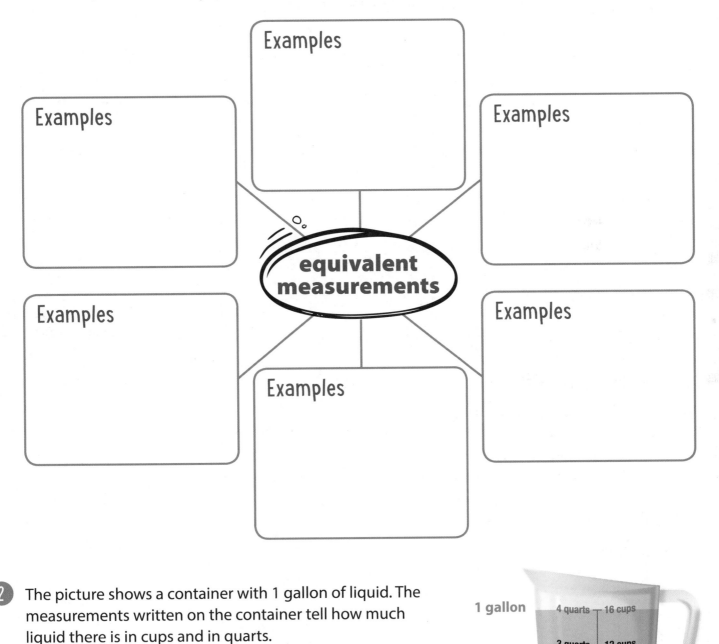

Examples

Examples

Examples

equivalent measurements

Examples

Examples

Examples

2 The picture shows a container with 1 gallon of liquid. The measurements written on the container tell how much liquid there is in cups and in quarts.

Use the picture to write the equivalent measurement units.

2 quarts = ... cups   12 cups = ... quarts

1 gallon = ... cups   8 quarts = ... gallons

1 gallon   4 quarts — 16 cups

3 quarts — 12 cups

2 quarts — 8 cups

1 quart — 4 cups

③ Solve the problem. Show your work.

Marc is filling 1-cup containers with juice. He has 5 gallons of juice. How many 1-cup containers can he fill? (1 gallon = 16 cups)

Solution ....

④ Check your answer. Show your work.

Develop Converting Larger Units to Smaller Units

Read and try to solve the problem below.

> In some parts of the world, travel distances on road signs and maps are given in kilometers. How many meters are there in 3.5 kilometers? (1 kilometer = 1,000 meters)

TRY IT

 Math Toolkit
- base-ten blocks
- number lines
- grid paper
- thousandths decimal place-value charts
- math reference sheet

DISCUSS IT

Ask your partner: Can you explain that again?

Tell your partner: I started by . . .

Explore one way to understand converting larger measurement units to smaller measurement units.

> **In some parts of the world, travel distances on road signs and maps are given in kilometers. How many meters are there in 3.5 kilometers? (1 kilometer = 1,000 meters)**

MODEL IT

You can use a table to help understand the problem.

The table below shows the relationship between meters and kilometers.

kilometers	1	2	3	4	5	6
meters	1,000	2,000	3,000	4,000	5,000	6,000

SOLVE IT

Use the information from the table to understand how to solve the problem.

The pattern in the table shows that the number of meters is always 1,000 times the number of kilometers.

kilometers	1	2	3	3.5	4	5	6
meters	1,000	2,000	3,000		4,000	5,000	6,000

To find the number of meters in 3.5 kilometers, multiply 3.5 by 1,000. Write the answer in the table.

CONNECT IT

Now you will use the problem from the previous page to help you understand how to convert larger measurement units to smaller measurement units.

1 Which is the smaller unit, *meters* or *kilometers*? ....
How do you know?

2 What operation do you use to convert from a larger measurement unit to a smaller

measurement unit? ....

3 3.5 kilometers = ... meters

4 Use what you learned about the relationship between meters and kilometers to complete the table below.

kilometers	0.8	1	1.85	2	2.03	3
meters		1,000		2,000		3,000

5 How many meters are in *k* kilometers?

6 There are 3 feet in 1 yard. Explain how you decide whether to multiply or divide by 3 if you need to convert yards to feet.

7 REFLECT

Look back at your **Try It**, strategies by classmates, and **Model It** and **Solve It**. Which models or strategies do you like best for converting larger units to smaller units? Explain.

....

....

....

Lesson 25 Convert Measurement Units   **515**

APPLY IT

Use what you just learned to solve these problems.

8 How many ounces are there in $4\frac{1}{2}$ pounds? Show your work.
(16 ounces = 1 pound)

Solution ....

9 How many millimeters are in 9.25 centimeters? Show your work.
(1 centimeter = 10 millimeters)

Solution ....

10 Ravi's fish tank can hold 65 liters of water. How many milliliters of water can the fish tank hold? (1 liter = 1,000 milliliters)

Ⓐ 0.065 milliliters

Ⓑ 6.5 milliliters

Ⓒ 6,500 milliliters

Ⓓ 65,000 milliliters

Practice Converting Larger Units to Smaller Units

Study the Example showing how to convert between meters and millimeters. Then solve problems 1–10.

EXAMPLE

How many millimeters are in 2.52 meters?

The table below shows the relationship between meters and millimeters.

meters (m)	1	2	3	4	5
millimeters (mm)	1,000	2,000	3,000	4,000	5,000

To find the number of millimeters in 2.52 meters, multiply 2.52 by 1,000.

$2.52 \times 1,000 = 2,520$

There are 2,520 millimeters in 2.52 meters.

1 Which is the larger unit, *meters* or *millimeters*? ....

2 How can you find how many millimeters are in 4.06 meters?

3 How many millimeters are in 4.06 meters? ....

4 Fill in the missing information in the table.

meters (m)	0.34	1	1.5	2	2.09	3	3.77	4
millimeters (mm)		1,000		2,000		3,000		4,000

5 What operation do you use to convert from a larger measurement unit to a smaller measurement unit? Explain why.

6 The pattern in the table shows that the number of centimeters is always 100 times the number of meters. Fill in the missing number of centimeters.

meters (m)	1	1.5	2	2.07	3	3.26	4
centimeters (cm)	100	150	200				

7 A football player runs for $13\frac{1}{2}$ yards. How many feet does he run? Show your work. (1 yard = 3 feet)

Solution ....

8 There are 24 hours in a day. If you want to convert days to hours, should you multiply or divide by 24? Explain.

9 Look at problem 8. How many hours are in $2\frac{1}{2}$ days? Show your work.

Solution ....

10 16 ounces is equivalent to 1 pound. A lion cub born at the zoo weighs $2\frac{1}{2}$ pounds. How many ounces does the lion cub weigh? Show your work.

Solution ....

Develop Converting Smaller Units to Larger Units

Read and try to solve the problem below.

> **How many quarts are equivalent to 6 cups? (1 quart = 4 cups)**

1 quart   1 cup

TRY IT

Math Toolkit
- fraction tiles
- fraction circles
- number lines
- grid paper
- math reference sheet

DISCUSS IT

Ask your partner: How did you get started?

Tell your partner: A model I used was . . . It helped me . . .

Explore one way to understand converting smaller measurement units to larger measurement units.

> **How many quarts are equivalent to 6 cups?**
> **(1 quart = 4 cups)**

MODEL IT

You can use a table to help understand the problem.

The table below shows the relationship between cups and quarts.

quarts	1	2	3	4	5	6
cups	4	8	12	16	20	24

SOLVE IT

Use the information from the table to understand how to solve the problem.

The pattern in the table shows that there are 4 cups in every quart.

quarts	1		2	3	4	5	6
cups	4	6	8	12	16	20	24

To find the number of quarts equivalent to 6 cups, divide by 4.

©Curriculum Associates, LLC   Copying is not permitted.

CONNECT IT
Now you will use the problem from the previous page to help you understand how to convert smaller measurement units to larger measurement units.

1 Which is a smaller unit, quarts or cups? ....

How do you know?

2 What operation do you use to convert from a smaller measurement unit to a

larger measurement unit? ....

3 6 cups = ... quarts

Write your answer in the table on the previous page. Explain your reasoning.

4 Use what you learned about the relationship between cups and quarts to complete the table below.

quarts		1		2		3		4
cups	2	4	5	8	9	12	15	16

5 One gallon is equivalent to 8 pints. Describe how to convert from pints to gallons. Explain your reasoning.

6 REFLECT

Look back at your **Try It**, strategies by classmates, and **Model It** and **Solve It**. Which models or strategies do you like best for converting smaller units to larger units? Explain.

....

....

....

APPLY IT

Use what you just learned to solve these problems. Use the Math Reference Sheet as necessary.

 How many kilometers is equal to 800 meters? Show your work.

Solution ....

8 How many yards are equal to 25 feet? Show your work.

Solution ....

9 Which of the following measures is equivalent to 3,300 grams?

Ⓐ 330 kilograms

Ⓑ 33 kilograms

Ⓒ 3.3 kilograms

Ⓓ 0.33 kilograms

Practice Converting Smaller Units to Larger Units

Study the Example showing how to convert between ounces and pounds.
Then solve problems 1–8.

EXAMPLE

How many pounds are equivalent to 56 ounces?

The table below shows the relationship between pounds and ounces.

pounds (lb)	1	2	3	4
ounces (oz)	16	32	48	64

To find the number of pounds equivalent to 56 ounces, divide by 16.

$$56 \div 16 = 3\frac{1}{2}$$

$3\frac{1}{2}$ pounds is equivalent to 56 ounces.

1 Which is the smaller unit, pounds or ounces? ....

2 What operation do you use to convert from a smaller measurement unit to a larger

measurement unit? ....

3 Look at the Example. Explain how you can use multiplication to check the answer.

4 Use the relationship between pounds and ounces complete the table.

pounds (lb)		1		2	
ounces (oz)	8	16	20	32	40

5   How many yards are equivalent to 38 feet? Show your work.
(1 yard = 3 feet)

Solution ....

6   How many meters are equivalent to 247 centimeters? Show your work.
(1 meter = 100 centimeters)

Solution ....

7   When converting between two measurement units, how can you tell which operation to use?

8   How many gallons are equivalent to 24 cups? Show your work.
(1 gallon = 4 quarts and 1 quart = 4 cups)

Solution ....

Refine Converting Measurement Units

Complete the Example below. Then solve problems 1–9 using the Math Reference Sheet as necessary.

EXAMPLE

How many liters are equivalent to 100 milliliters?

Look at how you could explain your work using conversions.

1 liter = 1,000 milliliters

Liters are larger than milliliters, so the number of liters will be less than the number of milliliters. Divide the number of milliliters by 1,000 or 10^3.

$100 \div 1,000 = 0.1$ because dividing by 10^3 changes the placement of the decimal point. The digit 1 from the hundreds place has a value of 0.1 in the quotient because it has moved three place values to the right.

Solution ....

> Use division, because milliliters are smaller than liters.
>
>

> **PAIR/SHARE**
> How can you check your answer?

APPLY IT

1 Jillian makes $10\frac{1}{2}$ gallons of lemonade to sell in 1-quart bottles. How many quarts of lemonade can she make? Show your work.

> How many quarts are in $\frac{1}{2}$ gallon?

> **PAIR/SHARE**
> Draw a picture or make a table to support your answer.

Solution ....

2 How many kilograms are equivalent to 450 grams? Show your work.

Will the number of kilograms be greater or less than 450?

PAIR/SHARE
Did you and your partner solve the problem the same way?

Solution ....

3 How many millimeters are in 180 meters?

Ⓐ 0.18 millimeter

Ⓑ 1.80 millimeter

Ⓒ 180,000 millimeters

Ⓓ 1,800,000 millimeters

Emily chose Ⓐ as the correct answer. How did she get that answer?

Which is a larger unit, millimeters or meters?

PAIR/SHARE
Does Emily's answer make sense?

4 A mining company digs 75 kilograms of silver. They plan to use 1 gram of silver in each special coin they make. How many grams are equivalent to 75 kilograms?

5 Five measurements are shown below. Write one of the measurements on each of the lines to create two true equations.

300 millimeters   30 meters   3,000 meters   3 kilometers   3,000 centimeters

.... = ...

.... = ...

6 Complete each conversion below. Show your work.

a. 3 feet + 7 inches = ... inches

b. 2 gallons − 5 quarts = ... quarts

c. 5 pounds − 38 ounces = ... ounces

d. 60 centimeters + 4 meters = ... centimeters

e. 2,000 meters + 5,000 meters = ... kilometers

f. 1 liter − 150 milliliters = ... milliliters

7 How many yards are equivalent to 1,000 feet?

Ⓐ $333\frac{1}{3}$ yards

Ⓑ $333\frac{1}{12}$ yards

Ⓒ $83\frac{4}{12}$ yards

Ⓓ 3,000 yards

8 Write each measurement below in the table under an equivalent measure, if possible. Some of the measurements may not have an equivalent measure.

$\frac{1}{2}$ quart   4 pints   16 cups $\frac{1}{4}$ gallon   8 pints

1 gallon	1 quart	1 pint

9 MATH JOURNAL

Rafael uses a ruler to measure his desk. It is 85 centimeters wide. If he measures the width of his desk in meters, will the number of meters be less than or greater than 85? What will the measure in meters be? Explain how you know.

✓ SELF CHECK Go back to the Unit 4 Opener and see what you can check off.

Solve Word Problems Involving Conversions

Dear Family,

This week your child is learning how to solve word problems that involve converting units of measurement.

Your child might see a problem like the one below.

Laura is making punch for a party. The recipe calls for $3\frac{1}{2}$ cups of lemonade per batch. Laura wants to make 10 batches of punch. How many gallons of lemonade will she need to buy?

1 cup   1 gallon

1 gallon = 16 cups

The picture shows how cups and gallons are related. You can see that gallons are larger units of measurement than cups.

The first step in solving the problem is to find how many cups are needed to make 10 batches of lemonade. Then you can convert cups to gallons.

- Multiply the number of cups needed for one batch by 10.

$$10 \times 3\frac{1}{2} = 10 \times \left(3 + \frac{1}{2}\right)$$
$$= 10 \times 3 + 10 \times \frac{1}{2}$$
$$= 30 + 5$$
$$= 35$$

35 cups are needed for 10 batches.

- Convert 35 cups to gallons. Divide the number of cups by 16.

$35 \div 16 = 2\ R\ 3$

35 cups is 2 gallons with 3 cups left over

The 3 cups left over means that Laura will need to buy another gallon of lemonade in addition to the 2 gallons. She will need to buy 3 gallons of lemonade in order to have enough to make 10 batches of punch.

Invite your child to share what he or she knows about solving word problems that involve converting units of measurement by doing the following activity together.

ACTIVITY USING CONVERSIONS IN WORD PROBLEMS

Do this activity with your child to solve word problems involving converting measurements.

Work with your child to make up and solve real-life problems involving converting units of measurement.

- Use the example below or use your own ideas. To convert units, you can use the equivalent units of measurement that are shown at the bottom of the page.

A sports-drink bottle holds 1 pint.

- Work together to create and solve problems about real-life situations.

Example: Sally is bringing a sports drink to a team party. The coach asks her to bring $2\frac{1}{2}$ gallons of the sports drink. How many of the sports-drink bottles shown above will Sally need to bring?

1 gallon = 16 cups
1 gallon = 4 quarts
1 gallon = 8 pints
1 quart = 4 cups
1 pint = 2 cups
1 quart = 2 pints

1 liter = 1,000 milliliters

1 kilometer = 1,000 meters
1 meter = 100 centimeters
1 centimeter = 10 millimeters

1 mile = 1,760 yards
1 mile = 5,280 feet
1 yard = 3 feet
1 foot = 12 inches

Answer to Example:

1 gallon = 8 pints; $8 \times 2\frac{1}{2} = 20$; Sally needs to bring 20 pints of the sports drink.

Since each bottle is 1 pint, she needs to bring 20 bottles.

Explore Solving Word Problems Involving Conversions

Previously, you converted among different measurement units. In this lesson, you will convert measurement units to solve multi-step, real-world problems. Use what you know to try to solve the problem below.

Ray finds a log that is 90 inches long. He cuts the log into 2-foot pieces of wood to sell as firewood at his store. How many pieces of wood can Roy sell at his store using this log?
(1 foot = 12 inches)

90 inches

TRY IT

Math Toolkit
• base-ten blocks
• number lines
• grid paper
• math reference sheet

DISCUSS IT

Ask your partner: Can you explain that again?

Tell your partner: I started by . . .

CONNECT IT

1 LOOK BACK

Explain how you found the number of 2-foot pieces of wood Roy will have to sell.

2 LOOK AHEAD

In the previous problem, you used more than one step to find a solution to a problem involving converting units of measure. You can start this type of problem in different ways. Consider this problem:

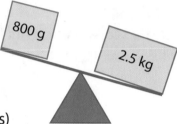

Look at the scale. How much more mass needs to be added to the left side in order to make the scale balance? (1 kilogram = 1,000 grams)

a. What should you do first to find how much more mass is needed to balance the scale?

b. Convert 2.5 kilograms to grams. What operation did you use? Convert 800 grams to kilograms. What operation did you use?

c. Choose one of the conversions from part b to solve the problem.

3 REFLECT

When you convert from grams to kilograms, do you end up with more units or fewer units? When you convert from kilograms to grams, do you end up with more units or fewer units? Why?

....

....

....

Prepare for Solving Word Problems Involving Conversions

1 Think about what you know about converting measurements. Fill in each box. Use words, numbers, and pictures. Show as many ideas as you can.

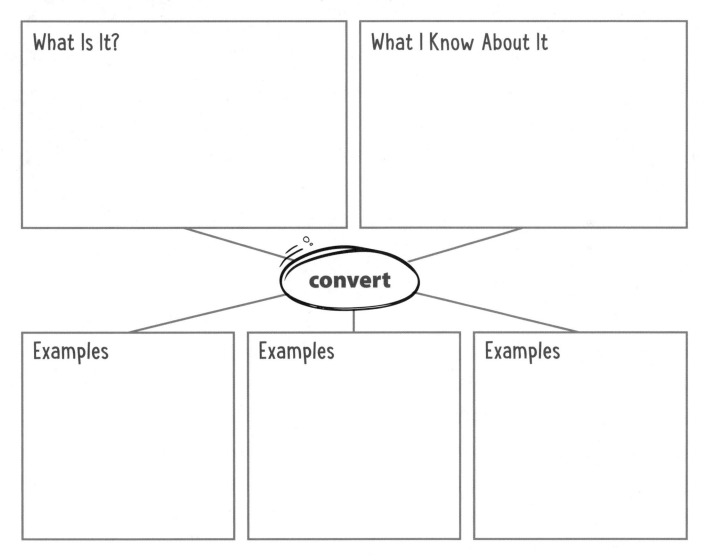

| What Is It? | What I Know About It |

convert

| Examples | Examples | Examples |

2 The statements **1 yard = 3 feet** and **1 foot = 12 inches** describe relationships among three units of length. How can you convert 5 yards to inches?

3) Solve the problem. Show your work.

Adela has a string that is 80 inches long. She cuts 3-foot pieces of the string to make necklaces. Each necklace will use one 3-foot piece. How many necklaces can Adela make using this string? (1 foot = 12 inches)

Solution ....

4) Check your answer. Show your work.

Develop Solving Multi-Step Word Problems with Conversions

Read and try to solve the problem below.

> Casey is making an exercise plan. She plans to walk a trail near her home 20 times each month. It takes 40 minutes to walk the trail. If Casey keeps the same pace, how many hours will she spend walking the trail each month? (1 hour = 60 minutes)

TRY IT

 **Math Toolkit**
- base-ten blocks
- number lines
- grid paper
- clocks
- math reference sheet

 **DISCUSS IT**

Ask your partner: How did you get started?

Tell your partner: I started by . . .

Explore different ways to understand converting a unit of time in order to solve a multi-step word problem.

> **Casey is making an exercise plan. She plans to walk a trail near her home 20 times each month. It takes 40 minutes to walk the trail. If Casey keeps the same pace, how many hours will she spend walking the trail each month?**
> **(1 hour = 60 minutes)**

PICTURE IT

You can use a picture to understand the relationship between hours and minutes.

1 hour = 60 minutes

$$\frac{40 \text{ minutes}}{60 \text{ minutes}} = \frac{4}{6} = \frac{2}{3}$$

40 minutes is $\frac{2}{3}$ of an hour, or $\frac{2}{3}$ hour.

MODEL IT

You can write an equation to find the number of minutes Casey will walk the trail in one month.

Casey walks the trail in 40 minutes. To find the total number of minutes walked, *m*, multiply the number of minutes by the number of times Casey will walk the trail.

$$m = 40 \times 20$$
$$= 800$$

Casey will spend 800 minutes walking the trail each month.

CONNECT IT
Now you will use the problem from the previous page to help you understand how to convert minutes to hours to solve a multi-step word problem.

1 Why do you need to convert units of time in order to solve the problem?

2 Look at **Picture It**. You can convert minutes to hours before you multiply. What part of an hour is 40 minutes? How do you know?

3 Show how to find the number of hours Casey will walk the trail using your answer to problem 2. Explain why this method works.

4 Look at **Model It**. What operation do you use to convert 800 minutes to hours? Explain why and solve the problem.

5 How are the solution methods from **Picture It** and **Model It** alike and different?

6 REFLECT

Look back at your **Try It**, strategies by classmates, and **Picture It** and **Model It**. Which models or strategies do you like best for solving word problems involving converting units of time? Explain.

....

....

....

APPLY IT

Use what you just learned to solve these problems.

7 Elijah's dog needs 8 ounces of food per day. Elijah buys dog food by the pound. How many pounds of food does Elijah need to buy to feed his dog for 2 weeks? Show your work. (16 ounces = 1 pound and 1 week = 7 days)

Solution ....

8 Mr. Rubens has $4\frac{1}{2}$ quarts of watercolor paint. His class is making a mural. Each of the 20 students in his class will get 1 cup of paint. Does he have enough paint for all of his students? Show your work. (1 quart = 4 cups)

Solution ....

9 A lemur at a zoo has a mass of 3 kilograms, 630 grams. The zookeeper records the lemur's mass in grams. What will the zookeeper write for the mass of the lemur? Show your work. (1 kilogram = 1,000 grams)

Solution ....

Practice Solving Multi-Step Word Problems with Conversions

Study the Example showing how to solve a word problem by converting units. Then solve problems 1–5.

EXAMPLE

Michael is planning a party for 30 people. He plans for each guest to drink 1 cup of juice. He has $2\frac{1}{2}$ gallons of juice. Does he have enough juice for the party?

1 gallon = 16 cups, so cups are a smaller measurement unit than gallons.

Michael multiplies $2\frac{1}{2}$ by 16 to find the number of cups of juice he has.

$$2\frac{1}{2} \times 16 = \left(2 + \frac{1}{2}\right) \times 16$$
$$= 2 \times 16 + \frac{1}{2} \times 16$$
$$= 32 + 8$$
$$= 40$$

There are 40 cups of juice.

40 > 30, so Michael has enough juice for the party.

1 Juanita has $3\frac{1}{4}$ pounds of sugar. How many ounces of sugar does she have? Explain how you know. (1 pound = 16 ounces)

2 Benjamin rode the train for 45 minutes. Then it took him another 30 minutes to walk to his friend's house. How many hours did he spend riding and walking to his friend's house? Explain how you know. (1 hour = 60 minutes)

3   Ms. Monet, the art teacher at Giverny School, has $3\frac{1}{2}$ quarts of liquid glue and 24 empty glue bottles that each hold 1 cup. Does she have enough glue to fill all of the bottles? Explain. (1 quart = 4 cups)

4   Ms. Monet gave $2\frac{1}{2}$ cups of red paint to each of her 20 students. How many quarts of red paint did she give out? Show your work. (1 quart = 4 cups)

Solution ....

5   Ms. Monet is combining 15 cups of green paint with 15 cups of white paint. She is pouring the paint mixture into empty quart bottles. How many quart bottles does she need? Explain. Show your work. (1 quart = 4 cups)

Solution ....

....

....

....

Develop Choosing a Unit to Solve a Word Problem

Read and try to solve the problem below.

> **Heather and Diego measure worms from their class compost bin. Heather measures a 3.5-centimeter worm and Diego measures a 28-millimeter worm. Which worm is longer? How much longer is the longer worm? (10 millimeters = 1 centimeter)**

TRY IT

 **Math Toolkit**
- base-ten blocks
- base-ten grid paper
- number lines
- centimeter rulers
- math reference sheet

DISCUSS IT

Ask your partner: Do you agree with me? Why or why not?

Tell your partner: I agree with you about . . . because . . .

Explore different ways to understand solving a word problem by choosing a unit to convert.

> **Heather and Diego measure worms from their class compost bin. Heather measures a 3.5-centimeter worm and Diego measures a 28-millimeter worm. Which worm is longer? How much longer is the longer worm? (10 millimeters = 1 centimeter)**

PICTURE IT

You can use a picture to help understand the relationship between centimeters and millimeters.

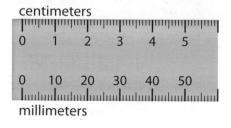

There are 10 millimeters in each centimeter.

MODEL IT

You can write equations to convert centimeters to millimeters or millimeters to centimeters.

To compare the lengths, the measurements need to be in the same unit.

Convert centimeters to millimeters:

There are 10 millimeters in each centimeter.

$$3.5 \times 10 = 35$$

3.5 centimeters is 35 millimeters.

Convert millimeters to centimeters:

There are 10 millimeters in each centimeter.

$$28 \div 10 = 2.8$$

28 millimeters is 2.8 centimeters.

CONNECT IT

Now you will use the problem from the previous page to help you understand how to solve the problem by choosing a unit to convert.

1 Why do you need to convert one of the units of measure to solve the problem?

2 Why do you multiply to convert centimeters to millimeters?

Why do you divide to convert millimeters to centimeters?

3 Who measured the longer worm? How much longer was it? Explain how you know.

4 Look at the problem wording again. Why can you give the answer in millimeters or centimeters?

5 REFLECT

Look back at your **Try It**, strategies by classmates, and **Picture It** and **Model It**. Which models or strategies do you like best for choosing a unit to convert? Explain.

....

....

....

APPLY IT

Use what you just learned to solve these problems. Refer to the Math Reference Sheet as necessary.

6 Steve and Tom each build a box. Who builds a box with a greater volume? How much greater is the volume? Show your work.

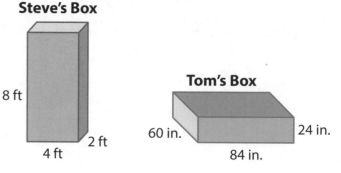

Steve's Box

8 ft
4 ft
2 ft

Tom's Box

60 in.
84 in.
24 in.

Solution ....

7 A tree in Kenji's backyard is 6.7 meters tall. A tree in Cho's backyard is 730 centimeters tall. Which tree is taller? How much taller? Show your work.

Solution ....

8 A rectangular coffee table is $1\frac{2}{3}$ yards long and 2 feet wide. Which of the following show the perimeter of the tabletop?

Ⓐ $3\frac{2}{3}$ yards

Ⓑ 14 feet

Ⓒ 7 feet

Ⓓ $\frac{14}{3}$ yards

Ⓔ $4\frac{2}{3}$ yards

Practice Choosing a Unit to Solve a Word Problem

Study the Example showing how to compare measurements in different units. Then solve problems 1–6.

EXAMPLE

Ryan and Layla measured the length of their hermit crabs. Ryan measured his crab to be 34 millimeters. Layla measured her crab to be 2.8 centimeters. Who has the longer crab? (1 centimeter = 10 millimeters)

34 millimeters

2.8 centimeters

It is easier to compare measurements in the same units. You can compare in millimeters or centimeters.

To compare the crabs in millimeters, convert the length of Layla's crab into millimeters. To convert from centimeters to millimeters, use multiplication:
2.8 centimeters × 10 = 28 millimeters
Layla's crab is 28 millimeters long.

    34 millimeters > 28 millimeters

Ryan has the longer crab.

1 Which is the smaller unit, centimeters or millimeters? ....

2 In the Example, multiplication was used to convert centimeters to millimeters. What operation would you use to convert millimeters to centimeters? ....

3 Look at the Example. Ryan and Layla's friend Jan also has a hermit crab. Jan measures her hermit crab to be 3.3 centimeters long.

   a. Who has the longer crab, Jan or Layla? ....

   b. Who has the longer crab, Jan or Ryan? ....
      Show your work.

Lesson 26 Solve Word Problems Involving Conversions   **545**

4   Geno's hamster Zippy ran in her hamster wheel for 48 seconds, stopped to drink water, and then ran in the wheel for another $2\frac{1}{2}$ minutes. How long did Zippy run in all? Show your work. (1 minute = 60 seconds)

Solution ....

5   Diego has two guinea pigs, Pia and Zia. Pia weighs $1\frac{3}{4}$ pounds. Zia weighs 32 ounces. Who weighs more? How much more? Show your work. (1 pound = 16 ounces)

Solution ....

6   The perimeter of a rectangular table is 18 feet. The table is 42 inches wide. Which of the following show the length of the table? (1 foot = 12 inches)

Ⓐ 6 feet

Ⓑ 60 inches

Ⓒ 66 inches

Ⓓ 5 feet

Ⓔ $5\frac{1}{2}$ feet

Refine Solving Word Problems Involving Conversions

Complete the Example below. Then solve problems 1–8, using the Math Reference Sheet as necessary.

EXAMPLE

Pierre is 53 inches tall. Pilar is 5 feet tall. Who is shorter? How much shorter is the shorter person?

Look at one way you could explain your work using conversions.

12 inches = 1 foot, so multiply 5 by 12.

5 × 12 = 60

60 − 53 = 7

Solution ....

The student used the relationship between feet and inches to solve the problem.

PAIR/SHARE
How could you answer this question in feet?

APPLY IT

1 Venell put together a model train with 25 train cars. Each train car is 80 millimeters long. How many meters long is Venell's model train if there are no gaps between the cars? Show your work.

Which is the larger unit, meters or millimeters?

PAIR/SHARE
There are 100 centimeters in 1 meter. How long is the train in centimeters?

Solution ....

2 Ed solved a puzzle $\frac{3}{4}$ minute faster than Brett. Brett solved the puzzle in 135 seconds. How long did it take Ed to solve the puzzle? Show your work.

How many seconds are in one minute?

Solution . . . .

PAIR/SHARE

How can you use a clock to find the number of seconds in $\frac{3}{4}$ minute?

3 Bennett exercises by lifting weights. He can lift 200 pounds 3 times without resting between lifts. Which equation shows a correct way to find the total number of ounces, *n*, he can lift without resting?

Ⓐ $n = (200 \times 3) \div 16$

Ⓑ $n = (200 \div 16) \times 3$

Ⓒ $n = (200 \times 3) \times 16$

Ⓓ $n = (16 \div 3) \times 200$

Jory chose Ⓐ as the correct answer. How did he get that answer?

Does Bennett lift a greater number of pounds or a greater number of ounces?

PAIR/SHARE

Does Jory's answer make sense?

4 A football field is marked every 5 yards. Garrett ran from the first mark to the eleventh mark. Which expression can you use to find the number of feet Garrett ran?

Ⓐ $(10 \times 5) \div 3$

Ⓑ $(10 \div 5) \div 3$

Ⓒ $(10 \times 5) \times 3$

Ⓓ 5×3

5 Mr. Wayne's class collected empty soda cans for a recycling project. Each of the 20 students had to collect 40 cans. Each can has a mass of 15 grams. How many kilograms of cans did the class collect to recycle?

Ⓐ 0.6 kilogram

Ⓑ 12 kilograms

Ⓒ 12,000 kilograms

Ⓓ 12,000,000 kilograms

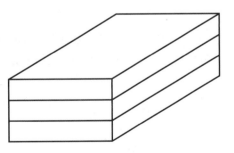

6 Susan is stacking boxes on a shelf. Each box is shaped like a rectangular prism and has a length of 2 feet, a width of 15 inches, and a height of 3 inches, as shown below at the left.

Susan will stack the boxes on top of each other, as shown below at the right. The space above the shelf is $1\frac{1}{2}$ yards high.

What is the greatest number of boxes that Susan can stack on the shelf?

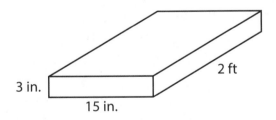

.... boxes

7 Emma keeps track of the time she spends on a report each week.

Week 1: $1\frac{1}{2}$ hours research, $\frac{3}{4}$ hour reading, and 45 minutes on outline

Week 2: $2\frac{1}{4}$ hours writing, 45 minutes editing, and $\frac{1}{2}$ hour on cover

Part A How much time did Emma spend on her report the first week? Show your work.

Solution

Part B How much more time did Emma spend on the report the second week than she spent the first week? Show your work.

Solution

8 **MATH JOURNAL**

Teresa has 800 milliliters of water. Sara has 5 liters of water. Without converting units, tell why Sara has more water than Teresa. Then show how much more water Sara has.

☑ **SELF CHECK** Go back to the Unit 4 Opener and see what you can check off.

Make Line Plots and Interpret Data

Dear Family,

This week your child is learning about line plots and about how to interpret data on line plots.

A **line plot** is a data display that shows data as marks above a number line. A line plot is useful for showing how data are grouped. The line plot below shows the weights of onions. Each onion is represented by an X on the line plot. Xs that are one above another represent onions that have the same weight. Weights are labeled beneath the number line.

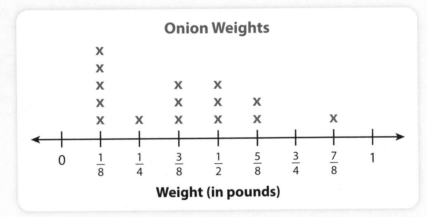

Onion Weights

Weight (in pounds)

The line plot shows how the data are grouped. You can describe the data by looking at the line plot. Most pieces of data on this line plot are grouped between $\frac{1}{8}$ and $\frac{1}{2}$.

You can also do mathematical operations with the data values to describe the data. For example, you can find the difference between the heaviest and lightest onions. The weights vary from $\frac{1}{8}$ pound to $\frac{7}{8}$ pound. The difference is $\frac{6}{8}$, or $\frac{3}{4}$, pound.

Using line plots can help your child ask and answer complex questions about data.

Invite your child to share what he or she knows about making line plots and interpreting data by doing the following activity together.

ACTIVITY MAKING A LINE PLOT

Do this activity with your child to make line plots and interpret data.

Materials centimeter ruler

Work with your child to make a line plot of the lengths of book covers.

- Gather several books. Measure the length of the cover of each book. Measure to the nearest centimeter. Use your own centimeter ruler or cut out and use the centimeter ruler below.

- Make a list of the lengths and use the data to make a line plot.

  - Use the number line below. Title the line plot "Lengths of Book Covers" and write the label "Length (in centimeters)" beneath the number line.

  - Decide what scale to use based on the measurements you collect. Then mark Xs to show the data.

- Describe how the data shown on the line plot are grouped.

- Do mathematical operations with the data values to describe the data. For example, find the difference between the length of the longest book cover and the length of the shortest book cover.

```
0   1   2   3   4   5   6   7   8   9   10  11  12  13  14  15  16
centimeters
```

Explore Making Line Plots and Interpreting Data

You have made and used line plots before. Now you will make line plots and use them to answer more complex questions about data. Use what you know to try to solve the problem below.

Learning Target

- Make a line plot to display a data set of measurements in fractions of a unit $\left(\frac{1}{2}, \frac{1}{4}, \frac{1}{8}\right)$. Use operations on fractions for this grade to solve problems involving information presented in line plots.

SMP 1, 2, 3, 4, 5, 6

Mrs. May's class weighs tomatoes of different sizes and types. They weigh each tomato to the nearest $\frac{1}{8}$ pound. The results are shown in the line plot below. What is the difference between the weights of the heaviest tomato and the lightest tomato?

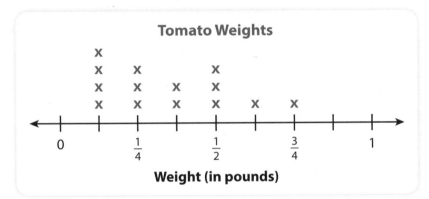

Tomato Weights

Weight (in pounds)

TRY IT

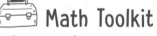 **Math Toolkit**

- fraction tiles
- fraction circles
- fraction bars
- number lines

DISCUSS IT

Ask your partner: Why did you choose that strategy?

Tell your partner: I knew ... so I ...

CONNECT IT

 LOOK BACK

What is the difference between the weights of the heaviest tomato and the lightest tomato? Explain how you know.

2 LOOK AHEAD

Graphing data on a line plot helps you get a "picture" of the data and how the data are spread out or grouped.

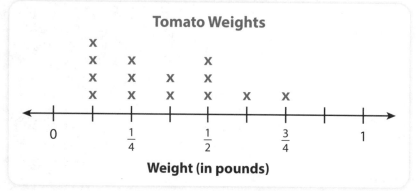

Tomato Weights

Weight (in pounds)

a. The scale of a line plot is the value represented by the distance between one tick mark and the next on the number line.

Counting up, how many tick marks does it take to get from 0 to 1? ....

What fraction of the whole is the distance between tick marks? ....

So, the scale is .... pound.

b. How many data values are recorded on the line plot? Explain how you know.

c. What do the four Xs above $\frac{1}{8}$ represent?

3 REFLECT

If the scale of the line plot is $\frac{1}{8}$, why are the numbers $\frac{1}{4}, \frac{1}{2}, \frac{3}{4}$, and 1 on the line plot?

....

Prepare for Making Line Plots and Interpreting Data

1 Think about what you know about line plots. Fill in each box. Use words, numbers, and pictures. Show as many ideas as you can.

Word	In My Own Words	Example
line plot		
scale		
data		

2 Look at the line plot. What is the scale? How do you know?

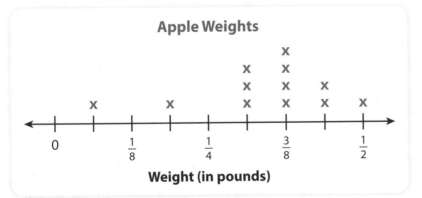

Apple Weights

Weight (in pounds)

3 Solve the problem. Show your work.

Mr. Lee's class weighs apples of different sizes and types. They weigh each apple to the nearest $\frac{1}{16}$ pound. The results are shown in the line plot below. What is the difference between the weights of the heaviest apple and the lightest apple?

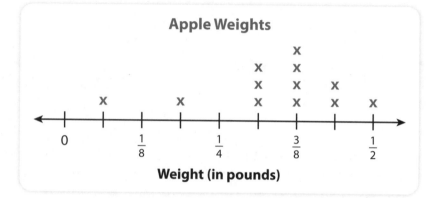

Apple Weights

Weight (in pounds)

Solution ....

4 Check your answer. Show your work.

Develop Making a Line Plot

Read and try to solve the problem below.

> Keira bought 12 different types of stickers to decorate her scrapbook. She measured the width, in inches, of each type of sticker and wrote down the results. Make a line plot to organize and display Keira's data.

Sticker Widths (in inches)		
$\frac{1}{4}$	$\frac{3}{4}$	$\frac{3}{8}$
$\frac{3}{4}$	$\frac{1}{4}$	$\frac{5}{8}$
$\frac{1}{8}$	$\frac{1}{2}$	$\frac{1}{2}$
$\frac{1}{2}$	1	1

TRY IT

Math Toolkit
- fraction tiles or circles
- fraction bars
- number lines
- rulers
- sticky notes

DISCUSS IT

Ask your partner: How did you get started?

Tell your partner: I started by . . .

Explore different ways to understand making a line plot.

> Keira bought 12 different types of stickers to decorate her scrapbook. She measured the width, in inches, of each type of sticker and wrote down the results. Make a line plot to organize and display Keira's data.

Sticker Widths (in inches)		
$\frac{1}{4}$	$\frac{3}{4}$	$\frac{3}{8}$
$\frac{3}{4}$	$\frac{1}{4}$	$\frac{5}{8}$
$\frac{1}{8}$	$\frac{1}{2}$	$\frac{1}{2}$
$\frac{1}{2}$	1	1

MODEL IT

List what you know and plan how to make the line plot.

- The fractions are in eighths, fourths, and halves.

- The narrowest sticker is $\frac{1}{8}$ inch. The widest sticker is 1 inch.

- The line plot will start at 0 and go up to 1 inch.

- The line plot will show an X for each of the 12 stickers.

- The line plot will have a title and scale label.

MODEL IT

Use your plan to start labeling and marking the line plot to display the data.

Draw a number line from 0 to 1. Choose an appropriate scale for the data.

Graph each data value. The line plot below shows the first row from Keira's list of sticker widths.

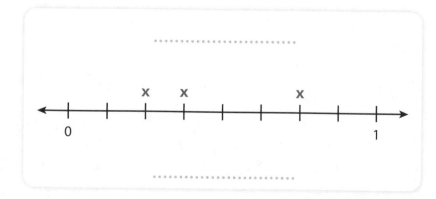

CONNECT IT
Now you will use the problem from the previous page to help you understand how to make a line plot.

1 Look at the first **Model It**. Why is it a good plan to go from 0 up to 1 inch for the line plot?

2 What scale is used for the line plot in the second **Model It**? Explain.

3 Why does this scale make sense for the data?

4 The tick marks in the second **Model It** are not labeled with fractions. Do they have to be? How can you locate data points with Xs when the tick marks are not labeled with numbers?

5 Complete the line plot in the second **Model It**. Include the rest of the data, a title above the line plot, and a label for the scale below the line plot.

6 How do you use a line plot to organize measurement data?

7 REFLECT

Look back at your **Try It**, strategies by classmates, and **Model Its**. Which models or strategies do you like best for making line plots? Explain.

....

....

....

APPLY IT

Use what you just learned to solve these problems.

8 Shawn records the lengths in inches of several bugs he collects for a science project. Complete the line plot of the data.

$1\frac{5}{8}$, $3\frac{1}{4}$, $1\frac{3}{4}$, $2\frac{7}{8}$, $1\frac{3}{4}$, $3\frac{1}{4}$, $1\frac{5}{8}$, $2\frac{3}{8}$, 1, $1\frac{3}{4}$

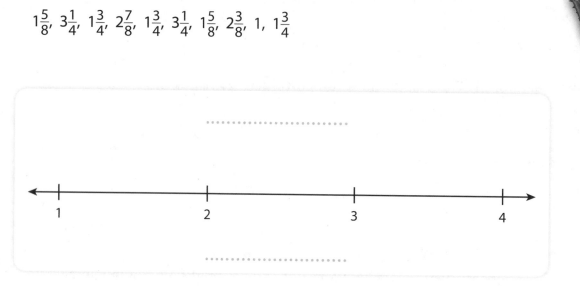

9 Dolores trains for a 5-mile race. She keeps track of the distances she runs each day, in miles, in a training log. Use the data to make a line plot. Show your work.

Distance Run Each Day (miles)							
	Mon	**Tues**	**Wed**	**Thurs**	**Fri**	**Sat**	**Sun**
Week 1	$7\frac{1}{4}$	5	$6\frac{1}{2}$	$5\frac{1}{2}$	5	7	6
Week 2	$4\frac{1}{4}$	$6\frac{1}{2}$	$5\frac{1}{2}$	5	$7\frac{1}{4}$	$6\frac{1}{4}$	$4\frac{3}{4}$

Practice Making Line Plots

Study the Example showing how to make a line plot. Then solve problems 1–4.

EXAMPLE

Rosa's grandfather gives her a box of old foreign coins. She measures the diameter of each coin. Then she makes a list that shows the diameters. How can Rosa show the data in a line plot?

Coin Diameters (inches)					
$\frac{3}{8}$	$\frac{3}{4}$	$\frac{7}{8}$	$\frac{5}{8}$	$\frac{3}{8}$	$\frac{3}{4}$
$\frac{7}{8}$	$\frac{7}{8}$	$\frac{5}{8}$	$\frac{7}{8}$	$\frac{3}{8}$	$\frac{7}{8}$

Begin making the line plot by marking a number line from 0 to 1 in eighths.

Make one X to stand for each coin in the table. The line plot below shows three of the 12 data values in Rosa's list.

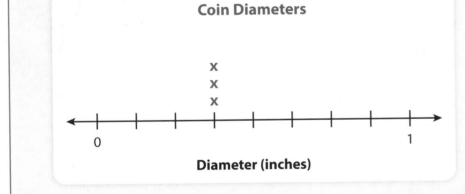

Coin Diameters

Diameter (inches)

1. Which data values do the three Xs Rosa draws represent?

2. Graph the rest of the data from the list in the Example on the line plot.

3 Gabe has a collection of stamps. He records the heights of the stamps in inches.

$\frac{1}{2}$, 1, $1\frac{1}{2}$, $2\frac{1}{2}$, 3, 2, 2, $\frac{1}{2}$, 1, 1, $2\frac{1}{2}$, 2, $1\frac{1}{2}$, 1, $2\frac{1}{2}$

Complete a line plot of Gabe's data. Label each tick mark for this line plot.

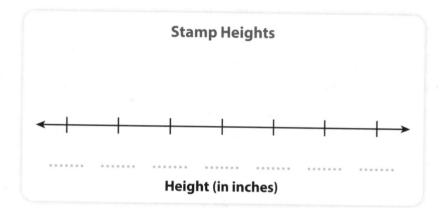

Stamp Heights

Height (in inches)

4 Gabe also records the widths of some of the stamps in inches.

$\frac{3}{4}$, 1, $1\frac{1}{2}$, $1\frac{1}{4}$, $1\frac{1}{2}$, 1, $1\frac{3}{4}$, $1\frac{3}{4}$, $1\frac{1}{2}$, $\frac{1}{2}$

Make a line plot of Gabe's data.

What scale did you use to make your line plot? Explain.

Vocabulary

scale (on a graph) the value represented by the distance between one tick mark and the next on a number line.

Develop Solving Problems Using Data in a Line Plot

Read and try to solve the problem below.

The line plot shows the lengths of songs, in minutes, on Ron's playlist.

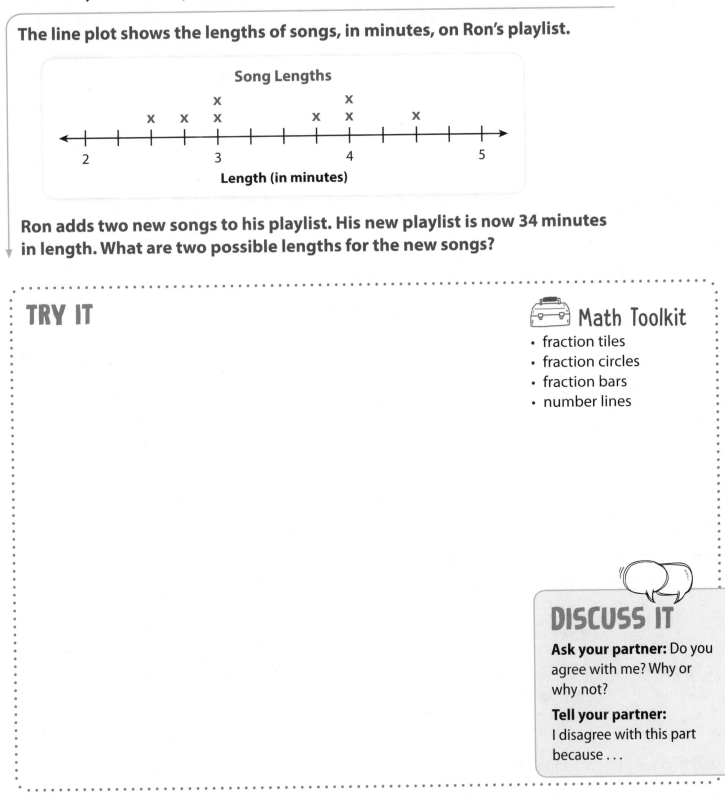

Ron adds two new songs to his playlist. His new playlist is now 34 minutes in length. What are two possible lengths for the new songs?

TRY IT

🧰 Math Toolkit
• fraction tiles
• fraction circles
• fraction bars
• number lines

DISCUSS IT

Ask your partner: Do you agree with me? Why or why not?

Tell your partner: I disagree with this part because . . .

Explore different ways to understand solving a problem using data from the line plot.

The line plot shows the lengths of songs, in minutes, on Ron's playlist.

Song Length

```
                        X               X
              X   X     X         X     X         X
      ←—+—+—+—+—+—+—+—+—+—+—+—+—+—→
        2       3           4           5
```

Length (in minutes)

Ron adds two new songs to his playlist. His new playlist is now 34 minutes in length. What are two possible lengths for the new songs?

PICTURE IT

You can use a picture to help understand the data in the problem.

Label the tick marks in the line plot to show the song lengths.

Song Lengths

```
                      X                 X
              X   X   X           X     X         X
      ←—+—+—+—+—+—+—+—+—+—+—+—+—+—→
        2  2¼  2½  2¾  3  3¼  3½  3¾  4  4¼  4½  4¾  5
```

Length (in minutes)

MODEL IT

You can use equations to help understand the problem.

Write an equation to find m, the length in minutes of Ron's original playlist.

$$m = 2\frac{1}{2} + 2\frac{3}{4} + 3 + 3 + 3\frac{3}{4} + 4 + 4 + 4\frac{1}{2}$$

Write an equation that shows how to find the total number of minutes, t, that the new songs add to the length of Ron's playlist.

$$t = 34 - m$$

Find two songs that add to the number of minutes, t.

CONNECT IT

Now you will use the problem from the previous page to help you understand how to solve a problem using data in a line plot.

1 How many minutes, *m*, is Ron's original playlist? Explain how you know.

2 How many minutes, *t*, do the two new songs add to Ron's playlist? Explain.

3 What are two possible lengths for the new songs? Is more than one correct answer possible? Explain.

4 How did the line plot help you solve the problem?

5 How did you use operations with fractions to solve the problem?

6 **REFLECT**

Look back at your **Try It**, strategies by classmates, and **Picture It** and **Model It**. Which models or strategies do you like best for solving problems using data in a line plot? Explain.

....

....

....

APPLY IT

Use what you just learned to solve these problems.

Renaldo collects 10 shells at the beach and weighs each of them. He uses the line plot below to display the data.

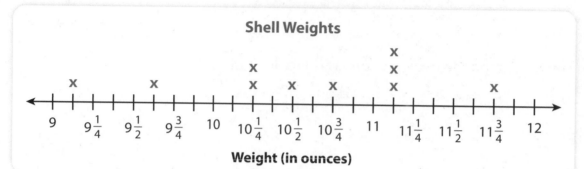

Shell Weights

Weight (in ounces)

 7 What is the difference between the weights of the lightest and heaviest shells Renaldo collected? Show your work.

Solution ....

8 What is the total weight of the shells Renaldo collected that weigh less than $10\frac{1}{2}$ ounces? Show your work.

Solution ....

9 What is the total weight of the shells Renaldo collected most often?

Ⓐ $11\frac{3}{4}$ ounces

Ⓑ $22\frac{1}{4}$ ounces

Ⓒ $33\frac{3}{8}$ ounces

Ⓓ $33\frac{3}{4}$ ounces

Practice Solving Problems Using Data in a Line Plot

Study the Example showing how to solve a problem using data in a line plot. Then solve problems 1–6.

EXAMPLE

Miguel has strips of colored tape that he uses to decorate his model planes. The line plot shows how many strips he has in several different lengths.

If Miguel places all of the $\frac{1}{4}$-inch strips in a row, how long is the line that he would make?

Tape Strip Lengths

```
                    x           x
            x       x           x
    x       x       x           x
    x       x       x   x       x
    x       x       x   x       x
    x       x       x   x       x
    x       x       x   x       x
    x       x       x   x       x
  <-+---+---+---+---+---+---+---+->
    0                           1
```

Length (in inches)

The tick marks divide the distance from 0 to 1 into eighths. The second tick mark to the right of 0 is $\frac{2}{8}$, or $\frac{1}{4}$.

There are six $\frac{1}{4}$-inch strips, and $6 \times \frac{1}{4} = \frac{6}{4}$, or $1\frac{1}{2}$. The line would be $1\frac{1}{2}$ inches long.

---

1 How long a line can Miguel make using all the $\frac{3}{8}$-inch strips? Show your work.

Solution ....

2 What is the difference in length between a line made with all the $\frac{3}{8}$-inch strips and a line made with all the $\frac{3}{4}$-inch strips? Show your work.

Solution ....

Use the data in the line plot to solve problems 3–6.

③ If Miguel uses 2 of each strip length that he has to make a line, how long would the line be? Show your work.

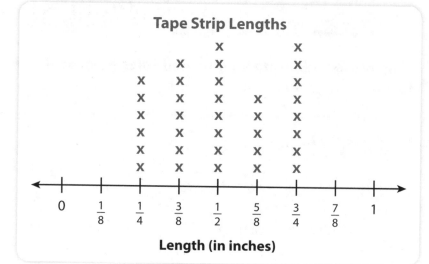

Tape Strip Lengths

Length (in inches)

Solution

④ Miguel adds another data value so that the difference between the longest and shortest strip lengths is $\frac{3}{4}$ inch. What tape length did Miguel add? Explain.

⑤ If Miguel makes a line with all of the $\frac{5}{8}$-inch strips, what is the total length in inches? Show your work.

Solution

⑥ How could Miguel use strips of different lengths to make a 4-inch line?

Refine Making Line Plots and Interpreting Data

Complete the Example below. Then solve problems 1–7.

EXAMPLE

The line plot shows the weights of the burgers Mel made for a cookout. How many pounds of meat did she use to make all the burgers?

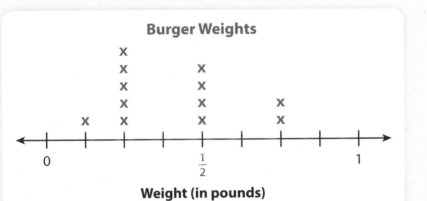

Burger Weights

Weight (in pounds)

Look at how you could use the data in the line plot.

One $\frac{1}{8}$-lb burger: $\frac{1}{8}$ Five $\frac{1}{4}$-lb burgers: $5 \times \frac{1}{4} = 1\frac{1}{4}$

Four $\frac{1}{2}$-lb burgers: $4 \times \frac{1}{2} = 2$ Two $\frac{3}{4}$-lb burgers: $2 \times \frac{3}{4} = 1\frac{1}{2}$

Total: $\frac{1}{8} + 1\frac{1}{4} + 2 + 1\frac{1}{2}$

Solution ....

The student multiplied the number of burgers of each weight by the weight and then added the amounts to find the total.

PAIR/SHARE
Check your partner's answer using addition instead of multiplication.

APPLY IT

1 Use the line plot in the Example. Mel cuts the smallest burger in half. What is the weight of the meat in each half? Show your work.

What operations could you use to solve the problem?

PAIR/SHARE
Draw a picture to show how Mel cut the burger.

Solution ....

2 An animal doctor's scale weighs animals to the nearest $\frac{1}{4}$ pound. The list below shows the weights, in pounds, of the last 10 dogs the animal doctor saw.

$$14\frac{1}{2}, \ 17\frac{1}{2}, \ 15\frac{1}{4}, \ 17\frac{1}{4}, \ 17\frac{1}{2}, \ 15\frac{1}{4}, \ 14\frac{1}{4}, \ 16, \ 14\frac{3}{4}, \ 15\frac{1}{4}$$

Create a line plot to show the data.

How should the line plot's scale be labeled to show these data?

PAIR/SHARE
How is your line plot the same as your partner's? How is it different?

3 Look at the line plot for problem 2. Which statement about the data is true?

Ⓐ The heaviest dog is $4\frac{1}{4}$ pounds heavier than the lightest dog.

Ⓑ The three lightest dogs weigh $43\frac{1}{2}$ pounds combined.

Ⓒ The three heaviest dogs weigh $52\frac{1}{2}$ pounds combined.

Ⓓ The 16-pound dog is closer in weight to the lightest dog than to the heaviest dog.

Michelle chose Ⓐ as the correct answer. How did she get that answer?

Read each statement carefully and check it against the data to see if it is true.

PAIR/SHARE
Does Michelle's answer make sense?

4 Juan drives a race car. The race tracks vary in length. To prepare for racing season, he records the lengths, in miles, of the tracks in the list shown below. Which line plot correctly shows the track data?

$$\frac{1}{4}, \frac{1}{2}, \frac{3}{8}, \frac{1}{2}, \frac{1}{4}, \frac{1}{2}, 1, 1\frac{1}{4}, \frac{3}{4}, \frac{1}{2}, \frac{7}{8}, \frac{1}{2}, \frac{3}{4}$$

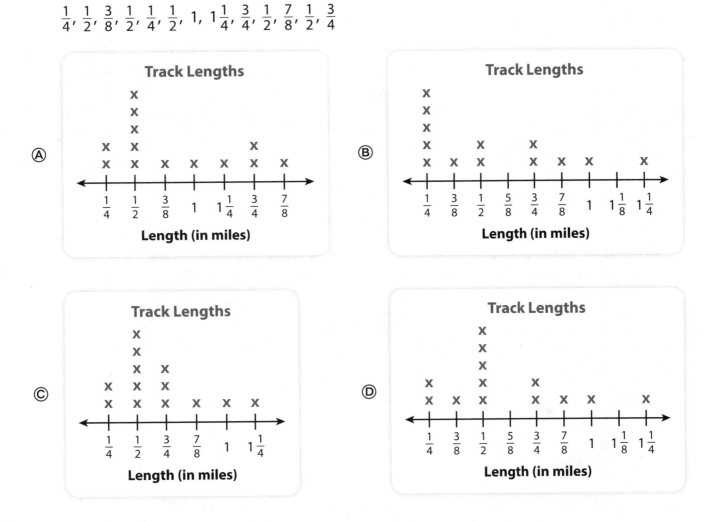

5 Look at the data for problem 4. Choose *True* or *False* for each statement.

	True	False
The longest track is 6 times the length of the shortest track.	Ⓐ	Ⓑ
The combined length of the three shortest tracks is $\frac{4}{8}$ mile.	Ⓒ	Ⓓ
The combined length of the three longest tracks is $3\frac{1}{8}$ miles.	Ⓔ	Ⓕ
Half the length of the shortest track is $\frac{1}{8}$ mile.	Ⓖ	Ⓗ

6 Sara owns Sara's Hardware. She made the line plot below to compare the fuel tank capacity of several lawn mowers she sells.

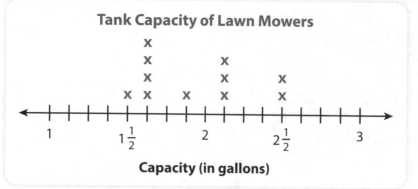

Part A What is the most common capacity of the mowers she sells? ....

Part B Marc buys the lawn mower with the smallest tank capacity. He uses 3 full tanks of gas mowing in the summer. How much fuel does he use? Show your work.

Solution ....

7 MATH JOURNAL

Jordan looks at the line plot above. He says the difference between the most common capacity and the least capacity is $\frac{1}{4}$ gallon. He says he knows the difference without subtracting. Explain Jordan's mistake. Then find the actual difference between the measurements.

☑ **SELF CHECK** Go back to the Unit 4 Opener and see what you can check off.

Understand Categories of Two-Dimensional Figures

Dear Family,

This week your child is exploring relationships among categories of two-dimensional figures.

You can group polygons, or closed figures with straight sides, by their **attributes**. Some attributes of polygons are the number of sides or angles they have.

When you place figures in a group, you can form a **category** and one or more **subcategories**. You can use a **hierarchy** to order groups of figures. The top of the hierarchy shows the category for the most general group. As you go down a hierarchy, you can see how the subcategories are related.

Diagrams can show the hierarchy of categories and subcategories. The **Venn diagram** at the right shows the relationship between polygons, quadrilaterals, and rectangles. The diagram shows that all rectangles are quadrilaterals but that not all quadrilaterals are rectangles. The diagram also shows that all quadrilaterals are polygons but that not all polygons are quadrilaterals.

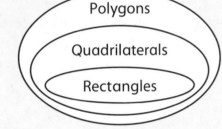

A **tree diagram** also can show relationships among two-dimensional figures. The tree diagram at the right shows the hierarchy of polygons from top to bottom. Polygons, the most general category, are shown at the top of the hierarchy. Rectangles, the most specific category, are shown at the bottom of the hierarchy.

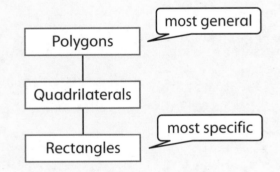

Invite your child to share what he or she understands about relationships among categories of two-dimensional figures by doing the following activity together.

ACTIVITY CATEGORIES OF TWO-DIMENSIONAL FIGURES

Do this activity with your child to understand categories of two-dimensional figures.

Work with your child to draw two-dimensional figures that share a common attribute.

- Use the dot paper below. The first person describes an attribute of a figure, and the second person draws and names the figure.

- Switch roles. The person who goes first now repeats the attribute that was said and adds another attribute to the description. The second person draws and names the figure.

- For example:

  - The first person says *a three-sided figure*. The second person draws and names a triangle.

  - Switch roles. The first person says *a three-sided figure with a right angle*. The second person draws and names a right triangle.

  - When you are finished, describe the category-subcategory relationship for your figures: Example: Right triangles are a subcategory of triangles.

Explore Categories of Two-Dimensional Figures

How can two-dimensional figures be grouped to show they are related?

Learning Target

• Understand that attributes belonging to a category of two-dimensional figures also belong to all subcategories of that category.

SMP 1, 2, 3, 4, 5, 6, 7

MODEL IT

Complete the problems below.

1 Polygons are described by their **attributes**, such as the number of sides or angles they have, and grouped into **categories** based on attributes they have in common.

In the space below, draw an example of a rectangle and an example of a square. Then complete the table by writing three attributes shared by all rectangles and three attributes shared by all squares.

Rectangles	Squares

2 **a.** What attribute do all squares have that not all rectangles have?

b. Circle the true statement below.

Every rectangle is a square.   Every square is a rectangle.

3 A **subcategory** is a category that shares all the attributes of a larger category. Are rectangles a subcategory of squares, or are squares a subcategory of rectangles?

DISCUSS IT

• Did you and your partner list the same attributes for rectangles and squares?

• I think rectangles and squares are subcategories of quadrilaterals because . . .

MODEL IT

Complete the problems below.

4 A **Venn diagram** uses ovals or other shapes to represent categories and to show how the categories are ordered in a **hierarchy,** or ranking, based on their attributes.

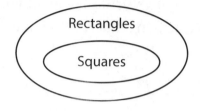

a. How does the Venn diagram at the right show that squares are a subcategory of rectangles?

b. What is an attribute of rectangles that is also an attribute of squares?

5 **a.** Use what you know about triangles to write the labels *Isosceles Triangles* and *Equilateral Triangles* in the Venn diagram below.

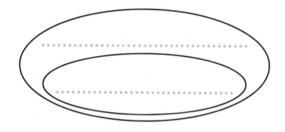

b. Use your Venn diagram to complete the statement below.

.... triangles are a subcategory of

.... triangles.

c. Describe two ways an equilateral triangle has the same attributes as an isosceles triangle.

DISCUSS IT

- How did you and your partner decide how to place isosceles and equilateral triangles in the Venn diagram?

- I think Venn diagrams are a good way to show the hierarchy of polygons because . . .

6 **REFLECT**

Based on your Venn diagram, is every equilateral triangle an isosceles triangle, or is every isosceles triangle an equilateral triangle? Explain.

Prepare for Categories of Two-Dimensional Figures

1 Think about what you know about two-dimensional figures. Fill in each box. Use words, numbers, and pictures. Show as many ideas as you can.

Word	In My Own Words	Example
attribute		
category		
subcategory		
Venn diagram		

2 Explain the category-subcategory relationships shown in the Venn diagram.

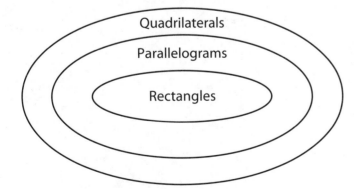

Lesson 28 Understand Categories of Two-Dimensional Figures   **577**

Complete the problems below.

3) Write three attributes shared by all rhombuses and three attributes shared by all squares.

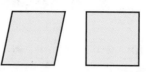

Rhombuses	Squares

4) What attribute do all squares have that not all rhombuses have?

5) Circle the true statement below.

Every rhombus is a square.   Every square is a rhombus.

6) Are rhombuses a subcategory of squares, or are squares a subcategory of rhombuses?

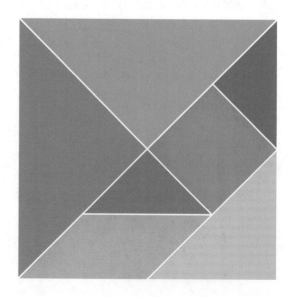

Develop Categories of Two-Dimensional Figures

MODEL IT: VENN DIAGRAMS

Try these two problems.

 A hierarchy orders categories from *most general* to *most specific*. Ovals A–D in this Venn diagram list attributes of four categories of quadrilaterals. Use the terms below to fill in the names of the subcategories from most general to most specific.

Rectangles   Squares   Parallelograms

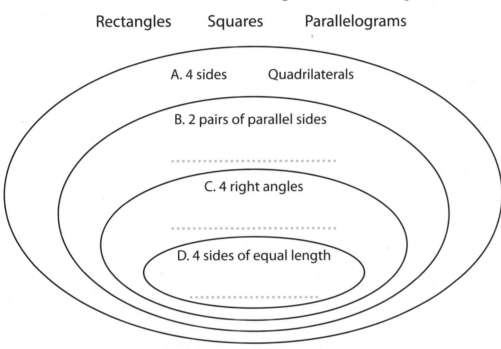

A. 4 sides   Quadrilaterals

B. 2 pairs of parallel sides

C. 4 right angles

D. 4 sides of equal length

2 Use the Venn diagram and what you know about quadrilaterals to complete the table. Fill in subcategory names for B–D and attributes for C and D.

Category/Subcategory	Attributes
A. Category: Quadrilaterals	4 sides
B. Subcategory:	4 sides 2 pairs of parallel sides
C. Subcategory:	
D. Subcategory:	

DISCUSS IT

• Compare your Venn diagram and table with your partner's diagram and table. How are they alike? How are they different?

• I think quadrilaterals is the most general category because . . .

MODEL IT: TREE DIAGRAMS

3 A **tree diagram** is a hierarchy diagram that connects categories and subcategories with lines to show how they are related. Write the terms below in the boxes of the tree diagram at the right to order the categories from most general to most specific.

Rectangles   Squares   Parallelograms

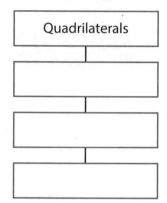

Quadrilaterals

CONNECT IT

Complete the problems below.

4 How are Venn diagrams and tree diagrams alike? How are they different?

DISCUSS IT

- How did you and your partner decide how to place the terms in the tree diagram?

- I think all rectangles are parallelograms because . . .

5 Use a Venn diagram or tree diagram to order the categories below from most general to most specific. Then explain why your order makes sense by describing the attributes the figures share.

Triangles   Polygons   Right Triangles

Practice with Categories of Two-Dimensional Figures

Study how the Example shows relationships among categories of two-dimensional figures. Then solve problems 1–5.

EXAMPLE

Give an example of how the Venn diagram below shows that one category of figures is a subcategory of another.

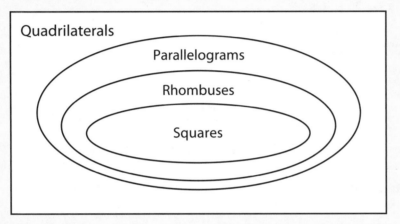

The Venn diagram shows that the region for parallelograms completely overlaps the region for quadrilaterals, so parallelograms are a subcategory of quadrilaterals. A parallelogram has all the attributes of a quadrilateral. A quadrilateral has 4 sides, and so does a parallelogram.

1 Complete each sentence using *all* or *some* to make each statement true.

a. Squares have .... of the attributes of rhombuses.

b. Rhombuses have .... of the attributes of parallelograms.

c. Parallelograms have .... of the attributes of rhombuses.

2 Name two attributes that squares and rhombuses always share.
Name an attribute they only sometimes share.

3 Use the tree diagram to complete each sentence. Use *all* or *some* to make each statement true.

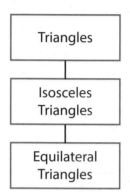

a. Isosceles triangles have .... of the attributes of equilateral triangles.

b. Equilateral triangles have .... of the attributes of isosceles triangles.

c. Triangles have .... of the attributes of isosceles triangles.

4 Name one attribute that isosceles and equilateral triangles always share. Name one attribute that they only sometimes share.

5 Look at the shape shown below. Which list of names for the shape is ordered from most general category to most specific subcategory?

Ⓐ quadrilateral, parallelogram, rectangle

Ⓑ quadrilateral, rectangle, parallelogram

Ⓒ quadrilateral, polygon, rectangle

Ⓓ rectangle, parallelogram, quadrilateral

Refine Ideas About Categories of Two-Dimensional Figures

APPLY IT
Complete these problems on your own.

1 EXPLAIN

A *regular polygon* has all sides of equal length and all angles of equal measure. Which shapes below are subcategories of regular polygons? Explain.

squares   pentagons   equilateral triangles   hexagons

2 ANALYZE

A tree diagram can use two lines to show subcategories that do not overlap. Jose drew these two diagrams to show how categories of triangles are related. Are his diagrams correct? Explain.

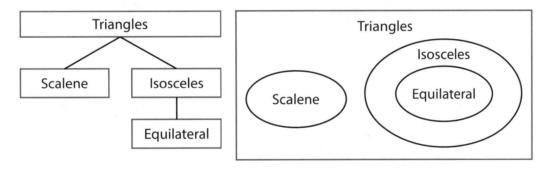

3 CREATE

Describe the attributes of a shape that is both a rectangle and a rhombus. Name the shape and use the grid to draw an example.

PAIR/SHARE
Discuss your solutions for these three problems with a partner.

Use what you have learned to complete problem 4.

4 Jake makes a tree diagram to show a hierarchy of polygons.

Part A Explain why Jake's tree diagram is not correct.
Then explain what changes are needed.

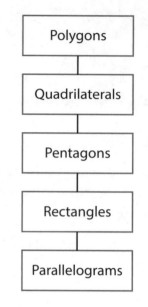

Part B Draw a tree diagram or Venn diagram to show
the hierarchy of the five categories in Part A.

5 MATH JOURNAL

Are rhombuses a subcategory of parallelograms or are
parallelograms a subcategory of rhombuses? Explain.

Classify Two-Dimensional Figures

Dear Family,

This week your child is continuing to make diagrams to classify two-dimensional figures.

Your child will continue to explore how Venn diagrams and tree diagrams can be used to show relationships among categories of two-dimensional figures.

Figures can be grouped into categories by their attributes or properties, such as the number of their sides and angles, the length of their sides, and the measure of their angles. Your child knows all figures in a category share at least one attribute. While subcategories share the attribute(s) of the broader category, figures in subcategories have additional specific properties.

Your child knows how to use Venn diagrams or tree diagrams to show that one category is a subcategory of another. Now your child will use more complex diagrams to classify figures. The Venn diagram below shows "Triangles" as the broader category. The labeled ovals represent subcategories of triangles.

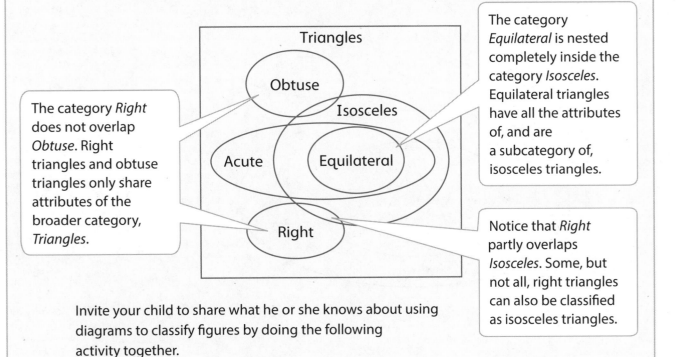

The category *Right* does not overlap *Obtuse*. Right triangles and obtuse triangles only share attributes of the broader category, *Triangles*.

The category *Equilateral* is nested completely inside the category *Isosceles*. Equilateral triangles have all the attributes of, and are a subcategory of, isosceles triangles.

Notice that *Right* partly overlaps *Isosceles*. Some, but not all, right triangles can also be classified as isosceles triangles.

Invite your child to share what he or she knows about using diagrams to classify figures by doing the following activity together.

ACTIVITY CLASSIFYING TWO-DIMENSIONAL FIGURES

Do this activity with your child to classify two-dimensional figures.

Work together with your child to describe how figures are classified in Venn diagrams.

- Look at the figures in the Venn diagrams below and talk about how the figures are related to each other.

- Work together to describe the attributes of the figures. Tell what attributes the figures do and do not share. The words in the box describe some attributes of figures that you might use in your discussion.

three sides	equilateral	isosceles
right angle	acute angle	obtuse angle
equal side lengths	different side lengths	

- Write category names in each oval to classify the shapes.

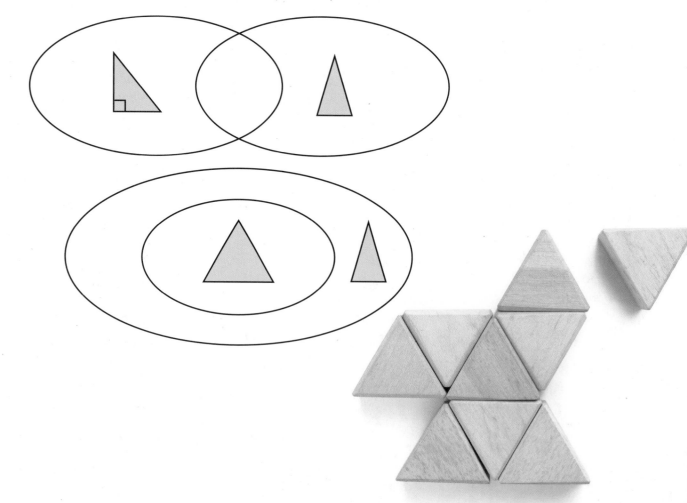

Explore Classifying Two-Dimensional Figures

Previously, you learned that attributes of a category are shared by its subcategories. Use what you know to try to solve the problem below.

> **Arrange the quadrilaterals shown below into a Venn diagram that shows a hierarchy of categories from most general to most specific. Label the categories represented by these shapes in your Venn diagram.**

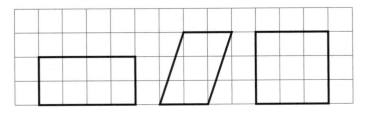

TRY IT

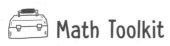 **Math Toolkit**
• geoboard
• rubber bands
• tracing paper
• grid paper
• rulers

DISCUSS IT

Ask your partner: Can you explain that again?

Tell your partner: I started by . . .

CONNECT IT

1 **LOOK BACK**

Explain how you organized the shapes in your Venn diagram.

2 **LOOK AHEAD**

In the Venn diagram below, the red and blue ovals represent subcategories of polygons. Three polygons are placed into the ovals, with one shape in both ovals.

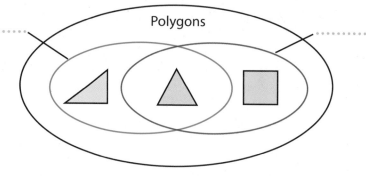

a. What property is shared by the two shapes in the red oval?

b. What property is shared by the two shapes in the blue oval?

c. Use your answers to parts a and b to write subcategory labels for each oval.

d. Why is the equilateral triangle inside of both the red and blue ovals?

3 **REFLECT**

In a Venn diagram, what is true about two categories represented by ovals that overlap without one oval being completely inside the other?

Prepare for Classifying Two-Dimensional Figures

1 Think about what you know about Venn diagrams. Fill in each box.
Use words, numbers, and pictures. Show as many ideas as you can.

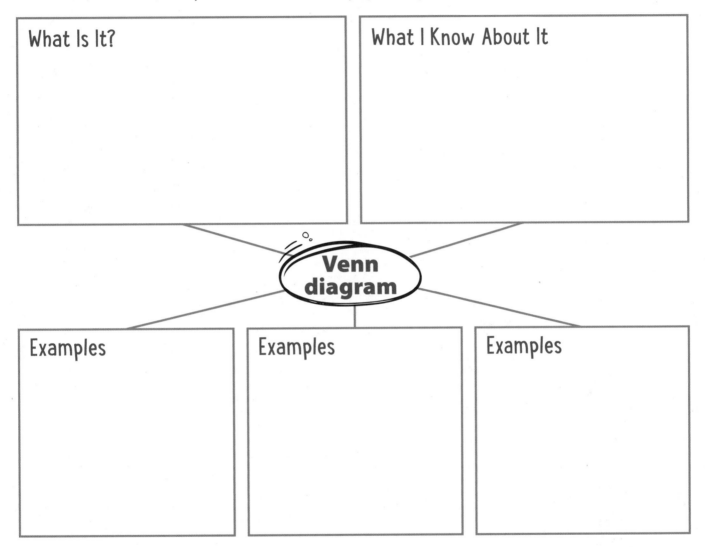

What Is It?	What I Know About It

Venn diagram

Examples	Examples	Examples

2 Look at the Venn diagram. Why is the square inside of
all the ovals?

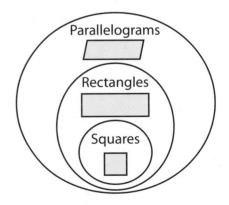

3 Solve the problem. Show your work.

Arrange the triangles below into the Venn diagram. Label each oval as a catgeory of triangles.

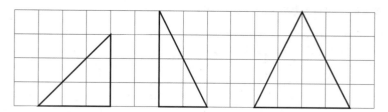

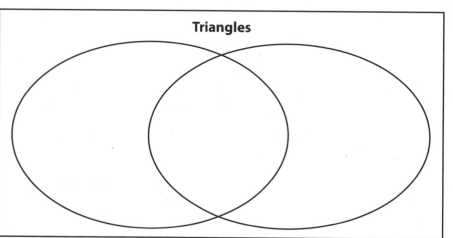

Triangles

4 Check your answer. Show your work.

Develop Classifying Two-Dimensional Figures

Read and try to solve the problem below.

Sort these shapes into the Venn diagram below to show the relationships among parallelograms, squares, rectangles, rhombuses, and quadrilaterals.

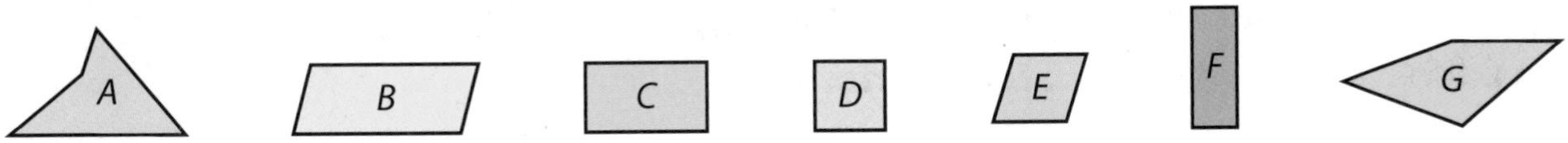

A   B   C   D   E   F   G

Use at least one shape in each region of the diagram. Classify the shapes by labeling each region with the category name.

TRY IT

🧰 **Math Toolkit**
- geoboard
- rubber bands
- tracing paper
- grid paper
- rulers

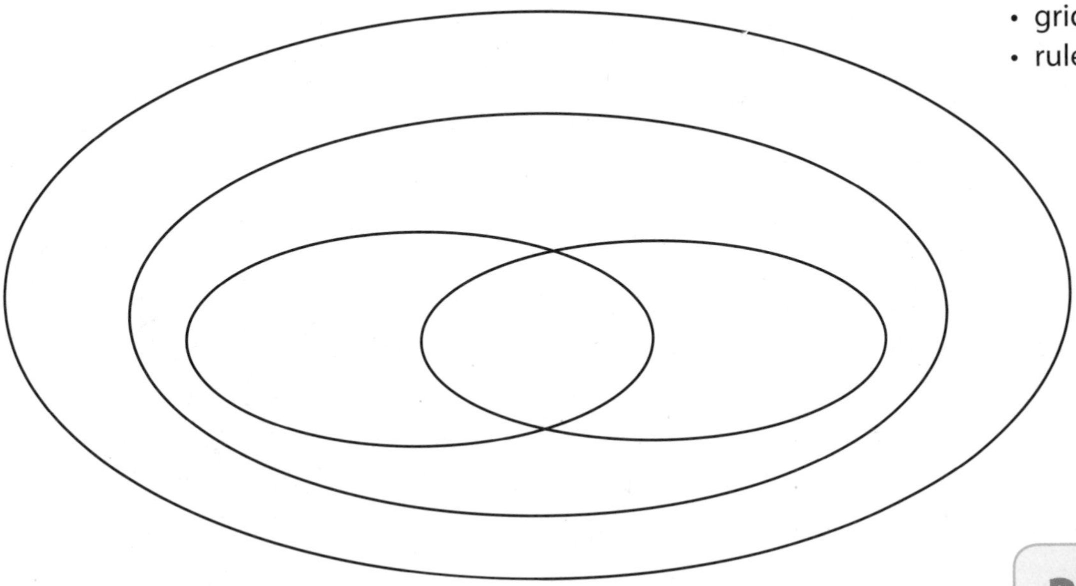

DISCUSS IT

Ask your partner: How did you get started?

Tell your partner: I knew ... so I ...

Explore ways to understand classifying two-dimensional figures using a Venn diagram.

> **Sort these shapes into a Venn diagram to show the relationships among parallelograms, squares, rectangles, rhombuses, and quadrilaterals.**
>
>
>
> **Use at least one shape in each region of the diagram. Classify the shapes by labeling each region with the category name.**

MODEL IT

You can use a table to compare properties of the categories of polygons.

Property	Parallelograms	Quadrilaterals	Rectangles	Rhombuses	Squares
4 sides	✕	✕	✕	✕	✕
2 pairs of parallel sides	✕		✕	✕	✕
2 pairs of sides of equal length	✕		✕	✕	✕
4 sides of equal length				✕	✕
4 right angles			✕		✕

MODEL IT

You can show the relationships among the categories with a Venn diagram.

Two regions of the Venn diagram are labeled and three of the shapes have been classified by placing them into the diagram.

Write the remaining category names and the letters for Figures C, D, E, and F in the diagram.

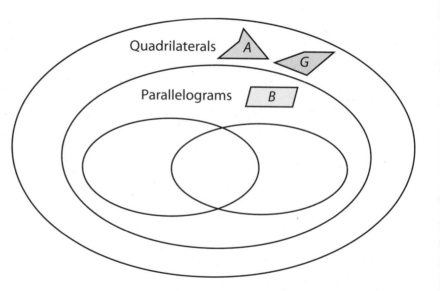

CONNECT IT

Now you will use the problem from the previous page to help you understand how to use Venn diagrams to classify two-dimensional figures.

1 Look at the Quadrilaterals column in the table and the placement of shapes *A* and *G* in the Venn diagram. Why are shapes *A* and *G* placed in the outermost oval?

2 Explain how the Venn diagram supports this statement: *All parallelograms are quadrilaterals, but not all quadrilaterals are parallelograms.*

3 Look at the table. Which categories share all the properties listed for parallelograms?

How is this shown in the Venn diagram?

4 Look at the table. Which properties are not shared by rectangles and rhombuses?

How is this shown in the Venn diagram?

5 Look at your Venn diagram. Why is Shape *D* inside all the ovals?

6 REFLECT

Look back at your **Try It**, strategies by classmates, and **Model Its**. Which models or strategies do you like best for classifying two-dimensional figures? Explain.

....

....

APPLY IT

Use what you just learned to solve these problems.

7 Mathematicians define trapezoids in two different ways:

- **Trapezoids** are quadrilaterals with *exactly one pair* of parallel sides.

- **Trapezoids** are quadrilaterals with *at least one pair* of parallel sides.

Write *exactly one pair* or *at least one pair* to show which definition of trapezoid was used to make each Venn diagram below.

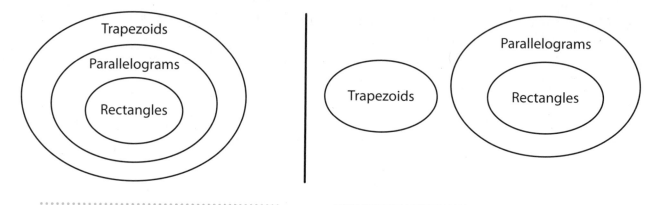

8 Sort these shapes into the Venn diagram, based on properties of having parallel sides and having perpendicular sides. Write category labels for the two ovals.

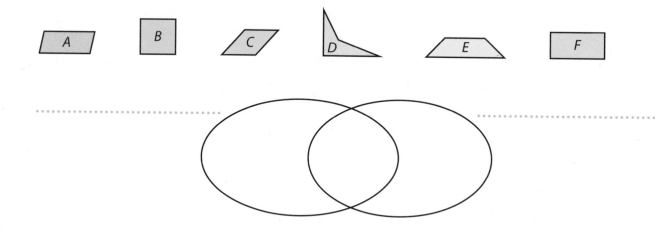

9 Which definition in problem 7 lets you classify shape *A* in problem 8 as a trapezoid? Explain.

Practice Classifying Two-Dimensional Figures

Study the Example showing how to use Venn diagrams to classify two-dimensional figures. Then solve problems 1–5.

EXAMPLE

You can use a Venn diagram to show the relationships between acute, right, obtuse, isosceles, and equilateral triangles.

You can plan your Venn diagram using a table describing properties of the triangles.

Triangle	Description
Acute	all acute angles
Right	2 acute angles and 1 right angle
Obtuse	2 acute angles and 1 obtuse angle
Isosceles	at least 2 sides of equal length
Equilateral	all sides equal length

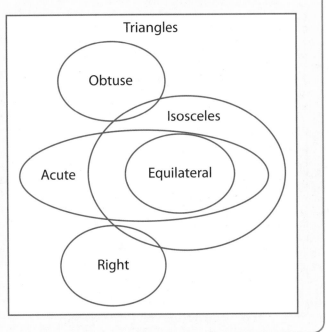

1   Look at the Venn diagram above. Can a right triangle ever be an equilateral triangle? Explain.

2 Look at the Venn diagram on the previous page. Write a statement about the relationship between acute triangles and isosceles triangles.

3 Look at the Venn diagram on the previous page. Write a statement about the relationship between acute triangles and equilateral triangles.

4 Draw a Venn diagram in the space below to show the relationships among the categories of isosceles, scalene, and equilateral triangles within the broader category, Triangles.

Triangles

5 Determine whether each statement is *True* or *False*. Draw a picture to help if needed.

	True	False
A scalene triangle is never isosceles.	Ⓐ	Ⓑ
A right triangle is sometimes equilateral.	Ⓒ	Ⓓ
A right triangle is never isosceles.	Ⓔ	Ⓕ
A scalene triangle can be a right, obtuse, or acute triangle.	Ⓖ	Ⓗ

Develop Classifying Two-Dimensional Figures with Tree Diagrams

Read and try to solve the problem below.

> Make a tree diagram to show the hierarchy of the following shapes based on their properties: rhombus, trapezoid, polygon, square, quadrilateral, rectangle, parallelogram. Use the exclusive definition of trapezoid in your diagram: a trapezoid is a quadrilateral with exactly one pair of parallel sides.
>
> Then, classify these shapes into as many categories as possible.

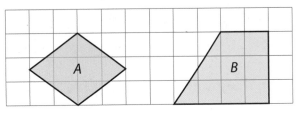

TRY IT

 Math Toolkit
- geoboard
- rubber bands
- tracing paper
- grid paper
- rulers

DISCUSS IT

Ask your partner: How did you get started?

Tell your partner: At first, I thought . . .

Explore ways to understand classifying two-dimensional figures using a tree diagram.

> Make a tree diagram to show the hierarchy of the following shapes based on their properties: rhombus, trapezoid, polygon, square, quadrilateral, rectangle, parallelogram. Use the exclusive definition of trapezoid in your diagram: a trapezoid is a quadrilateral with exactly one pair of parallel sides.
>
> Then, classify these shapes into as many categories as possible.

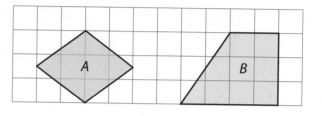

MODEL IT

You can use a Venn diagram to look at the hierarchy of the shapes.

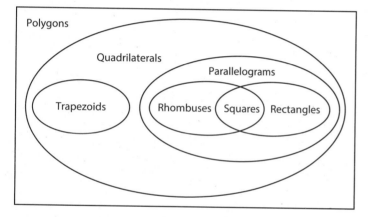

MODEL IT

You can show the hierarchy among shapes with a tree diagram.

This tree diagram has the most general category at the left (or top) and more specific categories as you go towards the right (or down). Each shape belongs in every category before it.

Write the remaining shape names in the diagram.

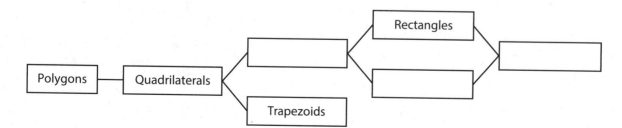

CONNECT IT

Now you will use the problem from the previous page to help you understand how to use tree diagrams to classify two-dimensional figures.

1 Look at the Venn Diagram. Which part of the diagram shows the most general category? Which part of the diagram shows the most specific category?

2 How is the tree diagram similar to the Venn diagram? How is it different?

3 How can you see all of the categories that a shape belongs to in a tree diagram? What are all of the categories that shape *A* belongs to?

4 Why do the branches that come off *Rectangles* and *Rhombuses* both lead to *Squares*?

5 Explain the relationship between the properties of categories when you move left or right (or up or down) in a tree diagram.

6 REFLECT

Look back at your **Try It**, strategies by classmates, and **Model Its**. Which models or strategies do you like best for classifying two-dimensional figures? Explain.

....

....

....

APPLY IT

Use what you just learned to solve these problems.

7 Cyrus made the following tree diagram to show the relationship among scalene triangles, equilateral triangles, and isosceles triangles. Is his diagram correct? Explain.

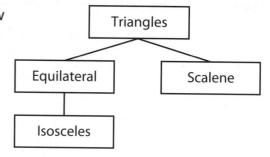

8 An equilateral triangle has three sides that have the same length. An equilateral triangle may also be called an equiangular triangle because each of the three angles has the same measure, 60°. Insert an additional category in the tree diagram for equiangular triangles. Explain.

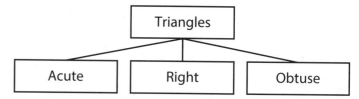

9 Look at the tree diagrams in the two problems above. Shape *E* has all sides the same length. What are all categories of triangles to which this triangle belongs? Explain.

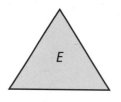

Practice Classifying Two-Dimensional Figures with Tree Diagrams

Study the Example showing how to use a tree diagram to classify two-dimensional figures. Then solve problems 1–5.

EXAMPLE

You can use a tree diagram to show the relationship between quadrilaterals, parallelograms, rectangles, squares, and rhombuses.

You can arrange your tree diagram using descriptions from a table of the properties of each quadrilateral.

Figure	Description
Quadrilateral	4 sides
Parallelogram	4 sides 2 pairs of parallel sides
Rhombus	4 sides 2 pairs of parallel sides 4 sides of equal length
Rectangle	4 sides 2 pairs of parallel sides 4 right angles
Square	4 sides 2 pairs of parallel sides 4 sides of equal length 4 right angles

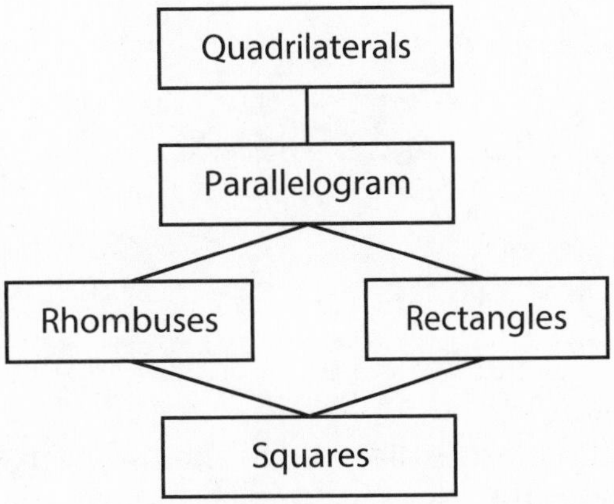

1. Look at the tree diagram above. Write a statement about the relationship between rhombuses and squares.

2 Look at the tree diagram on the previous page. Can a rhombus ever be a rectangle? Explain.

3 Draw a tree diagram to show the relationship among the following categories: polygons, pentagons, quadrilaterals, parallelograms, trapezoids, rectangles, and squares. Use the inclusive definition of trapezoid: *a quadrilateral with at least one pair of parallel sides*.

4 How would your tree diagram in the previous problem be different if you used the exclusive definition for trapezoid? Explain.

5 Determine whether each statement is *always*, *sometimes*, or *never* true. Use the inclusive definition for trapezoid.

	Always	Sometimes	Never
A square is a parallelogram.	Ⓐ	Ⓑ	Ⓒ
A trapezoid is a rectangle	Ⓓ	Ⓔ	Ⓕ
A pentagon is a parallelogram.	Ⓖ	Ⓗ	Ⓘ
A trapezoid is a square.	Ⓙ	Ⓚ	Ⓛ

Refine Classifying Two-Dimensional Figures

Complete the Example below. Then solve problems 1–8.

EXAMPLE

Hugo classified polygons based on properties of having exactly four sides and having all sides equal in length.

Look at how Hugo placed three figures in a tree diagram.

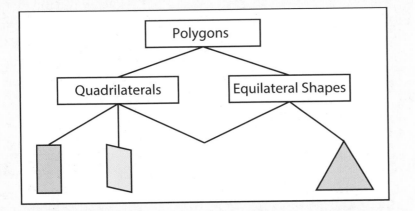

Draw a shape that belongs to both branches of the tree diagram. What is the name of the shape you drew?

Solution ....

What shape has four sides and all sides equal in length?

PAIR/SHARE
How can this tree diagram be shown with a Venn diagram?

APPLY IT

1 Draw a Venn diagram or a tree diagram to show the relationships among quadrilaterals, polygons, trapezoids, and hexagons. Then write a statement about the relationship between quadrilaterals and trapezoids. Show your work.

What is the most general category in your diagram?

PAIR/SHARE
What does your diagram show about hexagons and quadrilaterals?

2 Draw a Venn diagram or tree diagram to show the relationships among these polygons.

Polygon	Description
Quadrilateral	polygon with exactly 4 sides
Trapezoid	quadrilateral with exactly 1 pair of parallel sides
Parallelogram	quadrilateral with 2 pairs of parallel sides

The table contains one of the definitions of a trapezoid.

PAIR/SHARE
How would the diagram change if the description of the trapezoid used the definition *quadrilateral with at least one pair of parallel sides*?

3 Look at the Venn diagram below.

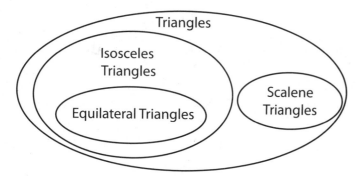

All triangles are three-sided polygons.

Which statement is true?

Ⓐ An equilateral triangle is always an isosceles triangle.

Ⓑ An isosceles triangle is always an equilateral triangle.

Ⓒ Scalene and isosceles triangles share no attributes.

Ⓓ The label inside the largest oval could be *Acute Triangles*.

Brad chose Ⓑ as the correct answer. How did he get that answer?

PAIR/SHARE
What would you say to Brad to help him understand his mistake?

4 Draw a tree diagram to show the relationships among triangles, quadrilaterals, isosceles triangles, and polygons.

5 Use the diagram in problem 4. Write two different statements that describe relationships among the shapes.

6 Could you add the two shapes below to your diagram in problem 4? If so, where would you put them? Name each shape as you explain your thinking.

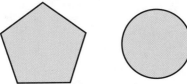

7 Saul drew a Venn diagram to show how rhombuses and squares are related. He used arrows to label each region with properties of shapes inside that region.

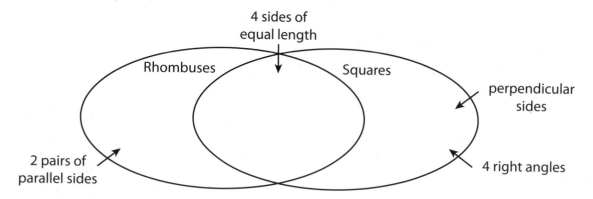

Part A Is Saul's Venn diagram correct? If not, what mistake did he make?

Part B Describe the relationship between rhombuses and squares.

8 MATH JOURNAL

A regular polygon has all sides of equal length. Sami says that all squares, equilateral triangles, and pentagons can be classified as regular polygons. Is Sami correct? Draw a Venn diagram and explain your thinking.

☑ **SELF CHECK** Go back to the Unit 4 Opener and see what you can check off.

Self Reflection

In this unit you learned to . . .

Skill	Lesson
Convert from one measurement unit to another, for example: 4 feet = 48 inches.	25, 26
Make a line plot of data represented as fractions of measurements.	27
Classify two-dimensional figures based on their properties, for example: a square is also a rhombus and a rectangle, but not all rhombuses and rectangles are squares.	28, 29
Use a Venn diagram and tree diagram to organize shapes that share the same properties.	29

Think about what you have learned.

Use words, numbers, and drawings.

1 One topic I could use in my everyday life is .... because . . .

2 A mistake I made that helped me learn was . . .

3 One thing I could do better is . . .

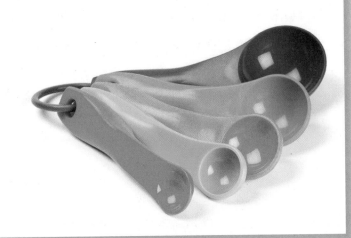

Work with Measurement and Data

Study an Example Problem and Solution

SMP 1 Make sense of problems and persevere in solving them.

Read this problem involving measurement. Then look at Sweet T's solution to this problem.

Salad Dressing

Sweet T needs to make salad dressing for an event. He knows that 2 gallons is not enough and 3 gallons is too much. Sweet T finds 2 quarts of vinegar and 2 gallons of oil in the cabinet. Read the salad dressing recipe.

Salad Dressing Recipe

- Mix equal parts of water, lemon juice, and vinegar.
- Add an amount of oil equal to the other three ingredients combined.
- Mix in your favorite herbs and spices and shake.

Sweet T wants to know how much water, lemon juice, vinegar, and oil he needs to make the dressing. He also wants to know how much oil and vinegar will be left over.

Read the sample solution on the next page. Then look at the checklist below. Find and mark parts of the solution that match the checklist.

✓ PROBLEM-SOLVING CHECKLIST

- ☐ Tell what is known.
- ☐ Tell what the problem is asking.
- ☐ Show all your work.
- ☐ Show that the solution works.

a. **Circle** something that is known.

b. **Underline** something that you need to find.

c. **Draw a box around** what you do to solve the problem.

d. **Put a checkmark** next to the part that shows the solution works.

SWEET T'S SOLUTION

Hi, I'm Sweet T. Here's how I solved this problem.

- **I know** the four different ingredients and how the amounts compare.

- **I have to decide** what units to use to find the amount of each ingredient and the amount left over. The information in the problem has both quarts and gallons. I think it will be easier to convert all amounts to cups.

  There are 16 cups in a gallon.   There are 4 cups in a quart.

  2 gallons = 2 × 16, or 32 cups   2 quarts = 2 × 4, or 8 cups

  3 gallons = 3 × 16, or 48 cups

  I can also use quarts, but I might end up using cups to find leftover amounts anyway.

- **Now I know** that the total amount is greater than 32 cups and less than 48 cups.

- **One way to think about** the amounts is that half of the dressing is oil and half is a combination of water, lemon juice, and vinegar. I'll look for half of a number between 33 and 47.

- **I'll use 36** for the total.

  $\frac{1}{2} \times 36 = 18$, so I need 18 cups of oil.

  Then divide by 3 to find the other amounts.

  18 ÷ 3 = 6, so I need 6 cups of each of the other ingredients.

  I multiplied 36 by $\frac{1}{2}$ but I also could have divided by 2.

- **I can check by adding.**

  18 cups + 6 cups + 6 cups + 6 cups = 36 cups

  36 > 32 and 36 < 48

- **Now I can write** the amount of each ingredient and find the leftovers.

  Amount for dressing   **Amount leftover**

  18 c oil   32 c − 18 c = 14 c leftover oil

  6 c vinegar   8 c − 6 c = 2 c leftover vinegar

  6 c water

  6 c lemon juice

  I used the abbreviation for cups since I had to write it so many times!

Try Another Approach

There are many ways to solve problems. Think about how you might solve the Salad Dressing problem in a different way.

Salad Dressing

Sweet T needs to make salad dressing for an event. He knows that 2 gallons is not enough and 3 gallons is too much. Sweet T finds 2 quarts of vinegar and 2 gallons of oil in the cabinet. Read the salad dressing recipe.

Salad Dressing Recipe

- Mix equal parts of water, lemon juice, and vinegar.
- Add an amount of oil equal to the other three ingredients combined.
- Mix in your favorite herbs and spices and shake.

Sweet T wants to know how much water, lemon juice, vinegar, and oil he needs to make the dressing. He also wants to know how much oil and vinegar will be left over.

PLAN IT

Answer these questions to help you start thinking about a plan.

A. How could you convert the ingredients to quarts to find a solution?

B. What are some total amounts of dressing that you could choose? Explain.

SOLVE IT

Find a different solution for the Salad Dressing problem. Show all your work on a separate sheet of paper.

You may want to use the Problem-Solving Tips to get started.

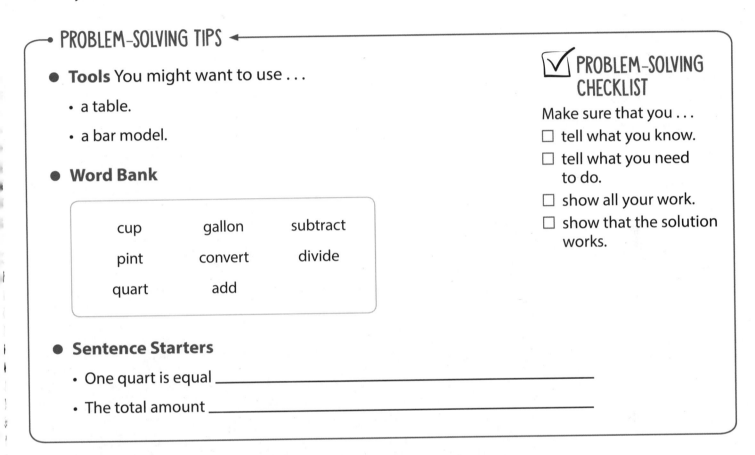

PROBLEM-SOLVING TIPS

- **Tools** You might want to use . . .
  - a table.
  - a bar model.

- **Word Bank**

cup	gallon	subtract
pint	convert	divide
quart	add	

- **Sentence Starters**
  - One quart is equal _____
  - The total amount _____

☑ PROBLEM-SOLVING CHECKLIST

Make sure that you . . .
- ☐ tell what you know.
- ☐ tell what you need to do.
- ☐ show all your work.
- ☐ show that the solution works.

REFLECT

Use Mathematical Practices As you work through the problem, discuss these questions with a partner.

- **Persevere** How can you use your answers to the **Plan It** questions to help choose a solution path?

- **Be Precise** Why should you label your numbers with units as you work through the solution?

DISCUSS MODELS AND STRATEGIES

Read the problem. Write a solution on a separate sheet of paper.
Remember, there can be lots of ways to solve a problem!

Desserts

Sweet T wants to make 4 different desserts for the event. He looks at his favorite recipes. He knows he only has $1\frac{6}{8}$ cups of flour and no time to buy more. Sweet T writes the amount of flour needed for each of the recipes below.

Almond Bites	$\frac{3}{8}$ cup
Cashew Dreams	$\frac{1}{2}$ cup
Chocolate Hugs	$\frac{1}{4}$ cup
Delish Cupcake	$\frac{5}{8}$ cup
Spiced Cookies	$\frac{3}{4}$ cup
Dream Pops	$\frac{2}{4}$ cup
Celebration Cake	$1\frac{1}{2}$ cups

Use a line plot to help Sweet T choose 4 desserts to make.

PLAN IT AND SOLVE IT

Find a solution to the Desserts problem.

- Make a line plot.

- Choose 4 desserts to make.

- Explain or show why your solution works.

You may want to use the Problem-Solving Tips to get started.

PROBLEM-SOLVING TIPS

- **Questions**

  - What will you use as labels on your line plot?

  - Can you use all the recipes?

- **Word Bank**

fraction	add	no more than
denominator	sum	compare
line plot		

 PROBLEM-SOLVING CHECKLIST

Make sure that you . . .
- ☐ tell what you know.
- ☐ tell what you need to do.
- ☐ show all your work.
- ☐ show that the solution works.

REFLECT

Use Mathematical Practices After you complete the task, choose one of these questions to discuss with a partner.

- **Use Models** How can you use a model to show that your solution works?

- **Make Sense of the Problem** How can the information in the problem help you choose 4 recipes?

Persevere On Your Own

Read the problems. Write a solution on a separate sheet of paper.

Backyard Barbecue

Sweet T is planning a barbecue for 50 people. There will be 2 different kinds of protein and 3 side dishes on the menu. Here are his choices, including amounts to estimate per person.

Protein

- Choose from ground beef, chicken, steak, or salmon.
- Estimate 6 to 8 ounces per person.

Sides

- Baked beans: 2 to 3 ounces per person
- Coleslaw: 3 to 4 ounces per person
- Potato salad: 4 to 5 ounces per person
- Grilled vegetables: 3 to 4 ounces per person
- Rice: 1 to 2 ounces per person

What food and how much of each should Sweet T make?

SOLVE IT

Suggest a menu for Sweet T.

- Choose the items for the menu.

- Tell how many pounds and ounces are needed for each dish. Explain.

REFLECT

Use Mathematical Practices After you complete the task, choose one of these questions to discuss with a partner.

- **Make Sense of Problems** What was the first step you took to find your solution? Why?

- **Reason Mathematically** What operations did you use to find your solution? Explain why.

Hierarchy Hit

Max makes a game to play at Sweet T's event. At random times in the game, a quadrilateral appears on the screen. Players smash the quadrilateral to score bonus points. When a shape is hit, it morphs into a different quadrilateral. It continues to morph into other quadrilaterals according to the rules below.

Hierarchy Hit Rules

- The morphing can go from the more general to more specific shape. Or it can go from the more specific to more general shape.
- There are at least three different quadrilaterals in the morphing sequence.

How could the quadrilaterals morph in Max's game?

SOLVE IT

Help Max design the game's hierarchy.

- Find quadrilaterals that will fit with the rules.
- Make a tree diagram that shows a hierarchy of quadrilaterals and their names.
- Draw an example of each quadrilateral.
- Explain why the order of shapes shows a hierarchy.

REFLECT

Use Mathematical Practices After you complete the task, choose one of these questions to discuss with a partner.

- **Use Models** How does the tree diagram you made show the hierarchy of shapes? Explain.

- **Be Precise** How does the most specific shape you drew fit in all of the other categories? Explain.

1 Mrs. Davis has 6 bowls of flour for a project. The line plot below shows the fraction of a cup of flour left in each bowl after the project is done.

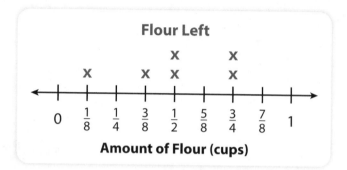

Flour Left

Amount of Flour (cups)

What is the total amount of flour left in the bowls after the project is done?

Ⓐ $\frac{12}{28}$ cup

Ⓑ $1\frac{3}{4}$ cups

Ⓒ 2 cups

Ⓓ 3 cups

2 Name one attribute that acute triangles and equilateral triangles always share. Name one attribute they only sometimes share.

3 How many feet are equivalent to 84 inches? Show your work.

Solution

4 Tanner and Jaylen are practicing for a track meet. Last week, Tanner ran 900 meters on each of 3 days. Jaylen ran 1.2 kilometers on each of 2 days. Which boy ran farther last week and by how much? Show your work.

Solution

5 Use the Venn diagram below to answer Part A and Part B.

Polygons

Quadrilaterals

Parallelogram

Rhombus

Rectangle

Square

Part A Use the Venn diagram. Decide if each statement is always true or sometimes true.
Choose *Always True* or *Sometimes True* for each statement.

	Always True	**Sometimes True**
A square is a polygon.	Ⓐ	Ⓑ
A quadrilateral is a rhombus.	Ⓒ	Ⓓ
A rectangle is a square.	Ⓔ	Ⓕ
A parallelogram is a quadrilateral.	Ⓖ	Ⓗ

Part B Lani wants to add this shape to the Venn diagram.

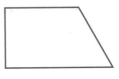

Where should she place the shape on the Venn diagram? Explain.

Solution

Performance Task

Answer the questions and show all your work on separate paper.

Ben and Cari are trying to solve the puzzle below.

Checklist
Did you . . .
- ☐ make a list?
- ☐ draw the figure on a grid?
- ☐ check your vocabulary?

Name That Shape

1. The figure is a quadrilateral.

2. The figure has a pair of parallel sides.

3. Three of the vertices are shown on the grid below.

What type of figure is it?

Ben thinks there is only one solution to the puzzle. Cari says there is more than one possible answer. Who do you think is right? Explain your reasoning. Then solve the puzzle. If you agree with Cari, find at least two possibilities for the figure's shape.

Now make your own geometry puzzle with three clues. Make sure your puzzle has only one answer and that it cannot be answered with only two clues.

REFLECT

Use Mathematical Practices After you complete the task, choose one of the following questions to answer.

- **Use Structure** How did you use the clues to solve the puzzle?

- **Be Precise** What did you think about when writing your own puzzle?

Vocabulary

Draw or write to show examples for each term. Then draw or write to show other math words in the unit.

category   a collection of objects grouped together based on attributes they have in common.

My Example

hierarchy   a ranking of categories based on attributes.

My Example

subcategory   a category within a larger category. It shares all the same attributes as the larger category. For example, parallelograms are a subcategory of quadrilaterals.

My Example

trapezoid (exclusive)   a quadrilateral with exactly one pair of parallel sides.

My Example

trapezoid (inclusive)   a quadrilateral with at least one pair of parallel sides.

My Example

tree diagram   a hierarchy diagram that connects categories and subcategories with lines to show how they are related.

My Example

Venn diagram a diagram that uses overlapping ovals (or other shapes) to show how sets of numbers or objects are related.

My Example

My Word: _____

_____

_____

My Example

My Word: _____

_____

_____

My Example

My Word: _____

_____

_____

My Example

My Word: _____

_____

_____

My Example

My Word: _____

_____

_____

My Example

Algebraic Thinking and the Coordinate Plane
Expressions, Graphing Points, Patterns and Relationships

☑ SELF CHECK

Before starting this unit, check off the skills you know below. As you complete each lesson, see how many more skills you can check off!

I can . . .	Before	After
Evaluate expressions, for example: $48 \div (6 + 10)$ has a value of 3.	☐	☐
Write a numerical expression to represent a phrase, for example: *subtract 5 from 12, then multiply by 4* can be written as $(12 - 5) \times 4$.	☐	☐
Write ordered pairs for points in the coordinate plane.	☐	☐
Graph points in the coordinate plane.	☐	☐
Find the vertical and horizontal distance between two points in the coordinate plane.	☐	☐
Graph quantities that represent real-world situations in the coordinate plane and interpret the coordinates of a point in terms of a real-world context.	☐	☐
Generate a numerical pattern using a rule.	☐	☐
Describe the relationship between corresponding terms of two number patterns.	☐	☐

Build Your Vocabulary

Math Vocabulary

Work with a partner to find the next number in each pattern. Identify the operation and write the rule for each pattern.

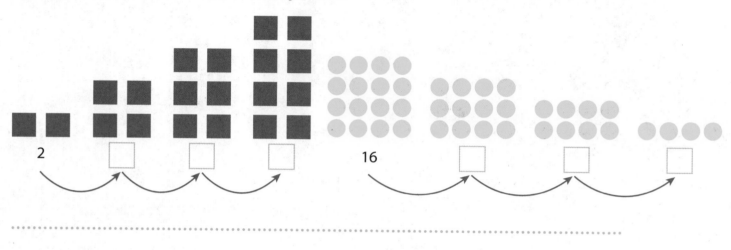

2 ☐ ☐ ☐   16 ☐ ☐ ☐

....

....

....

Academic Vocabulary

Place a check next to the academic words you know. Then use the words to complete the sentences.

☐ categorize   ☐ characterize   ☐ anticipate   ☐ concept

1 The .... of angles is important in geometry.

2 On a cloudy day, you can .... rain.

3 I will .... my books by genre: mystery, science fiction, and action adventure.

4 A pattern is .... by a recognizable arrangement that repeats.

Evaluate, Write, and Interpret Expressions

Dear Family,

This week your child is learning to evaluate, write, and interpret expressions.

When you **evaluate** an expression, you are finding the value of the expression. There are rules about the order in which you do the operations.

Your child might see an expression like this:

$$\frac{1}{2} \times (24 + 8)$$

To evaluate the expression, you first do the operation inside the parentheses. So, first add $24 + 8$. Then multiply that sum by $\frac{1}{2}$.

$$\frac{1}{2} \times (24 + 8)$$

$$\frac{1}{2} \times 32$$

$$16$$

The value of the expression is 16.

The same expression can be stated in words: *half of the sum of 24 and 8.*

Your child might also see a written phrase that describes an expression. He or she can write the expression using numbers and symbols:

15 minus the sum of 6 and 7 $15 - (6 + 7)$

Because you need to first find the sum $6 + 7$, there are parentheses around that part of the expression. To evaluate the expression, add 6 and 7 and subtract the sum from 15:

$$15 - (6 + 7)$$
$$15 - 13$$
$$2$$

Invite your child to share what he or she knows about evaluating and writing expressions by doing the following activity together.

ACTIVITY WRITING AND EVALUATING EXPRESSIONS

Do this activity with your child to write and evaluate expressions.

With your child, play a game called "Evaluate That Expression!"

- One person uses some of the math words in the box below to describe an expression in words and phrases.

sum	one less than	quotient
plus	product	difference
times	minus	divided by
triple	double	half

- The other person writes the expression using numbers and symbols. Remember to use parentheses if they are needed!

- Evaluate the expressions together. Take turns.

- Some examples of expressions:

  1. The sum of 8 and one less than 8

  2. Triple the difference of 5 and 2

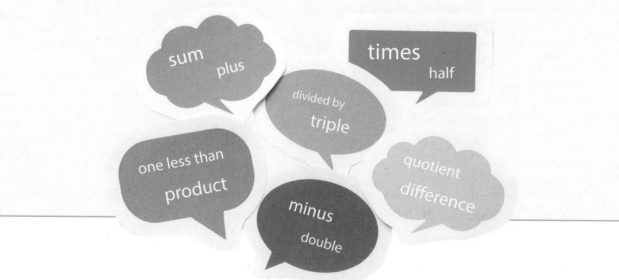

Answers: **1.** $8 + (8 - 1)$; **2.** $3 \times (5 - 2)$

Explore Evaluating, Writing, and Interpreting Expressions

You know that more than one operation may be needed to solve a multi-step problem. You also need to decide the order in which to do the steps. Use what you know to try to solve the problem below.

> **Maria and her friend go to a movie. At the snack stand, they each get a drink that costs $5 and a popcorn that costs $8. Maria pays for her friend. How much does Maria pay altogether?**

Learning Targets

- Use parentheses, brackets, or braces in numerical expressions, and evaluate expressions with these symbols.
- Write simple expressions that record calculations with numbers, and interpret numerical expressions without evaluating them.

SMP 1, 2, 3, 4, 5, 6, 7

TRY IT

Math Toolkit
- base-ten blocks
- counters
- number lines

DISCUSS IT

Ask your partner: Why did you choose that strategy?

Tell your partner: At first, I thought . . .

CONNECT IT

1 LOOK BACK

Explain how you found how much money Maria spent in all.

2 LOOK AHEAD

The problem on the previous page is a multi-step problem. It can be represented by an expression that contains **grouping symbols**—braces { }, brackets [ ], and parentheses ( ). When you **evaluate** an expression, you find the value of the expression. If an expression contains grouping symbols, you do the operation inside the grouping symbols first. The most commonly-used grouping symbols are parentheses.

To evaluate an expression, use the following rules, which are called the *order of operations*.

- First, do the operation inside grouping symbols.

- Next, multiply and divide from left to right.

- Last, add and subtract from left to right.

a. Evaluate $2 \times 5 + 8$.

b. Evaluate $2 \times (5 + 8)$.

c. How are the expressions in parts a and b the same? How are they different?

3 REFLECT

Can both expressions from problems 2a and 2b be used to find the amount of money Maria spent in all? Explain.

Prepare for Evaluating, Writing, and Interpreting Expressions

1 Think about what you know about evaluating expressions. Fill in each box. Use words, numbers, and pictures. Show as many ideas as you can.

Word	In My Own Words	Example
expression		
evaluate		
order of operations		

2 Explain the order of operations that you use to evaluate the expression $10 + (6 - 2) \times 2$.

3 Solve the problem. Show your work.

Ramon and his brother go to an amusement park. They each go on the Ferris wheel that costs $6 per ticket and a roller coaster that costs $9 per ticket. Ramon pays for all the tickets. How much does Ramon pay altogether?

Solution

4 Check your answer. Show your work.

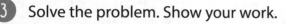

Develop Evaluating Expressions

Read and try to solve the problem below.

> **There are 32 people on a field trip to the aquarium. This includes 8 adults. The expression 6 × (32 − 8) represents the cost, in dollars, to buy the students but not the 8 adults a $6 souvenir poster. What is the total cost of the posters?**

TRY IT

🧰 **Math Toolkit**
- base-ten blocks
- counters
- number lines

DISCUSS IT

Ask your partner: How did you get started?

Tell your partner: A model I used was . . . It helped me . . .

Explore different ways to understand expressions with grouping symbols.

> **There are 32 people on a field trip to the aquarium. This includes 8 adults. The expression 6 × (32 − 8) represents the cost, in dollars, to buy the students but not the 8 adults a $6 souvenir poster. What is the total cost of the posters?**

PICTURE IT

You can use a picture to help understand how the expression represents the cost.

Think about what the posters for everyone and posters for students only would look like.

Each poster costs $6.

	$6	$6	$6	$6	$6	$6	$6	$6
32 people	$6	$6	$6	$6	$6	$6	$6	$6
	$6	$6	$6	$6	$6	$6	$6	$6
8 adults	$6	$6	$6	$6	$6	$6	$6	$6

6 × (32 − 8)

MODEL IT

You can use words to help understand how the expression represents the cost.

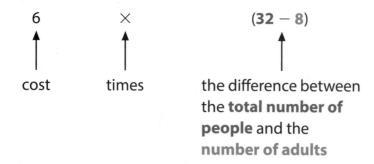

6	×	(32 − 8)
↑	↑	↑
cost	times	the difference between the **total number of people** and the number of adults

CONNECT IT

Now you will use the problem from the previous page to help you understand how to interpret and evaluate expressions with grouping symbols.

1 Using the order of operations, what are the steps in evaluating $6 \times (32 - 8)$? What is the total cost of the posters?

2 Suppose you omit the parentheses from the expression for the total cost of the posters. What is the value of the expression $6 \times 32 - 8$? Explain why the grouping symbols are needed for this problem.

3 Morgan says you can evaluate $6 \times (32 - 8)$ using three steps: multiply 32 by 6, multiply 8 by 6, and subtract the two products. Why does Morgan's method work?

4 Suppose the group also pays $75 for admission to the aquarium and that the cost for posters is $4 instead of $6. The expression that represents the total cost would be $75 + 4 \times (32 - 8)$. Evaluate the expression, explaining each of your steps.

5 REFLECT

Look back at your **Try It**, strategies by classmates, and **Picture It** and **Model It**. Which models or strategies do you like best for evaluating expressions with grouping symbols? Explain.

....

....

....

APPLY IT

Use what you just learned to solve these problems.

6 Evaluate $\frac{1}{3} \times [8 - 5] + 9$. Show your work.

Solution

7 Jake used the order of operations to evaluate the expression $(9 + 8) - 4 \times 3 - 2$. He says that the solution is 3. Natalie changes the location of the parentheses so that the expression reads $9 + 8 - 4 \times (3 - 2)$. Evaluate Natalie's expression. Show your work.

Solution

8 The numerical expression $\frac{1}{4} \times (7 \times 6 + 2) - 5$ is evaluated as shown.

Step 1: $\frac{1}{4} \times (7 \times 8) - 5$

Step 2: $\frac{1}{4} \times 56 - 5$

Step 3: $14 - 5$

Step 4: 9

In which step does a mistake first appear?

Ⓐ Step 1   Ⓑ Step 2

Ⓒ Step 3   Ⓓ Step 4

Practice Evaluating Expressions

Study the Example showing two ways to think about an expression that has parentheses. Then solve problems 1–5.

EXAMPLE

Ms. Nakos works 4 hours on Mondays and 8 hours on Tuesdays in the school library. During one week in May, she worked $\frac{1}{4}$ of her regular hours. Evaluate the expression $\frac{1}{4} \times (4 + 8)$ to find the number of hours she worked that week.

To understand the expression, you can use words.

$$\frac{1}{4} \qquad \times \qquad (4 + 8)$$

$$\uparrow \qquad \uparrow \qquad \uparrow$$

one   of   the sum of the
fourth   number of Monday
                    and Tuesday hours

Evaluate the expression.

$$\frac{1}{4} \times (4 + 8)$$

$$\frac{1}{4} \times 12$$

$$\frac{12}{4}$$

$$3$$

Ms. Nakos worked 3 hours that week.

1 Look at the expression in the Example. There are parentheses around $4 + 8$ to show that it is to be evaluated first. Are the parentheses necessary? Explain.

2 The expression $\frac{1}{2} \times (4 + 8)$ represents the number of hours Ms. Nakos works the last week of school. Evaluate the expression to find the number of hours she works that week.

....

Vocabulary

evaluate to find the value of an expression.

3×5 is 15.

3 Each day, Darius walks his dog 15 minutes in the morning and 25 minutes in the afternoon. Evaluate the expression 7 × (15 + 25) to find how many minutes Darius walks his dog each week. Show your work.

Solution

4 Evaluate the expression 9 + (21 − 6) ÷ 3. Show your work.

Solution

5 Sara has $50. While shopping, Sara chooses a shirt that costs $12 and a pair of pants that costs $26. The clothes are on sale. Sara only needs to pay half the regular price. Evaluate the expression $50 - \frac{1}{2} \times \{12 + 26\}$ to find how much money Sara has left after buying the clothes. Show your work.

Solution

Develop Writing and Interpreting Expressions

Read and try to solve the problem below.

> **Write a numerical expression to represent the following phrase.**
>
> *15 minus the sum of 6 and 7*

TRY IT

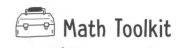 **Math Toolkit**
- counters
- base-ten blocks

 **DISCUSS IT**

Ask your partner: Do you agree with me? Why or why not?

Tell your partner: At first, I thought . . .

Explore different ways to understand writing numerical expressions.

> **Write a numerical expression to represent the following phrase.**
>
> *15 minus the sum of 6 and 7*

PICTURE IT
You can use a picture to help understand the problem.

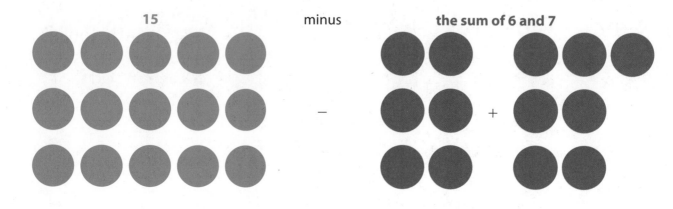

MODEL IT
You can think about what the words mean to help understand the problem.

15   minus   the *sum* of 6 and 7
            ↓   ↓

       Minus means   A *sum* is the result
       to subtract.   of addition. So, add
                                6 and 7.

CONNECT IT

Now you will use the problem from the previous page to help you understand how to write and interpret numerical expressions.

1 In the expression *15 minus the sum of 6 and 7*, do you add or subtract first? Why?

2 When you write a numerical expression, how can you show which operation to do first?

3 Write a numerical expression for *15 minus the sum of 6 and 7*. ....

4 Harper wrote the expression 15 − 6 + 7 to represent *15 minus the sum of 6 and 7*. Evaluate 15 − 6 + 7 and then explain why Harper's expression is incorrect.

5 Write a word phrase to show how to interpret Harper's expression, 15 − 6 + 7.

6 REFLECT

Look back at your **Try It**, strategies by classmates, and **Picture It** and **Model It**. Which models or strategies do you like best for writing expressions? Explain.

....

....

....

....

Lesson 30 Evaluate, Write, and Interpret Expressions   **637**

APPLY IT

Use what you just learned to solve these problems.

7 Draw a picture to show what the phrase *2 times the difference of 8 and 1* means. Then write an expression. Show your work.

Solution ....

8 Write an expression for the phrase *6 plus the quotient of 15 and 3*. Draw a picture to help, if needed. Show your work.

Solution ....

9 Which phrase correctly interprets the expression below?

$$24 - \frac{1}{2} \times (3 + 5)$$

Ⓐ Twenty-four plus half the sum of 3 and 5

Ⓑ Twenty-four minus a half of 3 and then add 5

Ⓒ Half the sum of 3 and 5 subtracted from 24

Ⓓ Half of 3 subtracted from 24 and then add 5

Practice Writing and Interpreting Expressions

**Study the Example showing how to write and interpret a numerical expression.
Then solve problems 1–8.**

EXAMPLE

Write a numerical expression for the phrase below.
  12 plus the quotient of 8 and 4

Think about what the words mean:

12 plus	the quotient of	8 and 4
↑	↑	↑
Plus means add.	A quotient is the result of division.	The numbers in the division operation

Since you add 12 *to the quotient* of 8 and 4, you need to first divide 8 by 4.
Use parentheses to show that you do the division first.

The numerical expression is 12 + (8 ÷ 4).

1. Draw a picture to show what the word phrase in the Example means.

   12 plus the quotient of 8 and 4

2. Suppose you wrote a numerical expression for the phrase *20 minus the product of 5 and 2*. To evaluate the expression, should you subtract or multiply first? Explain.

3   Write a numerical expression to represent *20 minus the product of 5 and 2.*
     Then evaluate your expression.

4   Complete the statement. *The value of 5 × (23,432 + 10,816) is ...*

     Ⓐ   one-fifth as large as 23,432 + 10,816.

     Ⓑ   five times as large as 23,432 + 10,816.

     Ⓒ   five more than 23,432 + 10,816.

     Ⓓ   five less than 23,432 + 10,816.

5   Write a numerical expression to represent *6 times the difference of 9 and 3.*
     Then evaluate your expression.

6   Write a word phrase for the expression 10 + (6 − 4).

7   Shana is doing a craft project using yarn and craft sticks. She has 5 green yarn
     pieces and 7 blue yarn pieces. She has 3 times as many craft sticks as yarn pieces.

     Which expression can you use to find the number of craft sticks Shana has?

     Ⓐ $5 + (7 \times 3)$

     Ⓑ $(5 + 7) \times 3$

     Ⓒ $(5 + 7) + 3$

     Ⓓ $5 \times (7 \times 3)$

8   Look at your answer to problem 7. Evaluate the expression to find
     the number of craft sticks Shana has.

Refine Evaluating, Writing, and Interpreting Expressions

Complete the Example below. Then solve problems 1–9.

EXAMPLE

Insert parentheses to make the following equation true.

$$15 - 7 - 2 = 10$$

Look at how you could show your work.

Try different placements of the parentheses.

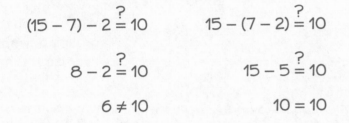

$$(15 - 7) - 2 \overset{?}{=} 10 \qquad 15 - (7 - 2) \overset{?}{=} 10$$

$$8 - 2 \overset{?}{=} 10 \qquad\qquad 15 - 5 \overset{?}{=} 10$$

$$6 \neq 10 \qquad\qquad\qquad 10 = 10$$

Solution ....

PAIR/SHARE
Why did the student write question marks above the equal signs? What does the equals sign with a slash through it mean?

APPLY IT

1 Aniyah sells bracelets and pairs of earrings at a craft fair. Each item sells for $8. Write a word phrase that describes the calculations you would do to find how much money Aniyah makes by selling 23 bracelets and 17 pairs of earrings. Then write and evaluate an expression to find how much money she makes. Show your work.

How many items will Aniyah sell altogether?

PAIR/SHARE
What other ways could you solve the problem?

Solution ....

2 Write numerical expressions for *the product of 3 and 2, plus 5* and *3 times the sum of 2 and 5.* Which expression has a greater value? Show your work.

The comma is a clue to where to put the grouping symbol. In this case, group the math that comes before the comma.

Solution ....

3 Which expression represents *the quotient of 2,375 and 125, plus 5?*

Ⓐ 2,375 ÷ (125 + 5)

Ⓑ 2,375 × 125 ÷ 5

Ⓒ (2,375 × 125) + 5

Ⓓ 2,375 ÷ 125 + 5

Jason chose Ⓐ as the correct answer. How did he get that answer?

What does the word "quotient" mean?

4 Kris ran 3 miles each day for 7 days in a row. One day, she ran an extra $\frac{1}{2}$ mile. Which expression represents how many miles Kris ran altogether?

Ⓐ $3 + 7 + \frac{1}{2}$

Ⓑ $3 \times 7 + \frac{1}{2}$

Ⓒ $3 \times 7 + 3\frac{1}{2}$

Ⓓ $\left(3 + \frac{1}{2}\right) \times 7$

5 Which expressions have a value of 8?

Ⓐ $3 \times 8 \div 4 + 2$

Ⓑ $3 \times (8 \div 4) + 2$

Ⓒ $(3 \times 8) \div (4 + 2)$

Ⓓ $(3 \times 8) \div 4 + 2$

Ⓔ $3 \times 8 \div (4 + 2)$

6 Which phrase is a correct interpretation of the expression below?

$$\frac{1}{2} \times [10 + 6] - [3 + 2]$$

Ⓐ Half of 10 plus 6 plus 3 and 2

Ⓑ The sum of 3 and 2 times half the sum of 10 and 6

Ⓒ The sum of 10 and 6 minus the sum of 3 and 2 times $\frac{1}{2}$

Ⓓ Half the sum of 10 and 6 minus the sum of 3 and 2

7 Insert parentheses into the expression below so that the value of the expression is 5. Show your work.

$$20 - 3 \times 4 + 1$$

Lesson 30 Evaluate, Write, and Interpret Expressions   **643**

8 Adam is 2 years old. His sister Lina is 1 year less than three times his age. Write a numerical expression for Lina's age.

···

9 Several expressions are shown below. Decide if the value of the expression is *less than*, *equal to*, or *greater than* 18. Write each expression in the correct category in the table.

$\frac{1}{5} \times (9 \times 2)$ $(9 \times 2) \times (4 - 3)$ $(9 \times 2) \div 3$ $22 - (9 \times 2)$

$(9 \times 2) + 7$ $4 \times \frac{1}{4} \times (9 \times 2)$ $1 \times (9 \times 2)$ $3 \times (9 \times 2)$

Less than 18	Equal to 18	Greater than 18

10 **MATH JOURNAL**

Without evaluating the expressions $8 \times 18{,}432 - 247$ and $8 \times (18{,}432 - 247)$, explain how you know which expression has a value that is 8 times a great as $18{,}432 - 247$.

☑ **SELF CHECK** Go back to the Unit 5 Opener and see what you can check off.

Understand the Coordinate Plane

Dear Family,

This week your child is exploring the coordinate plane.

Your child is learning to use ordered pairs of numbers to find a location on the coordinate plane and to identify locations on the coordinate plane with ordered pairs.

The **coordinate plane** at the right has two axes, the *x*-axis and the *y*-axis.

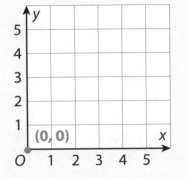

- The **x-axis** is a horizontal number line.

- The **y-axis** is a vertical number line.

- The axes intersect, or meet, at a point called the **origin**.

You can find any point on the coordinate plane if you know the *x*-coordinate and *y*-coordinate of the point. These coordinates are given in the **ordered pair** (*x*, *y*). The ordered pair (0, 0) tells where the origin is located. It marks a point on the coordinate plane. The point is located at 0 on the *x*-axis and 0 on the *y*-axis.

The ordered pair (3, 4) identifies point *J* on the coordinate plane at the right. Point *J* has an *x*-coordinate of 3 and a *y*-coordinate of 4. To locate point *J*, you start at the origin, move right 3 units on the *x*-axis, and move up 4 units.

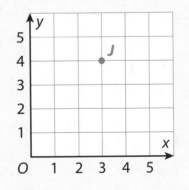

Invite your child to share what he or she knows about the coordinate plane by doing the following activity together.

ACTIVITY THE COORDINATE PLANE

Do this activity with your child to understand the coordinate plane.

Materials number cube

Work with your child to use ordered pairs to locate points in the coordinate plane.

- One person rolls a number cube to determine the *x*-coordinate of a point. The other person rolls the number cube to determine the *y*-coordinate.

- Write the coordinates in the table below in the row for point *A*. This is the ordered pair for point *A*.

  - *Example:* Roll a 2 and a 5 with the number cube. Write 2 in the *x* column and 5 in the *y* column of the table. The ordered pair for point *A* is (2, 5).

- Use the ordered pair to locate the point on the coordinate plane below. Describe where you begin, how many units you move, and in which direction you move to locate the point. Mark and label the point as point *A*.

- Repeat the activity three more times to determine coordinates for points *B*, *C*, and *D*.

- Look at the points on the coordinate plane and identify any patterns that you see. (For example, the points might form a line.) Talk about the location of one point in terms of another point. (For example, point *C* might be 2 units to the right and 3 units up from point *B*.) What other things do you notice about the points?

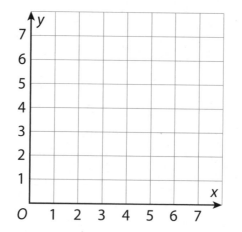

Point	x	y
A		
B		
C		
D		

Explore the Coordinate Plane

What does a point in the coordinate plane represent?

MODEL IT

Complete the problem below.

1 When a horizontal number line and a vertical number line are lined up so that the 0s intersect, a **coordinate plane** is formed.

Coordinate Plane

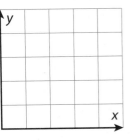

a. Label the numbers 1–4 on the **x-axis**, the horizontal number line.

b. Label the numbers 1–4 on the **y-axis**, the vertical number line.

c. Label the **origin**, the point where the x-axis and y-axis intersect, with the letter O.

DISCUSS IT

• Compare how you labeled the coordinate plane with how your partner labeled the coordinate plane. Are they the same? Are they different?

• I think a coordinate plane is like a number line because . . . I think a coordinate plane is different from a number line because . . .

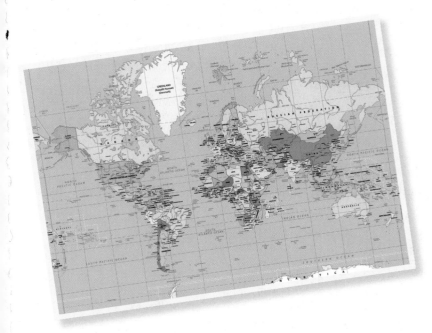

MODEL IT

Complete the problems below.

2 An **ordered pair** is a pair of numbers, called *coordinates*, that describes the location of a point in the coordinate plane. The coordinates of an ordered pair always appear in the same order: first the **x-coordinate** and then the **y-coordinate**.

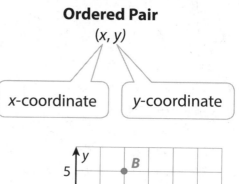

Ordered Pair
(x, y)

x-coordinate   y-coordinate

a. If you move only on grid lines, how can you get from the origin to point *B* in the fewest number of moves?

b. The ordered pair (2, 5) is a way to represent the location of point *B*. Use your answer to problem 2a to describe what the *x*-coordinate of an ordered pair tells you about the point's location and what the *y*-coordinate tells you about the point's location.

DISCUSS IT

• How can you and your partner figure out the ordered pair for point *C*?

• I know the *x*-coordinate of any point on the *y*-axis is 0 because . . .

c. What is the ordered pair for the origin, *O*? ....

3 REFLECT

Think about how you have heard the word *origin* used outside of math. Why do you think the point (0, 0) is called the *origin*?

....

....

....

Prepare for the Coordinate Plane

1 Think about what you know about the coordinate plane. Fill in each box. Use words, numbers, and pictures. Show as many ideas as you can.

Word	In My Own Words	Example
coordinate plane		
x-axis		
y-axis		
origin		
ordered pair		
x-coordinate		
y-coordinate		

2 From the origin, you move three units to the right and six units up to point *P*. What ordered pair tells the location of point *P*? ....

Solve.

3 Look at the coordinate plane below.

Coordinate Plane

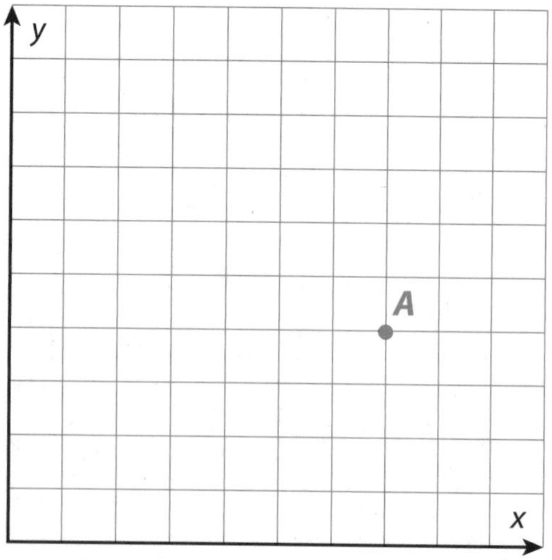

a. Label the origin with the letter O.

b. Label the numbers 1–9 on the x-axis.

c. Label the numbers 1–9 on the y-axis.

d. Explain what the ordered pair (7, 4) tells you about point A.

Develop Understanding of the Coordinate Plane

MODEL IT: THE COORDINATE PLANE

Try these two problems.

1 Points A, B, and C are graphed, or plotted, in the coordinate plane below. Use the graph to write the ordered pair for each point.

Point A ....

Point B ....

Point C ....

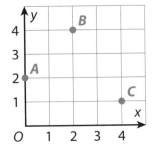

2 Plot the following points in the coordinate plane in problem 1. Label each point with its letter name.

Point D(1, 0)   Point E(3, 2)

DISCUSS IT

• Ask your partner to explain how he or she determined the location of points D and E.

• I think plotting points in the coordinate plane is like plotting points on a number line because . . .

• I think plotting points in the coordinate plane is different from plotting points on a number line because . . .

MODEL IT: TABLES

3 *x*- and *y*-coordinates can be organized in a table like the one below.

Point	A	B	C	D	E	F
x				1	3	4
y				0	2	3

a. Use the coordinate plane on the previous page to complete the table with the coordinates for points *A*, *B*, and *C*.

b. Use the coordinates given for point *F* in the table to graph point *F* in the coordinate plane on the previous page.

c. Explain how you can tell from the table which two points are located on the same vertical grid line in the coordinate plane.

DISCUSS IT

• Compare your answers to your partner's. Do you agree or disagree?

• Looking at points in a table helps me see . . .

CONNECT IT

Complete the problems below.

4 How do the coordinate plane and the table represent points? How are the *x*- and *y*-coordinates of a point shown in each model?

5 Plot point *A*(1, 4) and point *B*(3, 0) in the coordinate plane.

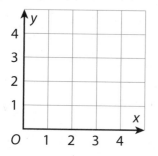

Practice with the Coordinate Plane

Study how the Example shows writing ordered pairs for points in the coordinate plane. Then solve problems 1–9.

EXAMPLE

Write ordered pairs for the origin and point *A* shown in the graph below.

The *x*-coordinate tells how many units from the origin the point is along the *x*-axis. It is the first number in the ordered pair.

The *y*-coordinate tells how many units from the origin the point is along the *y*-axis. It is the second number in the ordered pair.

Origin

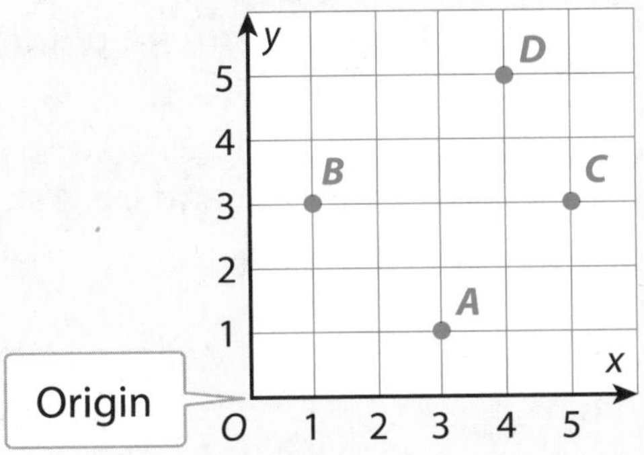

The ordered pair for the origin is (0, 0).
The ordered pair for point *A* is (3, 1).

1️⃣ Point *B* is .... unit(s) to the right of the origin and .... unit(s) up from the origin.

The ordered pair for point *B* is (........, ...).

2️⃣ Point *C* is .... unit(s) to the right of the origin and .... unit(s) up from the origin.

The ordered pair for point *C* is (........, ...).

3️⃣ Write the ordered pair for point *D*. Explain your answer.

4️⃣ Use the ordered pair (2, 3) to graph and label point *E* on the coordinate plane.

Vocabulary

coordinate plane
a two-dimensional space formed by two perpendicular number lines called axes.

ordered pair a pair of numbers, (*x*, *y*), that describes the location of a point in the coordinate plane, where the *x*-coordinate gives the point's horizontal distance from the origin, and the *y*-coordinate gives the point's vertical distance from the origin.

Use the table and coordinate plane for problems 5–7.

Point	A	B	C	D	E	F
x				3	4	5
y				4	4	2

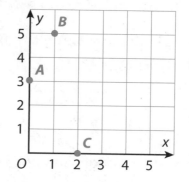

5 In the table, write the coordinates for points *A*, *B*, and *C*, shown in the coordinate plane above.

6 The coordinates for points *D*, *E*, and *F* are shown in the table. Plot and label the points in the coordinate plane.

7 Choose a point in the coordinate plane above. Describe its location compared to the origin.

Use the table and coordinate plane for problems 8 and 9.

Point	R	S	T
x	3	4	5
y	5	0	2

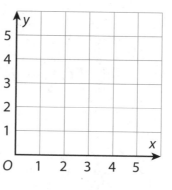

8 The coordinates for points *R*, *S*, and *T* are shown in the table. Plot and label the points in the coordinate plane.

9 Describe the location of point *T* compared to point *S* in the coordinate plane.

APPLY IT

Complete these problems on your own.

1 SHOW

Look at the table at the right. Plot and label points *M* and *N* in the coordinate plane below. Then write the ordered pairs for points *M* and *N* and describe how to move from (0, 0) to each point.

Point	x	y
M	1	4
N	5	2

2 ANALYZE

Irvin wrote the ordered pair (4, 3) for the location of point *J* in the coordinate plane at the right. Explain Irvin's error.

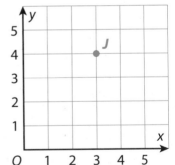

3 CREATE

Choose three points in the coordinate plane at the right to be the vertices of a triangle. Label the points with letters and draw the triangle. What are the ordered pairs for the vertices of your triangle?

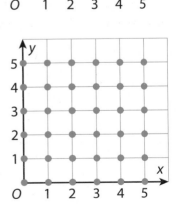

PAIR/SHARE

Discuss your solutions for these three problems with a partner.

Use what you have learned to complete problem 4.

4 **Part A** Use the coordinate plane below to complete the table.

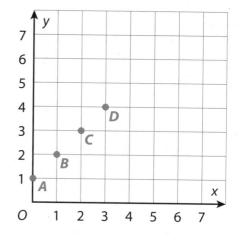

Point	x	y
A		
B		
C		
D		

Part B Describe a pattern you see formed by the points in the coordinate plane above. Then explain how the pattern is shown by the x- and y-coordinates in the table.

5 MATH JOURNAL

Graph and label point A(2, 3) and point B(3, 2) in the coordinate plane at the right. Then explain how you used the ordered pairs to decide where to place each point.

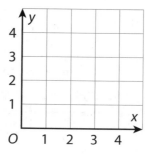

Represent Problems in the Coordinate Plane

Dear Family,

This week your child is learning to solve problems by graphing points in the coordinate plane.

Your child has already learned to use ordered pairs to locate and identify points in the coordinate plane. Now your child is learning how to solve problems involving points and figures in the coordinate plane.

Carla is saving money to buy a gift for her brother. The points in the coordinate plane below show Carla's savings. How many weeks does it take Carla to save $6?

You can solve the problem by using the axis titles to interpret the points. The x-axis represents the number of weeks that Carla has been saving money. The y-axis represents the amount of money that Carla has saved. To find the number of weeks it takes Carla to save $6, find the point with a y-coordinate of 6. The point is (3, 6), so it takes Carla 3 weeks to save $6.

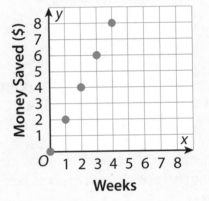

Your child is also learning to solve problems with plane figures graphed in the coordinate plane. For example, you can find the perimeter of the rectangle *EFGH* in the coordinate plane at the right by counting the number of units on each side to find the side lengths of the rectangle. Then add the lengths to find the perimeter.

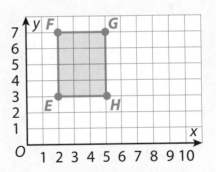

$$4 + 3 + 4 + 3 = 14$$

The perimeter of the rectangle is 14 units.

Invite your child to share what he or she knows about graphing points in the coordinate plane by doing the following activity together.

ACTIVITY GRAPHING A GEOMETRIC FIGURE

Do this activity with your child to graph a geometric figure in the coordinate plane.

Play a game to graph points and draw matching figures in coordinate planes with your child.

- Cut out the coordinate planes below or use separate paper, so each player can draw without the other player seeing.

- Player 1 chooses 4 points, marks them, and labels them *A*, *B*, *C*, and *D*. He or she should make sure that the other player does not see the marked points.

- Player 1 connects the points with lines to draw a figure with 4 sides, making sure that the other player does not see the 4-sided figure.

- Player 1 lists the *x*- and *y*-coordinates for each point in the table.

- Player 2 uses the table to graph the points in his or her own coordinate plane. He or she connects the points to form a 4-sided figure.

- Now players compare the figures in their coordinate planes. Are they the same?

Point	x	y
A		
B		
C		
D		

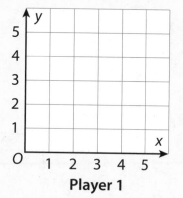

Player 1

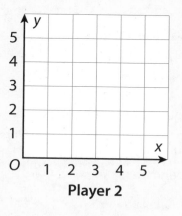

Player 2

Explore Representing Problems in the Coordinate Plane

Previously, you learned how to locate points in the coordinate plane. Use what you know to try to solve the problem below.

> On the graph below, points *S*, *M*, and *B* are three vertices of a square. Plot and label the fourth vertex, *G*, of the square. What are the *x*- and *y*-coordinates of *G*? How do you know?

Learning Target

- Represent real world and mathematical problems by graphing points in the first quadrant of the coordinate plane, and interpret coordinate values of points in the context of the situation.

SMP 1, 2, 3, 4, 5, 6, 7, 8

TRY IT

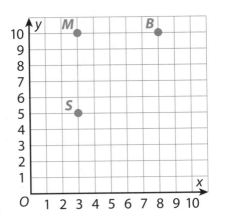

Math Toolkit
- geoboards
- rulers
- coordinate plane grid paper

DISCUSS IT

Ask your partner: Do you agree with me? Why or why not?

Tell your partner: I knew ... so I ...

CONNECT IT

 LOOK BACK

Explain how you determined the ordered pair for the fourth vertex, *G*, of the square.

2 LOOK AHEAD

On the previous page, you solved a problem about a geometric figure graphed in the coordinate plane. A coordinate plane graph can also be used to show relationships between two real-world quantities.

Mia works as a dog groomer at a pet store. The coordinate plane shows the relationship between the number of dogs Mia grooms and the number of hours she works.

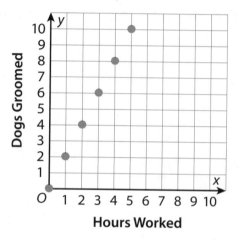

a. Use the titles on the axes to explain how to interpret a point on the graph.

b. How many dogs did Mia groom in 4 hours? How do you know?

c. What do the coordinates of the point located at (3, 6) represent in this situation?

3 REFLECT

What are some differences between the graphs in **Try It** and problem 2?

Prepare for Representing Problems in the Coordinate Plane

1   Think about what you know about the coordinate plane. Fill in each box. Use
    words, numbers, and pictures. Show as many ideas as you can.

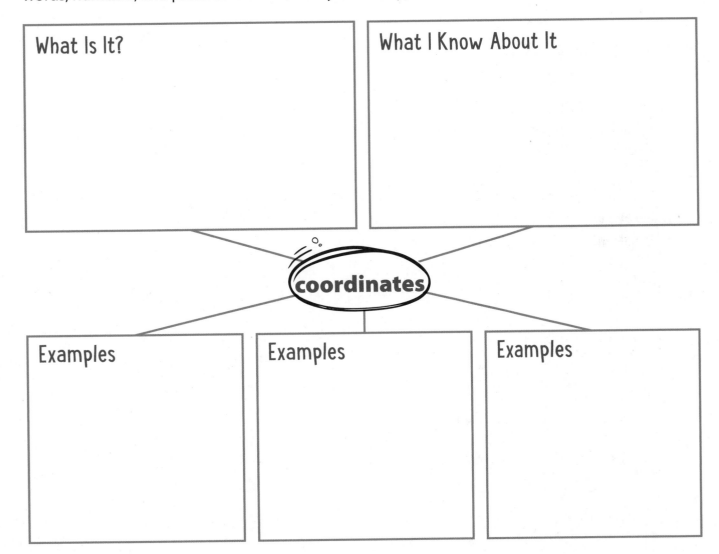

What Is It?

What I Know About It

coordinates

Examples

Examples

Examples

2   Write the ordered pair that gives the coordinates of each point.

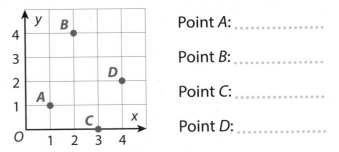

Point A: ....

Point B: ....

Point C: ....

Point D: ....

3 Solve the problem. Show your work.

Points *P*, *G*, and *R* are three vertices of a rectangle. Plot and label the fourth vertex, *A*, of the rectangle. What are the *x*- and *y*-coordinates of *A*? How do you know?

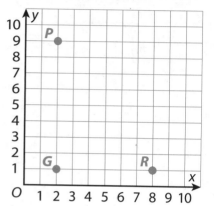

Solution

....

....

....

....

4 Check your answer. Show your work.

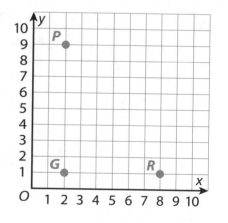

Develop Graphing Points and Finding Distances

Read and try to solve the problem below.

The coordinate plane shows the locations of buildings in Max's town. From the school, Max walks 3 units to the right and 5 units up to a park. Then he walks to the library, which is located at the point (1, 7).

- Graph and label points to show the locations of the park and the library. Write the ordered pair for the park.
- How many units does Max walk in all? Assume Max takes the shortest path along grid lines from the park to the library.

TRY IT

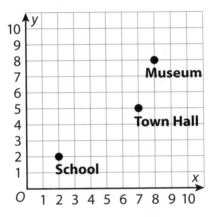

 Math Toolkit
- geoboards
- rulers
- coordinate plane grid paper

DISCUSS IT

Ask your partner: How did you get started?

Tell your partner: I also thought about . . .

Explore different ways to understand graphing points and finding distances in the coordinate plane.

> The coordinate plane shows the locations of buildings in Max's town. From the school, Max walks 3 units to the right and 5 units up to a park. Then he walks to the library, which is located at the point (1, 7).
> - Graph and label points to show the locations of the park and the library. Write the ordered pair for the park.
> - How many units does Max walk in all? Assume Max takes the shortest path along grid lines from the park to the library.

MODEL IT

You can use the graph to find the coordinates of Max's starting point.

Max starts walking from the school. The red and blue arrows on the graph show how to determine the coordinates for the school.

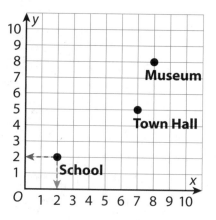

PICTURE IT

Plot points and show Max's path in the coordinate plane.

The blue arrows on the graph show the path Max takes from the school to the park, and then to the library.

Count the total number of units indicated by the arrows to find the number of units Max walks in all.

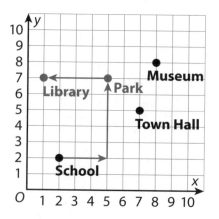

CONNECT IT

Now you will use the problem from the previous page to help you understand graphing points and finding distances in the coordinate plane.

1 Look at the coordinate plane in the first **Picture It**. Where does Max start walking? What is the ordered pair for this location?

2 Explain how to use the coordinates of the school to find the coordinates of the park. Then find the distance Max walks between these two locations.

3 How does the location of the park relate to the location of the library? Explain how to use the coordinate plane to find the distance Max walks between the park and the library.

4 The total distance Max walks is ....

5 Explain how you can use movements along grid lines to locate points and find distances in the coordinate plane.

6 REFLECT

Look back at your **Try It**, strategies by classmates, **Model It** and **Picture It**. Which models or strategies do you like best for solving problems about distance in the coordinate plane? Explain.

....

....

....

APPLY IT

Use what you just learned to solve these problems.

7 Julia plans a rectangular park using the coordinate plane below. To get from one corner of the park to another, Julia travels 3 units left and 6 units up. Draw arrows on the coordinate plane to show Julia's path. Write the coordinates for her start and end points.

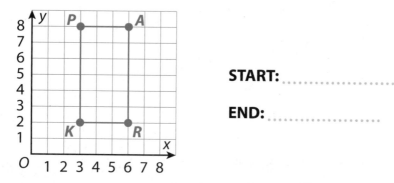

START: ....

END: ....

8 Use the coordinate plane in problem 7. What is the perimeter of rectangle *PARK*? Show your work.

Solution ....

9 Use the coordinate plane in problem 7. What is the length of Julia's path from point *R* to point *P* in the park?

Ⓐ 3 units

Ⓑ 6 units

Ⓒ 9 units

Ⓓ 18 units

Practice Graphing Points and Finding Distances

Study the Example that shows how to solve a measurement problem on a coordinate grid. Then solve problems 1–5.

EXAMPLE

The owner of an arcade plans to add a new game room. He draws a rectangle in the coordinate plane to represent the room. What is the area of the rectangle?

From point G to point A, go up 6 units.
From point A to point M, go right 5 units.
Length of $\overline{GA}$ is 6 units and length of $\overline{AM}$ is 5 units.

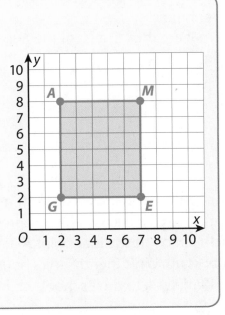

Area of a rectangle = length × width
Multiply the lengths of the sides to find the area of the rectangle: 6 × 5 = 30.
Area of rectangle *GAME* = 30 square units

1 Write ordered pairs for each vertex of rectangle *GAME* in the Example.

G (......................., ...)   A (......................., ...)

M (......................., ...)   E (......................., ...)

2 Find the lengths of $\overline{ME}$ and $\overline{EG}$. Explain how you can count to find the distance between points M and E and between points E and G.

3 What is the perimeter of rectangle *GAME*? Tell how you found your answer.

4 **a.** Plot and label the points K(2, 2), G(6, 2), and S(6, 5). Connect the points to form a triangle.

b. Which two sides of the triangle form a right angle?

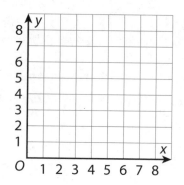

c. What are the lengths of the two sides that form the right angle?

5 The coordinate plane at the right models the streets of a city. Each grid line represents 1 city block. Jared's house is at point A. Jared walks 6 blocks up to his friend Kenji's house. Then Jared and Kenji walk to their school, which is located at (6, 9).

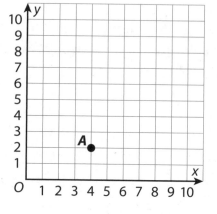

a. Graph point B to show the location of Kenji's house and point C to show the location of the school.

b. Write the ordered pair for each boy's house.

point A ....   point B ....

c. How many blocks does Jared walk in all from his house to school? Assume the boys take the shortest path from Kenji's house to school while staying on the city streets. Explain how you found your answer.

Develop Representing Relationships Between Quantities

Read and try to solve the problem below.

> Jenny has $20 saved in the bank. She earns $10 an hour washing cars and saves all her money. Graph points in the coordinate plane to show the relationship between the number of hours Jenny works and the total amount of money she has saved. Include the following in your graph:
> - titles for the *x*- and *y*-axes to show which quantity each axis represents.
> - points for 0, 1, 2, 3, 4, and 5 hours of work.

TRY IT

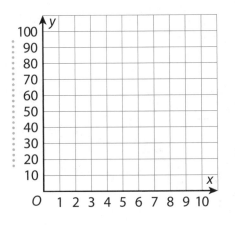

Math Toolkit
- counters
- geoboards
- rulers
- coordinate plane grid paper

DISCUSS IT

Ask your partner: Why did you choose that strategy?

Tell your partner: The strategy I used to find the answer was . . .

Explore different ways to understand how to use the coordinate plane to show relationships between quantities in the coordinate plane.

> Jenny has $20 saved in the bank. She earns $10 an hour washing cars and saves all her money. Graph points in the coordinate plane to show the relationship between the number of hours Jenny works and the total amount of money she has saved. Include the following in your graph:
> * titles for the *x*- and *y*-axes to show which quantity each axis represents.
> * points for 0, 1, 2, 3, 4, and 5 hours of work.

MODEL IT

You can use a table to model the relationship between the quantities.

The table shows the number hours Jenny works and the total amount of money she has saved.

Hours Worked	0	1	2	3	4	5
Total Saved ($)	20	30	40	50	60	70

PICTURE IT

You can graph points in the coordinate plane to model the relationship.

Use the data in the table to form ordered pairs to graph. The coordinate plane at the right shows points plotted for the first two columns of the table.

The ordered pair (**1**, **30**) is the ordered pair that represents the total the amount of money, **$30**, that Jenny will have saved after working **1** hour.

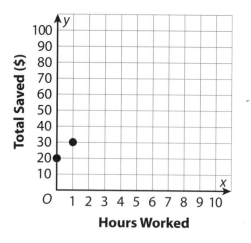

CONNECT IT

Now you will use the problem from the previous page to help you understand how to use the coordinate plane to show relationships between two quantities.

1 Look at the coordinate plane in **Picture It**.

What does the *x*-axis represent? ....

What does the *y*-axis represent? ....

2 Complete these ordered pairs, (*x*, *y*), where *x* is the number of hours Jenny works, and *y* is the total amount of money Jenny will have saved.

(0, ...)   (1, ...)   (2, ...)

(3, ...)   (4, ...)   (5, ...)

Plot the missing ordered pairs in the coordinate plane in **Picture It**.

3 How much money will Jenny have saved if she works for 5 hours? ....

Which point on the graph shows this? ....

4 How many hours does Jenny need to work to have saved $40? ....

Which point on the graph shows this? ....

5 How can you use the coordinate plane to represent relationships between two real-world quantities?

6 REFLECT

Look back at your **Try It**, strategies by classmates, **Model It**, and **Picture It**. Which models or strategies do you like best for graphing points to show relationships between quantities in the coordinate plane? Explain.

....

....

....

....

APPLY IT

Use what you just learned to solve these problems.

7 Ferran works in an ice cream store. He uses two scoops of ice cream for each ice cream cone he sells. Make a table of values and then graph the points on the coordinate plane to show the relationship between the number of ice cream cones Ferran sells and the number of scoops of ice cream he uses. Include the following in both the table and graph:

- titles to show which quantity is represented by x- and y-values
- data for 0, 1, 2, 3, and 4 ice cream cones.

Number of Ice Cream Cones, x					
........................, y					

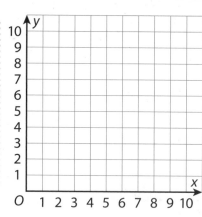

8 Use the table and graph in problem 7. Where would you put a point on the graph to show how many scoops of ice cream would be used for 5 cones? Explain your answer.

9 What does the point (2, 4) represent in the graph above?

Ⓐ 2 scoops of ice cream are used for 4 ice cream cones.

Ⓑ 6 scoops of ice cream are used in all.

Ⓒ 2 ice cream cones use 4 scoops of ice cream.

Ⓓ 8 scoops of ice cream are used in all.

Practice Representing Relationships Between Quantities

Study the Example showing how to use the coordinate plane to represent relationships between quantities. Then solve problems 1–6.

EXAMPLE

Holly is playing a crane game at the arcade. With each quarter, she gets 2 tries to grab a stuffed animal with the crane. Holly wants to show the relationship between the number of quarters and numbers of tries in a graph.

Make a table of x- and y-coordinates.

Number of Quarters, x	1	2	3	4	5
Number of Tries, y	2	4	6	8	10

Graph points (x, y) from the table.

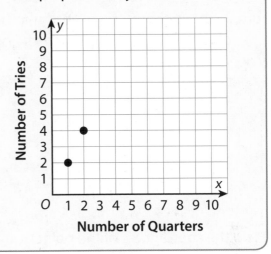

1 Use the table in the Example above. Finish plotting the points (x, y) in the coordinate plane.

2 What is the meaning of the ordered pair (3, 6) in this situation?

3 Use your graph in the Example. Describe moving from (1, 2) to (2, 4) and from (2, 4) to (3, 6) along grid lines. If you continue from point to point, what do you notice?

Use the coordinate plane to answer problems 4–6.

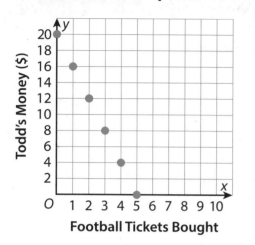

Todd's Money ($) vs. Football Tickets Bought

(4) The graph above shows the relationship between the money Todd has and the number of football tickets he buys. How much does each football ticket cost? How do you know? Explain.

(5) What do the coordinates of the point (3, 8) mean in this situation?

(6) Which point on the graph shows that Todd has run out of money? Explain.

Refine Representing Problems in the Coordinate Plane

Complete the Example below. Then solve problems 1–8.

EXAMPLE

The graph shows how Jaina's parents determine her weekly allowance. What does the point located at (3, 5) represent?

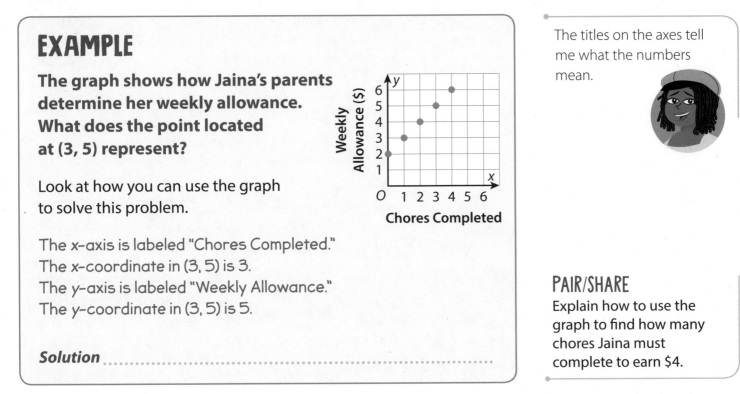

Look at how you can use the graph to solve this problem.

The *x*-axis is labeled "Chores Completed."
The *x*-coordinate in (3, 5) is 3.
The *y*-axis is labeled "Weekly Allowance."
The *y*-coordinate in (3, 5) is 5.

Solution ....

The titles on the axes tell me what the numbers mean.

PAIR/SHARE
Explain how to use the graph to find how many chores Jaina must complete to earn $4.

APPLY IT

1 Plot the points (4, 4), (8, 4), (3, 1), and (7, 1) in the coordinate plane. Use the points to draw two parallel, horizontal segments. Label the endpoints of one segment *A* and *B*. Label the endpoints of the other segment *C* and *D*. What is the distance between points *A* and *B*? What is the distance between points *C* and *D*?

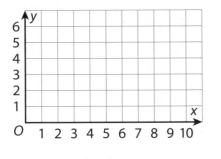

Are horizontal lines parallel to the *x*-axis or the *y*-axis?

Solution ....

PAIR/SHARE
What shape could have the four points as vertices?

2 What is the area of rectangle *EFGH* shown in the coordinate plane? Show your work.

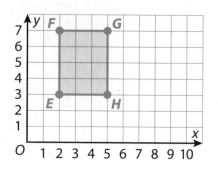

The formula for the area of a rectangle is $A = \ell \times w$.

PAIR/SHARE
Suppose the *x*-coordinates for points *G* and *H* each increase by 1. What kind of shape would this be? What would be the area of this shape?

Solution ....

3 Mr. Palmer uses the coordinate plane to design his bulletin board.

He moves *Rules* 2 units right and 3 units down. What ordered pair represents the new location of *Rules*?

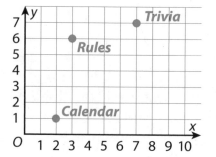

What is the ordered pair for the starting point?

Ⓐ (5, 3)

Ⓑ (1, 9)

Ⓒ (1, 3)

Ⓓ (5, 9)

Maya chose Ⓒ as the correct answer. How did she get that answer?

PAIR/SHARE
Does Maya's answer make sense?

4 The coordinate plane shows the relationship between the amount of water in the bathtub and the amount of time the faucet has been turned on. What do the coordinates of the point at (3, 6) represent in this situation?

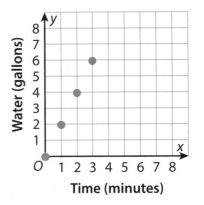

5 Use the coordinate plane from problem 4. How many minutes must the faucet be turned on for there to be 8 gallons of water in the bathtub?

Ⓐ 2 minutes

Ⓑ 4 minutes

Ⓒ 8 minutes

Ⓓ 10 minutes

6 Look at triangle *ABC*.

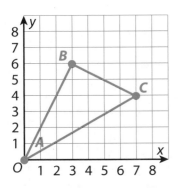

Which directions describe moving from point *C* to point *B*?

Ⓐ move 4 units right and 2 units down

Ⓑ move 2 units up and 4 units right

Ⓒ move 4 units left and 2 units down

Ⓓ move 2 units up and 4 units left

Lesson 32 Represent Problems in the Coordinate Plane   **677**

7. **Part A** Draw a rectangle in the coordinate plane below with one vertex at the origin and an area 20 of square units. Label the vertices of your rectangle R, S, T, U.

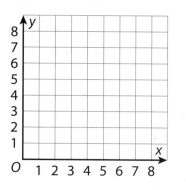

Part B Write the ordered pairs for the points R, S, T, and U.

Part C How do you know that the area of rectangle RSTU is 20 square units?

8. MATH JOURNAL

The coordinate plane shows the relationship between the number of bikes Harry repairs and the number of days he works at the bike shop. Describe two things you know from looking at points on the graph. Use coordinates in each of your descriptions.

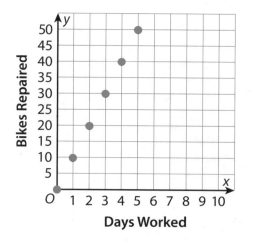

Days Worked

✓ SELF CHECK Go back to the Unit 5 Opener and see what you can check off.

Analyze Patterns and Relationships

Dear Family,

This week your child is learning to analyze patterns and relationships.

Your child is learning ways to describe how two number patterns are related. He or she might see a problem like this:

At the school fair, a box of raisins costs $2 and a box of nuts costs $4. How does the cost of a given number of boxes of raisins compare to the cost of the same number of boxes of nuts for 0, 1, 2, 3, or 4 boxes?

A diagram shows the number patterns for the raisins and the nuts:

+2 +2 +2 +2
0, 2, 4, 6, 8

+4 +4 +4 +4
0, 4, 8, 12, 16

You can list the numbers, or **terms,** of the pattern in a table and form ordered pairs of **corresponding terms**.

Look for a pattern. The second number in each ordered pair is twice the first number. For example, in the ordered pair (4, 8), 8 = 2 × 4.

Raisins, x	Nuts, y	Ordered Pair (x, y)
0	0	(0, 0)
2	4	(2, 4)
4	8	(4, 8)
6	12	(6, 12)
8	16	(8, 16)

Another way to see how the number patterns are related is to plot the ordered pairs on a graph.

The graph at the right shows a point for each ordered pair in the table. From point to point, the pattern is: move 2 to the right, move up 4.

Invite your child to share what he or she knows about analyzing number patterns and relationships by doing the following activity together.

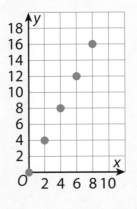

ACTIVITY ANALYZING PATTERNS

Do this activity with your child to analyze patterns and relationships.

Work with your child to show how the costs of two items are related.

- Together with your child, find the cost of your child's two favorite snacks. Round each to the nearest dollar. (*Example: A box of crackers costs $2 and a carton of ice cream costs $3.*)

- In the table, write the cost of 0, 1, 2, 3, 4, and 5 containers of each snack.

Snack 1: .... , x	Snack 2: .... , y	Ordered Pair (x, y)

- Together, plot the ordered pairs on the coordinate plane at the right and describe the relationship between the costs of the snacks.

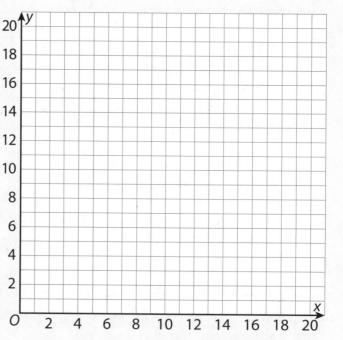

Explore Analyzing Patterns and Relationships

Previously you learned to identify and continue numerical patterns. Now you will describe the relationship between two patterns. Use what you know to try to solve the problem below.

Maria works at the snack stand at a basketball game. Each frozen yogurt costs $3, and each sandwich costs $6. Maria makes a list of the costs for buying 0, 1, 2, 3, 4, 5, or 6 frozen yogurts. She also makes a list of the costs for the same number of sandwiches.

• Show how Maria may have made her lists of costs.
• Write a sentence describing the rules used to make each list.

TRY IT

Math Toolkit
• counters
• base-ten blocks
• grid paper

DISCUSS IT

Ask your partner: Can you explain that again?

Tell your partner: A model I used was . . . It helped me . . .

CONNECT IT

1 LOOK BACK

How did you find the costs of yogurts and the costs of sandwiches?

2 LOOK AHEAD

In the previous problem, each list of costs forms a numerical pattern. The numbers in a pattern are called **terms**. A rule tells you how to move from one term in a pattern to the next. You can generate two related patterns using two different rules.

a. Maria also sells hot dogs for $5 each and pizzas for $10 each. Use the rules shown in the table to list the terms of two patterns.

Number of Items	Cost of Hot Dogs ($) Rule: add 5	Cost of Pizzas ($) Rule: add 10
0		
1		
2		
3		

b. Terms that are in the same position in two related patterns are called **corresponding terms**. What are the corresponding terms for the cost of 3 items in the two patterns you wrote in the table in part a?

3 REFLECT

How do the corresponding terms in problem 2b compare? Is this true for all pairs of corresponding terms in the table?

Prepare for Analyzing Patterns and Relationships

1 Think about what you know about patterns. Fill in each box.
Use words, numbers, and pictures. Show as many ideas as you can.

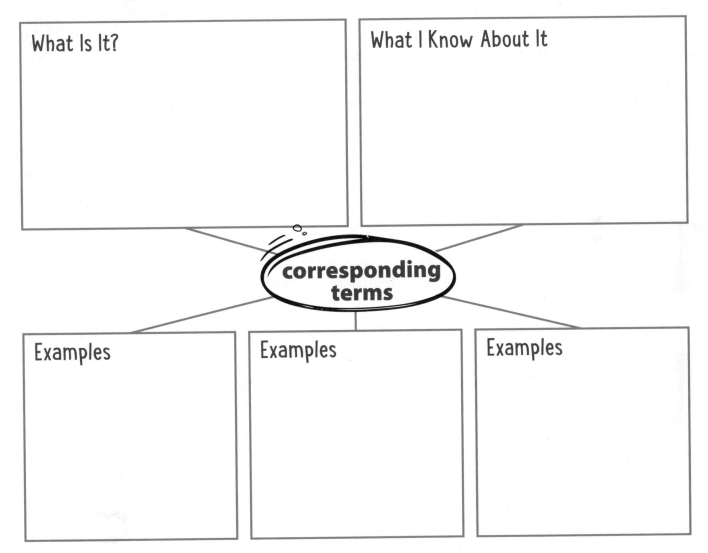

| What Is It? | What I Know About It |

corresponding terms

| Examples | Examples | Examples |

2 Look at the patterns. What are the corresponding terms?

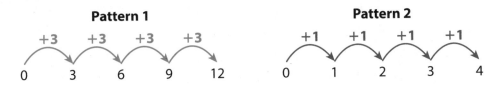

Pattern 1

+3 +3 +3 +3
0   3   6   9   12

Pattern 2

+1 +1 +1 +1
0   1   2   3   4

3 Solve the problem. Show your work.

Russell works at a gift shop. Each T-shirt costs $15, and each snow globe costs $5.
Russell makes a list of the costs for buying 0, 1, 2, 3, 4, 5, or 6 T-shirts. He also makes a list of the costs for the same number of snow globes.

- **Show how Russell may have made his list of the costs.**

- **Write a sentence describing the rules for each list.**

Solution ....

....

4 Check your answer. Show your work.

Develop Comparing Two Numerical Patterns

Read and try to solve the problem below.

> **In Level 1 of a video game, you earn 2 points for each monster you catch.**
> **In Level 2, you earn 8 points for each ghost you catch.**
> **Compare the number of points in Level 2 to the number of points in Level 1 if you catch 0, 1, 2, 3, 4, 5, or 6 monsters or ghosts.**

TRY IT

 **Math Toolkit**
- counters
- base-ten blocks
- grid paper

DISCUSS IT

Ask your partner: How did you get started?

Tell your partner: I didn't think about . . .

Explore different ways to understand relationships between two numerical patterns.

> In Level 1 of a video game, you earn 2 points for each monster you catch.
> In Level 2, you earn 8 points for each ghost you catch.
> Compare the number of points in Level 2 to the number of points
> in Level 1 if you catch 0, 1, 2, 3, 4, 5, or 6 monsters or ghosts.

PICTURE IT

You can use a diagram to show the terms of each pattern.

Level 1

Each monster caught earns **2 points**.

+2 +2 +2 +2 +2 +2

0   2   4   6   8   10   12

Level 2

Each ghost caught earns **8 points**.

+8 +8 +8 +8 +8 +8

0   8   16   24   32   40   48

MODEL IT

You can use a table to list the terms of each pattern.

Number Caught	Points in Level 1	Points in Level 2
0	0	0
1	2	8
2		
3		
4		
5		
6		

The total number of points in Level 1 increases by 2 for each monster caught.
The total number of points in Level 2 increases by 8 for each ghost caught.

CONNECT IT

Now you will use the problem from the previous page to help you understand how to identify relationships between two numerical patterns.

1 Look at **Picture It** on the previous page. Describe how the total number of points changes with each monster or ghost caught in Level 1 and Level 2.

Level 1 rule: ....

Level 2 rule: ....

2 Complete the table on the previous page.

3 Use the table to describe the relationship between the corresponding terms of the patterns.

4 Suppose the game has a third level. You get 10 points for each giant caught in Level 3. Explain how you could use the table to show how the points for catching a given number of monsters in Level 1 compares to catching the same number of giants in Level 3.

5 **REFLECT**

Look back at your **Try It**, strategies by classmates, and **Picture It** and **Model It**. Which models or strategies do you like best for representing patterns and identifying relationships between corresponding terms? Explain.

....

....

....

APPLY IT

Use what you just learned to solve these problems.

6 School magnets cost $4, and shirts cost $24. Write a pattern for the costs of 0–5 magnets and a second pattern for the costs of 0–5 shirts. How do the corresponding terms of the two patterns compare?

Solution ....

....

7 Tom and Ehrin write number patterns. Tom uses the rule "add 3" and starts at 12. Ehrin uses the rule "subtract 4" and starts at 26. Write the first five terms of their patterns. What number appears as a term in both patterns? Show your work.

Solution ....

8 The Lakeview Feed Store posts prices for two different types of grass seed by the square foot.

Number of Square Feet	0	1	2	3	4	5
Grass Seed A ($)	0	4	6	8	10	12
Grass Seed B ($)	0	8	12	16	20	24

Which sentences correctly compare the cost of a number of square feet of Grass Seed A and the cost of the same number of square feet of Grass Seed B?

Ⓐ The cost of Grass Seed A is one-half the cost of Grass Seed B.

Ⓑ The cost of Grass Seed A is two times the cost of Grass Seed B.

Ⓒ The cost of Grass Seed B is one-half the cost of Grass Seed A.

Ⓓ The cost of Grass Seed B is two times the cost of Grass Seed A.

Ⓔ The cost of Grass Seed A is always two dollars less than the cost of Grass Seed B.

Practice Comparing Two Numerical Patterns

Study the Example showing one way to identify relationships between two numerical patterns. Then solve problems 1–6.

EXAMPLE

The school store sells laces and decals in the school colors. Laces cost $1 each, and decals cost $5 each. Find the cost of laces and the cost of decals for selling 0, 1, 2, 3, 4, and 5 of each item.

Use a table to show the two patterns.

The pattern for the cost of laces follows the rule "add 1."
    0, 1, 2, 3, 4, 5

The pattern for the cost of decals follows the rule "add 5."
    0, 5, 10, 15, 20, 25

Number of Items	Cost of Laces ($)	Cost of Decals ($)
0	0	0
1	1	5
2	2	10
3	3	15
4	4	20
5	5	25

1   Look at the Example. What is the cost for 6 decals? Explain how you got your answer.

2   Look at the Example. How are the terms in the pattern for the cost of decals related to the corresponding terms in the pattern for the cost of laces?

3 Suppose school bookmarks cost $3 each. Complete the table to show how the terms in this pattern compare to the corresponding terms in the pattern for the cost of laces.

Number of Items	Cost of Laces ($)	Cost of Bookmarks ($)
0	0	0
1	1	3
2	2	
3	3	
4	4	
5	5	

4 Look at problem 3. How do the corresponding terms of the two patterns compare?

5 Look at problem 3. What is the rule for finding the cost of bookmarks?

6 Look at problem 3. If the table was continued, which two values could be corresponding terms for laces and bookmarks?

Ⓐ 8 and 21

Ⓑ 10 and 30

Ⓒ 12 and 36

Ⓓ 15 and 60

Ⓔ 16 and 24

Ⓕ 20 and 60

Vocabulary

term a number in a pattern.

corresponding terms terms that have the same position in two related patterns.

Develop Using a Graph to Compare Patterns

Read and try to solve the problem below.

The scouts are making model vehicles. They have a choice of making a model plane or a model boat.
- **The materials for each plane cost $2.**
- **The materials for each boat cost $4.**

Write two patterns to show the costs for making 0 to 4 of each type of vehicle. Graph points in the coordinate plane to show a relationship between corresponding terms of the patterns.

TRY IT

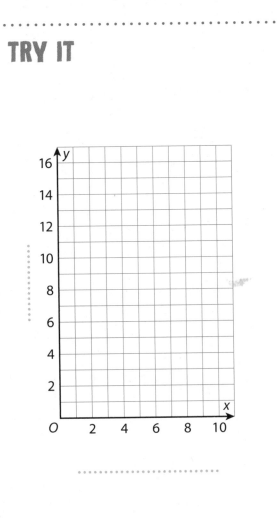

 **Math Toolkit**
- grid paper
- base-ten blocks

DISCUSS IT

Ask your partner: Do you agree with me? Why or why not?

Tell your partner: I knew . . . so I . . .

Explore ways to understand corresponding terms of patterns.

> **The scouts are making model vehicles.**
> **They have a choice of making a model plane or a model boat.**
> • **The materials for each plane cost $2.**
> • **The materials for each boat cost $4.**
> **Write two patterns to show the costs for making 0 to 4 of each**
> **type of vehicle. Graph points in the coordinate plane to show a**
> **relationship between corresponding terms of the patterns.**

MODEL IT

You can use a table to list the terms of the patterns.

List the cost of materials for 0, 1, 2, 3, and 4 planes and boats in a table. Then write the corresponding costs as ordered pairs.

Number Made	Cost of Planes ($), x	Cost of Boats ($), y	Ordered Pair (x, y)
0	0	0	(0, 0)
1	2	4	(2, 4)
2	4	8	(4, 8)
3	6	12	(6, 12)
4	8	16	(8, 16)

MODEL IT

You can use a graph to model the relationship between corresponding terms.

The coordinate plane shows the relationship between the cost of planes and cost of boats.

The first two ordered pairs from the table above are shown on the coordinate plane.

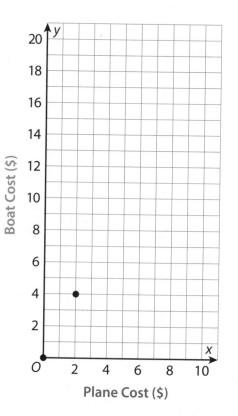

CONNECT IT

Now you will use the problem from the previous page to help you understand how to use a graph to show relationships between corresponding terms of patterns.

1 Look at the table in the first **Model It**. What does the ordered pair (4, 8) represent?

2 How do the corresponding terms in the ordered pair (4, 8) compare? Is this relationship true of all corresponding terms in the table?

3 The first two ordered pairs in the table are graphed in the coordinate plane in the second **Model It**. Plot the other three ordered pairs from the table on the graph.

4 Connect the points on the graph in the second **Model It**. Explain what you see.

5 Describe how to move along grid lines from one point to the next point to the right on your graph in the second **Model It**. How does your description relate to the rules for the patterns?

6 REFLECT

Look back at your **Try It**, strategies by classmates, and **Model Its**. Which models or strategies do you like best for how to use a graph to show relationships between corresponding terms of patterns. Explain.

....

....

....

APPLY IT

Use what you just learned to solve these problems.

7 Consider the two patterns below. Start each pattern with 0.

       Pattern A: add 1   **Pattern B:** add 3

Write five ordered pairs made up of corresponding terms from the two patterns. Plot the points in the coordinate plane to the right. Describe the relationship between the two patterns. Show your work.

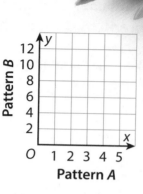

8 In the school store, pencils are sold in packages of 6. Write five ordered pairs made up of corresponding terms of these two patterns, based on selling 0 to 4 packages of pencils.

    Pattern A: number of packages sold

    Pattern B: number of pencils sold

Plot the points in the coordinate plane. Describe the relationship between the coordinates of the ordered pairs. Show your work.

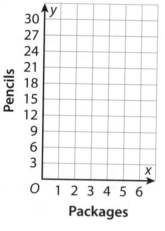

9 Madeline and Javier graphed ordered pairs using the terms from the patterns they made. Madeline made the number pattern 0, 1, 3, 5, 7, 9. Javier made a number pattern with terms that were three times the corresponding terms in Madeline's pattern. Which list shows the ordered pairs Madeline and Javier graphed?

  Ⓐ (0, 0) (1, 3) (3, 9) (5, 15) (7, 21) (9, 27)

  Ⓑ (0, 0) (1, 3) (3, 5) (5, 7) (7, 9) (9, 11)

  Ⓒ (0, 0) (1, 3) (3, 12) (5, 20) (7, 28) (9, 36)

  Ⓓ (0, 0) (3, 1) (9, 3) (15, 5) (7, 21) (9, 27)

Practice Using a Graph to Compare Patterns

Study the Example comparing two patterns on a graph. Then solve problems 1–6.

EXAMPLE

Luke compared a pattern with the rule "add 2" to a pattern with the rule "add 6."

He started at 0 and wrote the first three numbers of each pattern.
Add 2: **0, 2, 4**
Add 6: **0, 6, 12**

He wrote three ordered pairs.
   (0, 0)   **(2, 6)**   **(4, 12)**

Then he plotted the ordered pairs in the coordinate plane.

The first number in each ordered pair shows the location along the x-axis.

The second number in each ordered pair shows the location along the y-axis.

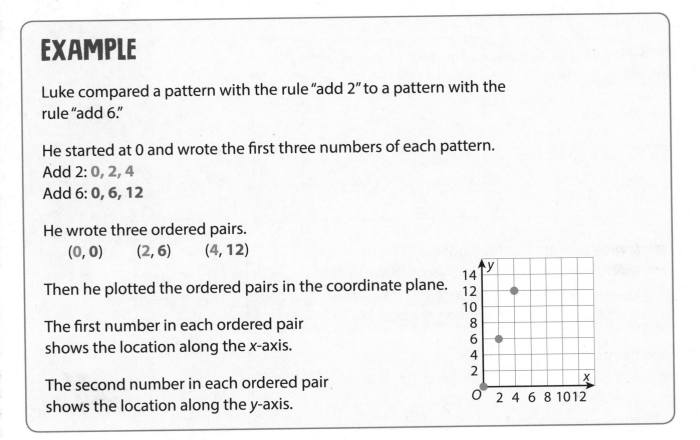

1. Look at the ordered pairs in the Example. Describe the relationship between corresponding terms of the two patterns.

2. Suppose you connect the points on the graph in the Example. What would the graph look like?

At a bake sale, cookies are sold in packages of 4 cookies each. Fruit bars are sold in packages of 2 fruit bars each.

3 Complete the table comparing the number of cookies and fruit bars sold for 0, 1, 2, and 3 packages.

Number of Packages	Number of Cookies, x	Number of Fruit Bars, y	Ordered Pair (x, y)
0	0	0	(0, 0)
1	4	2	(4, 2)
2			
3			

4 Use the coordinate plane at the right to graph the ordered pairs from the table in problem 3. What directions would you give someone to get from one point to the next point to the right on the graph?

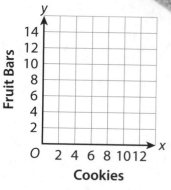

5 How do your directions relate to the rules for the patterns?

6 Graph the next two points in the coordinate plane following these rules:

Pattern A: Start at 1. Multiply by 3. Subtract 1.

Pattern B: Start at 1. Multiply by 4. Subtract 1.

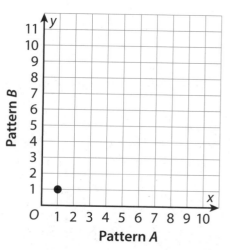

Refine Analyzing Patterns and Relationships

Study the Example below. Then solve problems 1–8.

EXAMPLE

Look at the following two number patterns.

> **Pattern A: 6, 5, 4, 3, 2, 1, 0**
>
> **Pattern B: 24, 20, 16, 12, 8, 4, 0**

What is the relationship between corresponding terms in the two patterns?

Look at how you could show your work using ordered pairs.

The first number is a term from Pattern A.
The second number is the corresponding term from Pattern B.

Ordered pairs: (6, 24), (5, 20), (4, 16), (3, 12), (2, 8), (1, 4), (0, 0)

Solution ....

....

The student wrote ordered pairs to identify a relationship between corresponding terms.

PAIR/SHARE
How are these patterns different from other patterns in this lesson?

APPLY IT

1 One pattern starts at 0 and has the rule "add 8." Another pattern starts at 0 and has the rule "add 4." Write each pattern of numbers. How do the corresponding terms in the patterns compare? Show your work.

How can you generate the patterns?

Solution ....

....

....

PAIR/SHARE
Does it matter how many terms you write for each pattern?

2 Identify the pattern in each column of the table. Complete the *x*- and *y*-columns of the table. Use those columns to write ordered pairs in the last column. Describe the relationship between corresponding terms in the patterns. Show your work.

x	*y*	Ordered Pair (*x*, *y*)
4	1	
8	2	
12	3	

What is the rule for each pattern?

Solution ....

....

PAIR/SHARE
Find the difference between the numbers in each ordered pair. Do you see another pattern?

3 The ordered pairs (2, 12), (3, 18), and (4, 24) are formed by corresponding terms in two patterns. How do the terms of the pattern of *y*-coordinates compare to the corresponding terms of the pattern of *x*-coordinates?

Ⓐ 10 more

Ⓑ 2 times as much

Ⓒ $\frac{1}{6}$ times as much

Ⓓ 6 times as much

Mike chose Ⓒ as the correct answer. How did he get that answer?

What rule works for all the ordered pairs?

PAIR/SHARE
Does Mike's answer make sense?

4 Look at the patterns below. Choose *True* or *False* for each statement.

Pattern A: 3, 6, 9, 12, 15, 18, . . .

Pattern B: 18, 36, 54, 72, 90, 108, . . .

	True	False
The rule for Pattern A is "multiply by 2."	Ⓐ	Ⓑ
The rule for Pattern B is "add 18."	Ⓒ	Ⓓ
Each term in Pattern A is 6 times the corresponding term in Pattern B.	Ⓔ	Ⓕ
Each term in Pattern B is 3 times the corresponding term in Pattern A.	Ⓖ	Ⓗ

5 Cindy and Dawn make these number patterns.

Cindy's rule: Start at 4. Multiply by 2.

Dawn's rule: Start at 28. Subtract 4.

Write the first five terms of their patterns. Are there two corresponding terms that are the same? Explain. Show your work.

Solution ....

6 The table shows the terms of a pattern of *x*-coordinates and a pattern of *y*-coordinates. What two rules were used to make the patterns?

x-coordinate	0	1	2	3	4
y-coordinate	0	5	10	15	20

Ⓐ Add 4, Add 5

Ⓑ Add 1, Add 5

Ⓒ Add 1, Add 4

Ⓓ Add 4, Add 8

7 **Part A** Use the rules "add 2" and "add 5" to make two patterns that each begin with 0. Use the patterns to complete the table.

Add 2, x	Add 5, y	Ordered Pair (x, y)

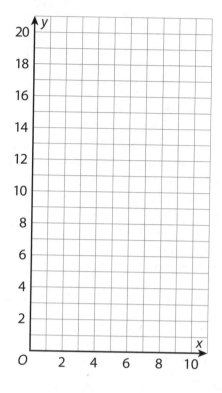

Part B Graph the ordered pairs and connect the points. What do you see?

Part C Describe the relationship between the corresponding terms of the patterns.

8 MATH JOURNAL

Use the graph of corresponding terms of Pattern *A* and Pattern *B*. Write the first 5 terms of each pattern. Explain how you found the terms.

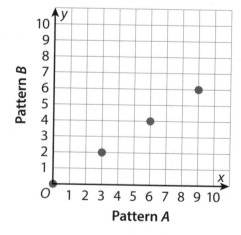

☑ SELF CHECK Go back to the Unit 5 Opener and see what you can check off.

In this unit you learned to . . .

Skill	Lesson
Evaluate expressions, for example: 48 ÷ (6 + 10) has a value of 3.	30
Write a numerical expression to represent a phrase, for example: *subtract 5 from 12, then multiply by 4* can be written as (12 − 5) × 4.	30
Write ordered pairs for points in the coordinate plane.	31, 32
Graph points in the coordinate plane.	31, 32, 33
Find the vertical and horizontal distance between two points in the coordinate plane.	32
Graph quantities that represent real-world situations in the coordinate plane and interpret the coordinates of a point in terms of a real-world context.	32
Describe the relationship between corresponding terms of two number patterns.	33
Generate a numerical pattern using a rule.	33

Think about what you have learned.

Use words, numbers, and drawings.

1 The most important topic I learned is 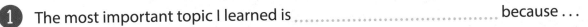 because . . .

2 Something I know well is . . .

3 A question I still have is . . .

Work with Coordinates and Patterns

Study an Example Problem and Solution

SMP 1 Make sense of problems and persevere in solving them.

Read this problem involving shapes and the coordinate plane. Then look at Max's solution to this problem.

Octagon Trap

Max is working on a new video game, *Shape Shake-Up*. He uses a coordinate plane to represent the screen. It helps him decide where to place graphics. Read one of Max's ideas.

Game Idea

- A shape that looks like a "C" traps players.
- The shape's perimeter is 14 to 16 units. Its area is 6 to 8 square units.
- The shape is located more than 2 units above the *x*-axis and more than 2 units to the right of the *y*-axis.

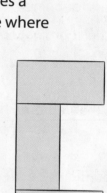

Draw a shape in the coordinate plane that works with Max's game idea and explain why it works. Label each vertex with an ordered pair.

Read the sample solution on the next page. Then look at the checklist below. Find and mark parts of the answer that match the checklist.

✓ PROBLEM-SOLVING CHECKLIST

- ☐ Tell what is known.
- ☐ Tell what the problem is asking.
- ☐ Show all your work.
- ☐ Show that the solution works.

a. **Circle** something that is known.

b. **Underline** something that you need to find.

c. **Draw a box around** what you do to solve the problem.

d. **Put a checkmark** next to the part that shows the solution works.

MAX'S SOLUTION

- **I know** the choices for area and perimeter of the shape. I need to find the lengths of sides that can make an area and perimeter that work.

- **I can try different lengths for the sides.**
  There are 8 sides.
  Their lengths must have a sum of 14 to 16.
  It looks like I should try numbers close to 2.

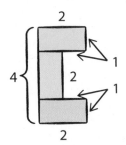

- **I'll check** that the perimeter works.
  $4 + (3 \times 2) + (1 \times 4) = 14$

- **I'll check** that the area works.
  $(2 \times 1) + (2 \times 1) + (2 \times 1) = 6$

  The shape has a perimeter of 14 units and an area of 6 square units.

- **Now I can plot the shape in the coordinate plane.**
  I'll put the bottom left vertex at (3, 3) so I know it is more than 2 units from each axis.

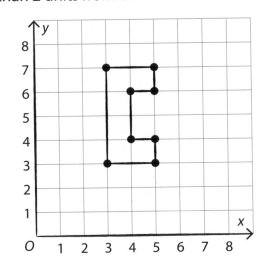

> Hi, I'm Max. Here's how I solved this problem.

> First I tried a shape that was 5 units wide and 5 units tall, but that was much too big.

> After I put a corner at (3, 3), I counted right 2, up 1, left 1, up 2, and so on to draw the whole shape.

Try Another Approach

There are many ways to solve problems. Think about how you might solve the Octagon Trap problem in a different way.

Octagon Trap

Max is working on a new video game, *Shape Shake-Up*. He uses a coordinate plane to represent the screen. It helps him decide where to place graphics. Read one of Max's ideas.

Game Idea

- A shape that looks like a "C" traps players.
- The shape's perimeter is 14 to 16 units. Its area is 6 to 8 square units.
- The shape is located more than 2 units above the *x*-axis and more than 2 units to the right of the *y*-axis.

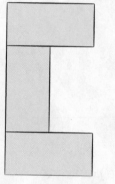

Draw a shape in the coordinate plane that works with Max's game idea and explain why it works. Label each vertex with an ordered pair.

PLAN IT

Answer these questions to help you start thinking about a plan.

A. How can you make a different "C" shape?

B. What are some different locations you can use on the grid?

SOLVE IT

Find a different solution for the Octagon Trap problem. Show all your work on a separate sheet of paper.

You may want to use the Problem-Solving Tips to get started.

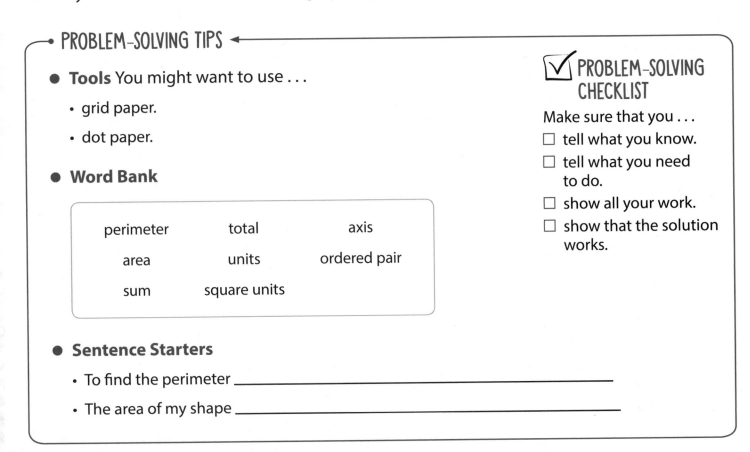

PROBLEM-SOLVING TIPS

- **Tools** You might want to use . . .
  - grid paper.
  - dot paper.

- **Word Bank**

perimeter	total	axis
area	units	ordered pair
sum	square units	

- **Sentence Starters**
  - To find the perimeter _____
  - The area of my shape _____

☑ PROBLEM-SOLVING CHECKLIST

Make sure that you . . .
- ☐ tell what you know.
- ☐ tell what you need to do.
- ☐ show all your work.
- ☐ show that the solution works.

REFLECT

Use Mathematical Practices As you work through the problem, discuss these questions with a partner.

- **Use Models** How can a sketch help you solve this problem?

- **Use Tools** Will a ruler be helpful for this problem? Explain how it can help, or explain why not.

Discuss Models and Strategies

Read the problem. Write a solution on a separate sheet of paper. Remember, there can be lots of ways to solve a problem!

Rectangle Maze

One screen in Max's game has a maze of rectangles. Players try to move through the maze. The rectangles start in a certain location, but they move both left and right and up and down. Max will decide the starting location for each rectangle.

Max's Notes

- Show 5 rectangles.
- Put one rectangle near the middle of the screen.
- Put other rectangles on all 4 sides of the middle rectangle.
- Other rectangles must have either an area that is half of the area or a perimeter that is half of the perimeter of the middle rectangle.
- Each shape must be a distance of at least 1 unit from the middle rectangle on all sides.

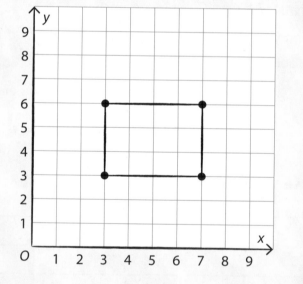

Where should Max put the other 4 rectangles?

PLAN IT AND SOLVE IT

Find a solution to the Rectangle Maze problem.

- Draw the other 4 rectangles.

- Label the vertices of all shapes with ordered pairs.

- Explain why your shapes work with Max's notes.

You may want to use the Problem-Solving Tips to get started.

REFLECT

Use Mathematical Practices As you work through the problem, discuss these questions with a partner.

- **Be Precise** How can you find the area and perimeter of a rectangle in the coordinate plane?

- **Use Models** What expressions can you write to find half of the perimeter and half of the area of the given rectangle?

Persevere On Your Own

Read the problems. Write a solution on a separate sheet of paper.

The Plunging Parallelogram

In Max's game, a parallelogram starts at the top of the screen and zigzags down to the bottom. Read Max's design notes.

Max's Design Notes

- The parallelogram has all right angles.
- The sides are at least 2 units long.
- The game starts with one vertex located at (10, 10).
- The game ends when one vertex is located at (0, 0).

What points should Max use as the parallelogram's vertices?
What path can the shape take to get to the bottom of the screen?

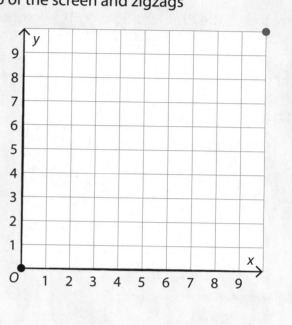

SOLVE IT
Help Max draw the parallelogram.

- Plot points and draw the parallelogram at its starting point.

- Give the coordinates of each vertex.

- Plot points and draw the parallelogram at its ending point.

- Describe a path the shape could follow to get to the bottom of the screen. Use directional words and numbers of units in your description.

REFLECT

Use Mathematical Practices After you complete the task, choose one of these questions to discuss with a partner.

- **Critique Reasoning** Does the path your partner described work? Why or why not?

- **Be Precise** What are all the different names that can be used to describe Max's shape?

Game Booklets

Max is printing instruction booklets for his game. Max is deciding what size booklets to print. He needs 4 pages for the instructions, but with 8 pages he could include hints. Max will sell a booklet at twice the printing cost. The money he has left after paying the printer is his *profit*.

Printing Costs
- $1.50 for each 4-page booklet.
- $2.00 for each 8-page booklet.

Max thinks that he can sell more booklets at a lower price. But he thinks he might make more profit with higher-price booklets. Here are Max's sales estimates.

- I can sell 280 to 300 of the 4-page booklet.
- I can sell 250 to 280 of the 8-page booklet.

About how much profit might Max make selling the booklets? How many pages should the booklets be?

SOLVE IT
Help Max decide whether to make 4-page or 8-page booklets.

- Choose a number of 4-page and 8-page booklets from Max's sales estimates.

- Use these numbers to write and evaluate expressions that show how much profit Max will make after paying for the booklets to be printed.

- Recommend a booklet length and support your recommendation.

REFLECT
Use Mathematical Practices After you complete the task, choose one of these questions to discuss with a partner.

- **Make an Argument** How did you support your recommendation?

- **Reason Mathematically** How did you choose the number of 4-page booklets and 8-page booklets?

1 What are the coordinates of point *C*?

Ⓐ (2, 6)

Ⓑ (3, 5)

Ⓒ (6, 2)

Ⓓ (6, 6)

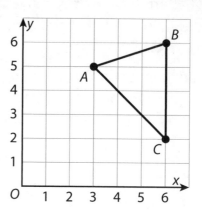

2 Look at the coordinate plane at the right.

Which statements about the points in the coordinate plane are true? Choose all the correct answers.

Ⓐ The *x*-coordinate of point *S* is 4.

Ⓑ The *x*-coordinate of point *T* is 4.

Ⓒ The *y*-coordinate of point *R* is 4.

Ⓓ Point *S* and point *T* have the same *x*-coordinate.

Ⓔ Point *R* and point *S* have the same *y*-coordinate.

3 Decide if the value of each expression is less than, equal to, or greater than 30.

Choose *Less Than*, *Equal To*, or *Greater Than* for each expression.

	Less Than	Equal To	Greater Than
$3 \times 5 \times 6$	Ⓐ	Ⓑ	Ⓒ
$5 \times (6 - 3)$	Ⓓ	Ⓔ	Ⓕ
$\frac{1}{2} \times (6 \times 5)$	Ⓖ	Ⓗ	Ⓘ
$4 \times \frac{1}{4} \times (6 \times 5)$	Ⓙ	Ⓚ	Ⓛ
$(10 \times 6) \times (5 - 4)$	Ⓜ	Ⓝ	Ⓞ
$(5 \times 6) \div (4 - 3)$	Ⓟ	Ⓠ	Ⓡ

4 Zhen makes two different number patterns. Pattern *A* starts at 0 and has the rule "add 12." Pattern *B* starts at 0 and has the rule "add 6." Write the first five terms of each pattern. How are the corresponding terms related? Show your work.

Solution ....

5 Justin designs a plan for a local park using the coordinate plane shown. He includes a water fountain in his design. The water fountain is located 2 units to the right and 3 units down from point *A*. Decide if each statement about the location of the water fountain is true.

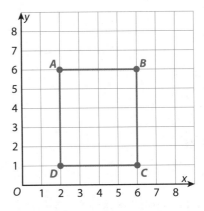

Choose *True* or *False* for each statement.

	Yes	No
The location of the water fountain is (2, 3).	Ⓐ	Ⓑ
You can get to the water fountain from point *C* by going 2 units to the left and 2 units up.	Ⓒ	Ⓓ
The location of the water fountain is (4, 3).	Ⓔ	Ⓕ
The location of the water fountain is closer to the origin than point *B*.	Ⓖ	Ⓗ

6 Insert parentheses into the expression below so that the value of the expression is 6. Show your work.

$2 \times 12 \div 3 + 1$

7 Asim is 7 years old. His mother is 3 years less than 5 times his age. Write a numerical expression to represent his mother's age.

....

Performance Task

Answer the questions and show all your work on separate paper.

Your friend Sophie has asked you to check her math homework. She sends you a text message with the expressions she evaluated and the values she found. Unfortunately, she didn't include any parentheses in her message.

Copy each equation below. If the equation is true as written, write a check mark (✓) next to it. If the equation is not true, insert parentheses to make the equation true.

$6 + 5 \times 3 - 1 = 32$ $\qquad$ $12 \div 2 + 4 \times 5 = 10$ $\qquad$ $15 - 3 + 4 \times 2 = 20$

$6 + 5 \times 3 - 1 = 16$ $\qquad$ $12 \div 2 + 4 \times 5 = 26$ $\qquad$ $15 - 3 + 4 \times 2 = 1$

Then write a message to Sophie explaining why she needed to include the parentheses in order for you to check her homework.

REFLECT

Use Mathematical Practices After you complete the task, choose one of the following questions to answer.

- **Be Precise** How did you decide where to insert the parentheses in each equation?

- **Use Structure** Consider the expression $6 + 7 \times 5 - 2$. Would you rewrite it as $6 + (7 \times 5) - 2$? Why or why not?

Checklist

Did you . . .

☐ check your calculations?

☐ use order of operations?

☐ use complete sentences?

Vocabulary

Draw or write to show examples for each term.

coordinate plane a two-dimensional space formed by two perpendicular number lines called *axes*.

My Example

corresponding terms terms that have the same position in two related patterns. For example, the second term in one pattern and the second term in a related pattern are corresponding terms.

My Example

evaluate to find the value of an expression.

My Example

grouping symbol a symbol, such as braces { }, brackets [ ], or parentheses ( ), used to group parts of an expression that should be evaluated before others.

My Example

ordered pair a pair of numbers, (x, y), that describes the location of a point in the coordinate plane, where the x-coordinate gives the point's horizontal distance from the origin, and the y-coordinate gives the point's vertical distance from the origin.

My Example

origin the point $(0, 0)$ in the coordinate plane where the x-axis and y-axis intersect.

My Example

terms   the numbers or shapes in a pattern.

My Example

x-axis   the horizontal number line in the coordinate plane.

My Example

x-coordinate   the first number in an ordered pair. It tells the point's horizontal distance from the origin.

My Example

y-axis   the vertical number line in the coordinate plane.

My Example

y-coordinate   the second number in an ordered pair. It tells the point's vertical distance from the origin.

My Example

My Word: ....

....

....

My Example

Cumulative Practice

Name: _____

Set 1: Decimal Place Value

Fill in the blanks.

1 0.4 = ... × 10

2 0.06 = ... ÷ 10

3 10 times 0.25 is ....

4 $\frac{1}{10}$ of 0.07 is ....

5 0.9 is .... of 9.

6 10 times .... is 0.06.

7 The value of the 3 in 0.13 is .... of the value of the 3 in 0.3.

8 The value of the 4 in 4.2 is .... times the value of the 4 in 0.402.

9 The value of the 9 in 0.19 is .... times the value of the 9 in 0.449.

Set 2: Powers of 10

Complete the equations.

1 4.3 × 100 = ...

2 0.055 × 10^4 = ...

3 0.004 × 10^2 = ...

4 66 ÷ 100 = ...

5 0.1 ÷ 10^1 = ...

6 45 ÷ 10^3 = ...

Complete the equations. Fill in each blank with a power of 10 in exponential form.

7 2.2 × .... = 220

8 40 ÷ .... = 0.04

9 0.07 × .... = 700

10 .... × 0.75 = 75

11 24 ÷ .... = 2.4

12 160 ÷ .... = 0.016

Set 3: Compare Decimals

Write <, >, or = in each circle to compare the numbers.

1 42.5 ◯ 42.05

2 3.6 ◯ 3.60

3 0.24 ◯ 0.244

4 0.4 ◯ 0.364

5 65 ◯ 65.3

6 1.075 ◯ 1.65

Set 4: Read and Write Decimals

Write each number in standard form in problems 1–6.

1 Thirteen and four tenths

....

2 Eight and twenty-two hundredths

....

3 Six hundred and seven thousandths

....

4 Seventy-five thousandths

....

5 $2 \times 10 + 4 \times \frac{1}{10} + 3 \times \frac{1}{1,000}$

....

6 $8 \times \frac{1}{100} + 9 \times \frac{1}{1,000}$

....

Write each number in word form in problems 7–9.

7 6.047

8 50.12

9 0.305

Set 5: Round Decimals

Round to the nearest whole number for problems 1–3.

1 26.48

2 0.533

3 5.615

....

Round to the nearest tenth for problems 4–6.

4 2.154

5 15.98

6 0.064

....

Round to the nearest hundredth for problems 7–9.

7 84.167

8 18.062

9 9.509

....

Set 6: Add and Subtract Decimals

Add. Show your work.

1 3.14 + 0.59

2 10.205 + 0.41

3 16 + 0.09 + 2.51

Subtract. Show your work.

4 2.15 − 1.84

5 15 − 0.67

6 4.754 − 3.62

Set 7: Add Fractions

Add. Show your work.

1 $\frac{1}{5} + \frac{3}{4}$

2 $\frac{5}{6} + \frac{1}{12}$

3 $1\frac{3}{4} + \frac{2}{3}$

4 $1\frac{4}{5} + 4\frac{3}{8}$

Set 8: Subtract Fractions

Subtract. Show your work.

1 $\frac{4}{9} - \frac{2}{5}$

2 $\frac{7}{3} - \frac{1}{2}$

3 $3\frac{1}{9} - 1\frac{5}{6}$

4 $3\frac{7}{10} - 2\frac{1}{6}$

Set 9: Multiply and Divide Multi-Digit Numbers

Multiply. Show your work.

1
$$\begin{array}{r} 1{,}516 \\ \times \quad 24 \\ \hline \end{array}$$

2
$$\begin{array}{r} 377 \\ \times \quad 15 \\ \hline \end{array}$$

3
$$\begin{array}{r} 471 \\ \times \quad 28 \\ \hline \end{array}$$

Divide. Show your work.

4 $936 \div 18$

5 $1{,}034 \div 22$

6 $19\overline{)2109}$

Cumulative Practice

Name: _____

Set 1: Multiply Decimals by Whole Numbers

Multiply. Show your work.

1 2.21 × 4

2 3.60 × 5

3 8 × 0.75

Set 2: Multiply Decimals

Multiply. Show your work.

1 0.2 × 0.6

2 0.4 × 0.03

3 5.5 × 0.6

4 0.5 × 1.2

5 2.1 × 1.3

6 4 × 1.5

Set 3: Divide Decimals

Divide. Show your work.

1 5 ÷ 0.5

2 4.9 ÷ 7

3 4.8 ÷ 0.6

4 1.82 ÷ 13

5 3.6 ÷ 0.09

6 3.3 ÷ 1.5

Set 4: Fractions as Division

Write a division expression equivalent to each fraction or mixed number for problems 1–6.

1 $\frac{5}{2}$ ....

2 $\frac{7}{15}$ ....

3 $\frac{2}{6}$ ....

4 $3\frac{1}{3}$ ....

5 $7\frac{3}{4}$ ....

6 $2\frac{3}{7}$ ....

Write each quotient as a fraction for problems 7–9.

7 $5 \div 9$ ....

8 $15 \div 4$ ....

9 $1 \div 20$ ....

Write each quotient as a mixed number for problems 10–12.

10 $8 \div 3$ ....

11 $15 \div 14$ ....

12 $24 \div 5$ ....

Set 5: Multiply Fractions

Multiply for problems 1–6.

1 $\frac{5}{6} \times \frac{1}{3} =$ ....

2 $\frac{1}{8} \times \frac{4}{5} =$ ....

3 $\frac{5}{6} \times \frac{1}{6} =$ ....

4 $\frac{3}{3} \times \frac{1}{3} =$ ....

5 $\frac{3}{4} \times \frac{2}{3} =$ ....

6 $\frac{5}{8} \times \frac{3}{4} =$ ....

Find the area for problems 7 and 8. Show your work.

7 A square with side length $\frac{5}{8}$ ft. What is the area of the square?

8 A rectangle with length $\frac{9}{5}$ inches and width $\frac{2}{3}$ inches. What is the area of the rectangle?

Set 6: Multiplication as Scaling

Fill in the blanks with *less than*, *greater than*, or *equal to*.

1 $6 \times \frac{1}{3}$ is .... 6.

2 $\frac{1}{4} \times \frac{3}{4}$ is .... $\frac{1}{4}$.

3 $\frac{5}{3} \times \frac{1}{4}$ is .... $\frac{5}{3}$.

4 $\frac{5}{3} \times \frac{1}{4}$ is .... $\frac{1}{4}$.

5 $\frac{1}{6} \times \frac{5}{5}$ is .... $\frac{1}{6}$.

6 $\frac{9}{4} \times 2$ is .... 2.

Set 7: Multiply Fractions in Word Problems

Write a multiplication equation to represent and solve each problem. Show your work.

1 Chris had $\frac{3}{4}$ of a jug of milk left. He used $\frac{2}{5}$ of it to bake a cake. How much of the jug of milk did he use in his cake?

2 Tiana lives $\frac{5}{8}$ mile away from school. She walks halfway to school. How many miles does she walk?

3 Kaya does homework for $2\frac{2}{3}$ hours. She spends $\frac{1}{4}$ of this time doing her science homework. How much times does she spend doing her science homework?

4 Nick has a rope that is $3\frac{1}{4}$ yards long. He cuts off a piece of the rope so that it is now $\frac{5}{9}$ as long as the original rope. What is the length of his rope now?

5 Kevin writes two stories for English class. His first story is $5\frac{1}{3}$ pages long. His second story is $\frac{3}{4}$ as long as the first. How long is Kevin's second story?

Set 8: Divide with Unit Fractions

Divide.

1 $3 \div \frac{1}{3} =$ ....

2 $\frac{1}{5} \div 5 =$ ....

3 $\frac{1}{8} \div 2 =$ ....

4 $4 \div \frac{1}{6} =$ ....

5 $10 \div \frac{1}{4} =$ ....

6 $\frac{1}{3} \div 8 =$ ....

Write and solve the division equation that matches the question.

7 What is $\frac{1}{3}$ divided into 7 equal parts?

8 How many groups of $\frac{1}{4}$ are in 9?

Set 9: Divide Unit Fractions in Word Problems

Write a division equation to represent and solve each problem. Show your work.

1 Diego has $\frac{1}{4}$ of a book left to read. There are 6 chapters left. Each chapter is the same length. What fraction of the book is each chapter?

2 Morgan has 8 cups of cereal. She fills some bowls with $\frac{1}{2}$ cup of cereal each. How many bowls does she use?

3 A marathoner can run a mile in $\frac{1}{6}$ hour. How many miles can she run in 3 hours?

4 Zaid has a ribbon that is $\frac{1}{3}$ yard long. He cuts it into 9 pieces of equal length. How long is each piece of ribbon?

5 It takes Isadora's dog 5 days to eat $\frac{1}{3}$ of a bag of dog food. Her dog eats the same amount each day. How much of the original bag of dog food does her dog eat each day?

Set 10: Add and Subtract Fractions

Add or subtract. Show your work.

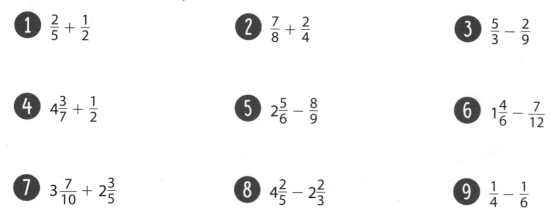

1 $\frac{2}{5} + \frac{1}{2}$

2 $\frac{7}{8} + \frac{2}{4}$

3 $\frac{5}{3} - \frac{2}{9}$

4 $4\frac{3}{7} + \frac{1}{2}$

5 $2\frac{5}{6} - \frac{8}{9}$

6 $1\frac{4}{6} - \frac{7}{12}$

7 $3\frac{7}{10} + 2\frac{3}{5}$

8 $4\frac{2}{5} - 2\frac{2}{3}$

9 $\frac{1}{4} - \frac{1}{6}$

Cumulative Practice

Name: _____

Set 1: Multiply Decimals

Multiply. Show your work.

1 5×0.4

2 9×0.12

3 3.4×0.07

Set 2: Divide Decimals

Divide. Show your work.

1 $6.4 \div 8$

2 $14 \div 0.7$

3 $1.8 \div 0.9$

Set 3: Multiply Fractions to Find Area

Find the area of each shape. Show your work.

1 A rectangle with length $\frac{3}{5}$ in. and width $\frac{3}{4}$ in. What is its area?

2 A rectangle with length $2\frac{1}{2}$ cm and width $1\frac{2}{3}$ cm. What is its area?

Set 4: Multiply Fractions in Word Problems

Write and solve a multiplication equation to solve each problem. Show your work.

1 Kira's purple scarf is $3\frac{1}{2}$ feet long. Her red scarf is $1\frac{1}{3}$ times as long as her purple scarf. How many feet long is Kira's red scarf?

2 Jim has $\frac{1}{3}$ of a box of cereal. He eats $\frac{1}{3}$ of the remaining cereal. What fraction of the original whole box of cereal did Jim eat?

3 Becca exercises for $1\frac{1}{2}$ hours. She dances for $\frac{5}{6}$ of the time she spends exercising. How much time does Becca spend dancing?

4 Vicente usually walks $1\frac{3}{5}$ miles to school. If he takes a new short-cut, he will walk $\frac{3}{4}$ as far as usual. How far will Vicente walk to school if he takes the short-cut?

Set 5: Divide Unit Fractions in Word Problems.

Write and solve a division equation to solve each problem. Show your work.

1 A bag of tennis balls contains 4 balls and weighs $\frac{1}{2}$ lb. Each tennis ball has the same weight. What is the weight of one tennis ball?

2 A group of students wrote a 2-page report. The students in the group each wrote $\frac{1}{3}$ of a page. How many students were in the group?

3 Iesha has 3 gallons of water. She fills glasses with $\frac{1}{10}$ gallon each. How many glasses can she fill?

Set 6: Add and Subtract Decimals

Add or subtract. Show your work.

1 $5.09 + 6.5$

2 $1.95 + 4.5$

3 $2.1 + 0.07 + 21.60$

4 $6 - 0.06$

5 $3.13 - 2.53$

6 $7.56 - 2.2$

7 $0.9 + 0.64$

8 $60.2 - 6.02$

9 $12 + 4.5 + 0.82$

Set 7: Add and Subtract Fractions

Add or subtract. Show your work.

1 $\frac{1}{4} + \frac{3}{8}$

2 $6\frac{7}{9} - 3\frac{2}{3}$

3 $\frac{4}{5} - \frac{1}{2}$

4 $1\frac{1}{3} + 2\frac{3}{4}$

5 $3\frac{2}{5} + 2\frac{3}{10}$

6 $7\frac{3}{7} - 5\frac{1}{2}$

7 $1\frac{2}{3} - \frac{5}{6}$

8 $5\frac{1}{3} + 4\frac{8}{12}$

9 $\frac{1}{2} - \frac{1}{9}$

Set 8: Volume

Find the volume of each figure. Show your work.

1. What is the volume of a rectangular prism with length 2 feet, width 4 feet, and height 10 feet?

2. What is the volume of a cube with a side length of 5 centimeters?

3. What is the volume of a rectangular prism with height 12 inches and a base with an area of 2 square inches?

4. What is the volume of the solid figure?

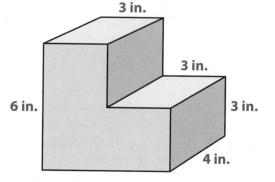

Set 9: Multiply and Divide Multi-Digit Numbers

Multiply. Show your work.

1.
$$\begin{array}{r} 615 \\ \times\ 21 \\ \hline \end{array}$$

2.
$$\begin{array}{r} 984 \\ \times\ \ 7 \\ \hline \end{array}$$

3.
$$\begin{array}{r} 1{,}279 \\ \times\ \ \ 26 \\ \hline \end{array}$$

Divide. Show your work.

4. $47\overline{)893}$

5. $15\overline{)1{,}650}$

6. $22\overline{)3{,}080}$

Glossary/Glosario

English	Español	Example/Ejemplo
Aa		

acute angle an angle that measures more than 0° but less than 90°.

ángulo agudo ángulo que mide más de 0° pero menos de 90°.

---

acute triangle a triangle that has three acute angles.

triángulo acutángulo triángulo que tiene tres ángulos agudos.

---

addend a number being added.

sumando número que se suma.

$24 + 35 = 59$

addends

---

algorithm a set of routine steps used to solve problems.

algoritmo conjunto de pasos que se siguen rutinariamente para resolver problemas.

```
     17 R 19
31)546
   -31↓
    236
   -217
     19
```

AM the time from midnight until before noon.

a. m. el tiempo que transcurre desde la medianoche hasta el mediodía.

AM **7:20**

---

angle a geometric shape formed by two rays, lines, or line segments that meet at a common point.

ángulo figura geométrica formada por dos semirrectas, rectas o segmentos de recta que se encuentran en un punto.

English	Español	Example/Ejemplo
area the amount of space inside a closed two-dimensional figure. Area is measured in square units such as square centimeters.	**área** cantidad de espacio dentro de una figura bidimensional cerrada. El área se mide en unidades cuadradas, como los centímetros cuadrados.	Area = 4 square units
array a set of objects arranged in equal rows and equal columns.	**matriz** conjunto de objetos agrupados en filas y columnas iguales.	
associative property of addition when the grouping of three or more addends is changed, the total does not change.	**propiedad asociativa de la suma** cambiar la agrupación de tres o más sumandos no cambia el total.	$(2 + 3) + 4 \ = \ 2 + (3 + 4)$
associative property of multiplication changing the grouping of three or more factors does not change the product.	**propiedad asociativa de la multiplicación** cambiar la agrupación de tres o más factores no cambia el producto.	$(2 \times 4) \times 3$ $\quad$ $2 \times (4 \times 3)$
attribute any characteristic of an object or shape, such as number of sides or angles, lengths of sides, or angle measures.	**atributo** característica de un objeto o una figura, como el número de lados o ángulos, la longitud de los lados o la medida de los ángulos.	attributes of a square: • 4 square corners • 4 sides of equal length
axis a horizontal or vertical number line that determines a coordinate plane. The plural form is *axes*.	**eje** recta numérica horizontal o vertical que determina un plano de coordenadas.	

Bb

base (of a power) in a power, the number that is used as a repeated factor.	**base (de una potencia)** en una potencia, el número que se usa como factor repetido.	8^2

English	Español	Example/Ejemplo
base (of a prism) one side of a prism, usually considered to be the side shown as the bottom of the prism. In the volume formula $V = b \times h$, b represents the area of the base of the prism.	**base (de un prisma)** lado de un prisma (por lo general, el lado inferior). En la fórmula de volumen $V = b \times a$, b representa el área de la base del prisma.	base
base ten a ten-digit number system in which the value of a digit depends on its place. The value of each place is 10 times the value of the place to the right and $\frac{1}{10}$ of the value of the place to the left.	**base diez** sistema numérico en el que el valor de un dígito depende de su valor posicional. El valor de cada posición es 10 veces el valor de la posición que está a la derecha y $\frac{1}{10}$ del valor de la posición que está a la izquierda.	
benchmark fraction a common fraction that you might compare other fractions to.	**fracción de referencia** fracción común que se puede comparar con otras fracciones.	$\frac{1}{4}$, $\frac{1}{2}$, $\frac{2}{3}$, and $\frac{3}{4}$ are often used as benchmark fractions.

Cc

English	Español	Example/Ejemplo
capacity the amount a container can hold. Capacity can be measured in the same units as liquid volume.	**capacidad** cantidad que cabe en un recipiente. La capacidad se mide en las mismas unidades que el volumen líquido.	2 liters 1 liter capacity of 2 liters
category a collection of objects grouped together based on attributes they have in common.	**categoría** grupo de objetos clasificados según atributos que tienen en común.	Quadrilaterals ← category Parallelograms Rectangles Squares ← subcategory
centimeter (cm) a unit of length. There are 100 centimeters in 1 meter.	**centímetro (cm)** unidad de longitud. 100 centímetros equivalen a 1 metro.	Your little finger is about 1 **centimeter** (cm) across.

English	Español	Example/Ejemplo
closed figure a two-dimensional figure that begins and ends at the same point.	**figura cerrada** figura bidimensional que comienza y termina en el mismo punto.	Closed figure Open figure
column a vertical line of objects or numbers, such as in an array or table.	**columna** línea vertical de objetos, como las de una matriz o una tabla.	
common denominator a number that is a common multiple of the denominators of two or more fractions.	**denominadores communes** número que es común múltiplo de los denominadores de dos o más fracciones.	$2 \times 3 = 6$, so 6 is a common denominator for $3\frac{1}{2}$ and $1\frac{1}{3}$.
commutative property of addition changing the order of addends does not change the total.	**propiedad conmutativa de la suma** cambiar el orden de los sumandos no cambia el total.	$3 + 4 \quad = \quad 4 + 3$
commutative property of multiplication changing the order of the factors does not change the product.	**propiedad conmutativa de la multiplicación** cambiar el orden de los factores no cambia el producto.	$3 \times 2 \quad = \quad 2 \times 3$
compare to decide if numbers, amounts, or sizes are *greater than*, *less than*, or *equal to* each other.	**comparar** determinar si un número, una cantidad o un tamaño es *mayor que, menor que* o *igual a* otro número, otra cantidad u otro tamaño.	$3.37 > 3.096$
compose to make by combining parts. You can put together numbers to make a greater number or shapes to make a new shape.	**componer** combinar partes para formar algo. Se pueden combinar números para formar un número mayor o figuras para formar otra figura.	50° 50° 50° The three 50° angles compose the larger angle.
composite number a number that has more than one pair of factors.	**número compuesto** número que tiene más de un par de factores.	16 is a composite number.

English	Español	Example/Ejemplo
convert to write an equivalent measurement using a different unit.	**convertir** expresar una medida equivalente en una unidad diferente.	5 feet = 60 inches
coordinate plane a two-dimensional space formed by two perpendicular number lines called *axes*.	**plano de coordenadas** espacio bidimensional formado por dos rectas numéricas perpendiculares llamadas *ejes*.	**Coordinate Plane**
corresponding terms terms that have the same position in two related patterns. For example, the second term in one pattern and the second term in a related pattern are corresponding terms.	**términos correspondientes** términos que tienen la misma posición en dos patrones relacionados. Por ejemplo, el segundo término de un patrón y el segundo término de un patrón relacionado son términos correspondientes.	Pattern A: 6, **9**, 12, 15, 18 Pattern B: 12, **18**, 24, 30, 36
cubic unit the volume of a unit cube.	**unidad cúbica** el volumen de un cubo con aristas de 1 unidad de longitud.	
cup (c) a unit of liquid volume in the customary system. 4 cups is equal to 1 quart.	**taza (tz)** unidad de volumen líquido del sistema usual. 4 tazas equivalen a 1 cuarto.	

English	Español	Example/Ejemplo

customary system the measurement system commonly used in the United States that measures length in inches, feet, yards, and miles; liquid volume in cups, pints, quarts, and gallons; and weight in ounces and pounds.

sistema usual sistema de medición comúnmente usado en Estados Unidos. La longitud se mide en pulgadas, pies, yardas, y millas; el volumen líquido, en tazas, pintas, cuartos, y galones; y el peso, en onzas y libras.

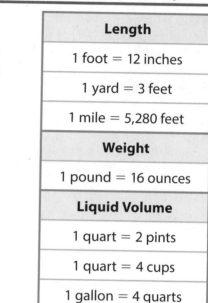

Length		
1 foot = 12 inches		
1 yard = 3 feet		
1 mile = 5,280 feet		
Weight		
1 pound = 16 ounces		
Liquid Volume		
1 quart = 2 pints		
1 quart = 4 cups		
1 gallon = 4 quarts		

Dd

data a set of collected information. Often numerical information such as a list of measurements.

datos conjunto de información reunida. A menudo es información numérica, tal como una lista de mediciones.

earthworm lengths (in inches):
$4\frac{1}{2}$, 5, 5, 5, $5\frac{1}{4}$, $5\frac{1}{4}$, $5\frac{1}{4}$, 6, $6\frac{1}{4}$

decimal a number containing a decimal point that separates a whole from fractional place values (tenths, hundredths, thousandths, and so on).

número decimal número que contiene un punto decimal que separa la posición de las unidades de las posiciones fraccionarias (décimas, centésimas, milésimas, etc.).

1.293

decimal point the dot used in a decimal that separates the ones place from the tenths place.

punto decimal punto que se usa en un número decimal para separar la posición de las unidades de la posición de las décimas.

1.65
↑
decimal point

decompose to break into parts. You can break apart numbers and shapes.

descomponer separar en partes. Se pueden separar en partes números y figuras.

$\frac{3}{8} = \frac{1}{8} + \frac{1}{8} + \frac{1}{8}$

degree (°) a unit of measure for angles. There are 360° in a circle.

grado (°) unidad de medida para ángulos. Hay 360° en un círculo.

There are 360° in a circle.

English	Español	Example/Ejemplo
denominator the number below the line in a fraction that tells the number of equal parts in the whole.	**denominador** número que está debajo de la línea de una fracción. Dice cuántas partes iguales hay en el entero.	$\dfrac{2}{3}$
difference the result of subtraction.	**diferencia** el resultado de la resta.	$\begin{array}{r} 16.75 \\ -\ 15.70 \\ \hline \mathbf{1.05} \end{array}$
digit a symbol used to write numbers.	**dígito** símbolo que se usa para escribir números.	The digits are 0, 1, 2, 3, 4, 5, 6, 7, 8, and 9.
dimension length in one direction. A figure may have one, two, or three dimensions.	**dimension** longitud en una dirección. Una figura puede tener una, dos o tres dimensiones.	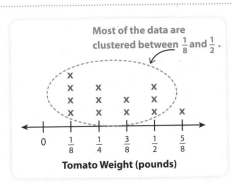 5 in. 2 in. 3 in.
distribution how spread out or how clustered pieces of data are.	**distribución** qué tan esparcidos o agrupados están los datos.	Most of the data are clustered between $\frac{1}{8}$ and $\frac{1}{2}$. Tomato Weight (pounds)
distributive property when one of the factors of a product is written as a sum, multiplying each addend by the other factor before adding does not change the product.	**propiedad distributiva** cuando uno de los factores de un producto se escribe como suma, multiplicar cada sumando por el otro factor antes de sumar no cambia el producto.	$2 \times (3 + 6) = (2 \times 3) + (2 \times 6)$
divide to separate into equal groups and find the number in each group or the number of groups.	**divisor** separar en grupos iguales y hallar cuántos hay en cada grupo o el número de grupos.	$2{,}850 \div 38 = 75$
dividend the number that is divided by another number.	**dividendo** el número que se divide por otro número.	$15 \div 3 = 5$

English	Español	Example/Ejemplo
division an operation used to separate a number of items into equal-sized groups.	**división** operación que se usa para separar una cantidad de objetos en grupos iguales.	**Division** $12 \div 3 = 4$ total number of groups number in each group
divisor the number by which another number is divided.	**divisor** el número por el que se divide otro número.	$15 \div 3 = 5$

Ee

English	Español	Example/Ejemplo
edge a line segment where two faces meet in a three-dimensional shape.	**arista** segmento de recta donde se encuentran dos caras de una figura tridimensional.	edge
elapsed time the amount of time that has passed between a start time and an end time.	**tiempo transcurrido** tiempo que ha pasado entre el momento de inicio y el fin.	The elapsed time from 2:00 PM to 3:00 PM is 1 hour.
equal having the same value, same size, or same amount.	**igual** que tiene el mismo valor, el mismo tamaño o la misma cantidad.	$25 + 15 = 40$ $25 + 15$ **is equal to** 40.
equal sign (=) a symbol that means *is the same value as.*	**signo de igual** (=) símbolo que significa *tiene el mismo valor que.*	$12 + 4 = 16$
equation a mathematical statement that uses an equal sign (=) to show that two expressions have the same value.	**ecuación** enunciado matemático que tiene un signo de igual (=) para mostrar que dos expresiones tienen el mismo valor.	$25 - 15 = 10$
equilateral triangle a triangle that has all three sides the same length.	**triángulo equilátero** triángulo que tiene los tres lados de igual longitud.	8 in. 8 in. 8 in.

English	Español	Example/Ejemplo
equivalent fractions two or more different fractions that name the same part of a whole or the same point on a number line.	**fracciones equivalentes** dos o más fracciones diferentes que nombran la misma parte de un entero y el mismo punto en una recta numérica.	$\dfrac{2}{4} = \dfrac{1}{2}$ $\dfrac{5}{10} = \dfrac{1}{2}$
estimate (noun) a close guess made using mathematical thinking.	**estimación** suposición aproximada que se hace usando el razonamiento matemático.	$28 + 21 = ?$ $30 + 20 = 50$ 50 is an estimate of the sum.
estimate (verb) to make a close guess based on mathematical thinking.	**estimar / hacer una estimación** hacer una suposición aproximada usando el razonamiento matemático.	$415 \div 20$ is about 21.
evaluate to find the value of an expression.	**evaluar** hallar el valor de una expresión.	The expression $48 \div (6 + 10)$ has a value of 3.
even number a whole number that always has 0, 2, 4, 6, or 8 in the ones place. An even number of objects can be put into pairs or into two equal groups without any leftovers.	**número par** número entero que siempre tiene 0, 2, 4, 6, o 8 en la posición de las unidades. Un número par de objetos puede agruparse en pares o en dos grupos iguales sin que queden sobrantes.	20, 22, 24, 26, and 28 are even numbers.
expanded form a way to write a number to show the place value of each digit.	**forma desarrollada** manera de escribir un número para mostrar el valor posicional de cada dígito.	$34.56 = 3 \times 10 + 4 \times 1 + 5 \times \frac{1}{10} + 6 \times \frac{1}{100}$
exponent the number in a power that tells how many times to use the base as a factor in repeated multiplication.	**exponente** el número de una potencia que dice cuántas veces debe multiplicarse la base.	8^2

English	Español	Example/Ejemplo
expression one or more numbers, unknown numbers, and/or operation symbols that represents a quantity.	**expresión** uno o más números, números desconocidos, o símbolos de operaciones que representan una cantidad.	3×4 or $5 + b$

Ff

English	Español	Example/Ejemplo
face a flat surface of a solid shape.	**cara** superficie plana de una figura sólida.	← face
fact family a group of related equations that use the same numbers, but in a different order, and two different operation symbols. A fact family can show the relationship between addition and subtraction or between multiplication and division.	**familia de datos** grupo de ecuaciones relacionadas que tienen los mismos números, ordenados de distinta manera, y dos símbolos de operaciones diferentes. Una familia de datos puede mostrar la relación que existe entre la multiplicación y la división.	$5 \times 4 = 20$ $4 \times 5 = 20$ $20 \div 4 = 5$ $20 \div 5 = 4$
factor a number that is multiplied.	**factor** número que se multiplica.	$4 \times 5 = 20$ factors
factor pair two numbers that are multiplied together to give a product.	**pares de factores** dos números que se multiplican para obtener un producto.	$4 \times 5 = 20$ factor pair
factors of a number whole numbers that multiply together to get the given number.	**factores de un número** números enteros que se multiplican para obtener el número dado.	$4 \times 5 = 20$ 4 and 5 are factors of 20.
foot (ft) a unit of length in the customary system. There are 12 inches in 1 foot.	**pie (ft)** unidad de longitud del sistema usual. Un pie equivale a 12 pulgadas.	12 inches = 1 foot

English	Español	Example/Ejemplo
formula a mathematical relationship that is expressed in the form of an equation.	**formula** relación matemática que se expresa en forma de ecuación.	$A = \ell \times w$

Gg

English	Español	Example/Ejemplo
gallon (gal) a unit of liquid volume in the customary system. There are 4 quarts in 1 gallon.	**galón (gal)** unidad de volumen líquido del sistema usual. 1 galón es igual a 4 cuartos.	4 quarts = 1 gallon
gram (g) a unit of mass in the metric system. A paper clip has a mass of about 1 gram. There are 1,000 grams in 1 kilogram.	**gramo (g)** unidad de masa del sistema métrico. Un clip tiene una masa de aproximadamente 1 gramo. 1,000 gramos equivalen a 1 kilogramo.	1,000 grams = 1 kilogram
greater than symbol (>) a symbol used to compare two numbers when the first is greater than the second.	**símbolo de mayor que (>)** símbolo que se usa para comparar dos números cuando el primero es mayor que el segundo.	$3.37 > 3.096$
grouping symbols a symbol, such as braces { }, brackets [ ], or parentheses ( ), used to group parts of an expression that should be evaluated before others.	**símbolos de agrupación** símbolos, tales como las llaves { }, los corchetes [ ], o los paréntesis ( ), que se usan para agrupar partes de una expresión que deben evaluarse antes que otras.	$3 + (5 \times 3) = 3 + 15$ $3 + \{5 \times 3\} = 3 + 15$ $3 + [5 \times 3] = 3 + 15$

Hh

English	Español	Example/Ejemplo
hexagon a polygon with exactly 6 sides and 6 angles.	**hexágono** polígono que tiene exactamente 6 lados y 6 ángulos.	
hierarchy a ranking of categories based on attributes.	**jerarquía** clasificación por categorías basada en atributos.	Quadrilaterals / Parallelograms / Rectangles / Squares
hour (h) a unit of time. There are 60 minutes in 1 hour.	**hora (h)** unidad de tiempo. 1 hora equivale a 60 minutos.	60 minutes = 1 hour

English	Español	Example/Ejemplo
hundredths the parts formed when a whole is divided into 100 equal parts.	**centésimos (fracciones)/ centésimas (decimales)** partes que se forman cuando un entero se divide en 100 partes iguales.	

Ii

English	Español	Example/Ejemplo
inch (in.) a unit of length in the customary system. There are 12 inches in 1 foot.	**pulgada (pulg.)** unidad de longitud del sistema usual. 12 pulgadas equivalen a 1 pie.	The length of a quarter is about 1 **inch** (in.).
inequality a mathematical statement that uses an inequality symbol (< or >) to show the relationship between expressions with different values.	**desigualdad** enunciado matemático en el que se usa un signo de desigualdad (< o >) para mostrar que dos expresiones tienen valores diferentes.	$3.275 > 3.240$ $3.240 < 3.275$
inverse operations operations that undo each other. For example, addition and subtraction are inverse operations, and multiplication and division are inverse operations.	**operación inversa** operaciones que se anulan unas a otras. Por ejemplo, la suma y la resta son operaciones inversas, y la multiplicación y la división son operaciones inversas.	$3{,}000 \div 10 = 300$ $300 \times 10 = 3{,}000$
isosceles triangle a triangle that has at least two sides the same length.	**triángulo isósceles** triángulo que tiene al menos dos lados de igual longitud.	8 in. 8 in. 6 in.

Kk

English	Español	Example/Ejemplo
kilogram (kg) a unit of mass in the metric system. There are 1,000 grams in 1 kilogram.	**kilogramo (kg)** unidad de masa del sistema métrico. 1 kilogramo equivale a 1,000 gramos.	1,000 grams = 1 kilogram

English	Español	Example/Ejemplo
kilometer (km) a unit of length in the metric system. There are 1,000 meters in 1 kilometer.	**kilómetro (km)** unidad de longitud del sistema métrico. 1 kilómetro equivale a 1,000 metros.	1 kilometer = 1,000 meters

Ll

English	Español	Example/Ejemplo
length measurement that tells the distance from one point to another, or how long something is.	**longitud** medida que indica la distancia de un punto a otro, o cuán largo es un objeto.	length
less than symbol (<) a symbol used to compare two numbers when the first is less than the second.	**símbolo de menor que (<)** símbolo que se usa para comparar dos números cuando el primero es menor que el segundo.	$3.096 < 3.37$
line a straight row of points that goes on forever in both directions.	**recta** fila recta de puntos que continúa infinitamente en ambas direcciones.	
line of symmetry a line that divides a shape into two mirror images.	**eje de simetría** recta que divide una figura en dos imágenes reflejadas.	
line plot a data display that shows data as marks above a number line.	**diagrama de puntos** representación de datos en la cual se muestran los datos como marcas sobre una recta numérica.	**Sea Lion Lengths**
line segment a straight row of points that starts at one point and ends at another point.	**segmento de recta** fila recta de puntos que comienza en un punto y termina en otro punto.	A B
liquid volume the amount of space a liquid takes up.	**volumen líquido** cantidad de espacio que ocupa un líquido.	When you measure how much water is in a bucket, you measure liquid volume.
liter (L) a unit of liquid volume in the metric system. There are 1,000 milliliters in 1 liter.	**litro (l)** unidad de volumen líquido del sistema métrico. 1 litro equivale a 1,000 mililitros.	1,000 milliliters = 1 liter

English	Español	Example/Ejemplo

Mm

mass the amount of matter in an object. Measuring the mass of an object is one way to measure how heavy it is. Units of mass include the gram and kilogram.

masa cantidad de materia que hay en un objeto. Medir la masa de un objeto es una manera de medir qué tan pesado es. El gramo y el kilogramo son unidades de masa.

The mass of a paper clip is about 1 gram.

---

meter (m) a unit of length in the metric system. There are 100 centimeters in 1 meter.

metro (m) unidad de longitud del sistema métrico. 1 metro es igual a 100 centímetros.

100 centimeters = 1 meter

---

metric system the measurement system that measures length based on meters, liquid volume based on liters, and mass based on grams.

sistema métrico sistema de medición. La longitud se mide en metros; el volumen líquido, en litros; y la masa, en gramos.

Length
1 kilometer = 1,000 meters
1 meter = 100 centimeters
1 meter = 1,000 millimeters

Mass
1 kilogram = 1,000 grams

Volume
1 liter = 1,000 milliliters

---

mile (mi) a unit of length in the customary system. There are 5,280 feet in 1 mile.

milla unidad de longitud del sistema usual. 1 milla equivale a 5,280 pies.

5,280 feet = 1 mile

---

milliliter (ml) a unit of liquid volume in the metric system. There are 1,000 milliliters in 1 liter.

mililitro (ml) unidad de volumen líquido del sistema métrico. 1,000 mililitros equivalen a 1 litro.

1,000 milliliters = 1 liter

---

millimeter (mm) a unit of length in the metric system. There 1,000 millimeters in 1 meter.

milímetro (mm) unidad de longitud del sistema métrico. 1,000 milímetros equivalen a 1 metro.

1,000 millimeters = 1 meter

English	Español	Example/Ejemplo
minute (min) a unit of time. There are 60 minutes in 1 hour.	**minuto (min)** unidad de tiempo. 60 minutos equivalen a 1 hora.	60 minutes = 1 hour
mixed number a number with a whole number part and a fractional part.	**número mixto** número con una parte entera y una parte fraccionaria.	$2\frac{3}{8}$
multiple the product of a given number and any other whole number.	**múltiplo** producto de un número y cualquier otro número entero.	4, 8, 12, 16, and so on, are multiples of 4.
multiplication an operation used to find the total number of items in a given number of equal-sized groups. See also *multiplicative comparison*.	**multiplicación** operación que se usa para hallar el número total de objetos en un número dado de grupos de igual tamaño. Ver también la *comparación multiplicativa*.	**Multiplication** $3 \times 4 = 12$ **number of groups** **number in each group** **total**
multiplicative comparison a comparison that tells how many times as many.	**comparación multiplicative** comparación que dice cuántas veces una cantidad es otra cantidad.	$\frac{1}{2} \times 6 = 3$ tells that 3 is $\frac{1}{2}$ as many as 6, and that 3 is 6 times as many as $\frac{1}{2}$.
multiply to repeatedly add the same number a certain number of times. Used to find the total number of items in equal-sized groups.	**multiplicar** sumar el mismo número una y otra vez una cierta cantidad de veces. Se multiplica para hallar el número total de objetos que hay en grupos de igual tamaño.	42 36 30 24 18 12 6 $7 \times 6 = 42$

Nn

numerator the number above the line in a fraction that tells the number of equal parts that are being described.	**numerador** número que está encima de la línea de una fracción. Dice cuántas partes iguales se describen.	$\frac{2}{3}$

English	Español	Example/Ejemplo

Oo

obtuse angle an angle that measures more than 90° but less than 180°.

ángulo obtuso ángulo que mide más de 90° pero menos de 180°.

---

obtuse triangle a triangle that has one obtuse angle.

triángulo obtusángulo triángulo que tiene un ángulo obtuso.

---

odd number a whole number that always has 1, 3, 5, 7, or 9 in the ones place. An odd number of objects cannot be put into pairs or into two equal groups without a leftover.

número impar número entero que siempre tiene el dígito 1, 3, 5, 7, o 9 en el lugar de las unidades. Los números impares no pueden ordenarse en pares o en dos grupos iguales sin sobrantes.

21, 23, 25, 27, and 29 are odd numbers.

---

operation a mathematical action such as addition, subtraction, multiplication, or division.

operación acción matemática como la suma, la resta, la multiplicación y la división.

$15 + 5 = 20$
$20 - 5 = 15$
$4 \times 6 = 24$
$24 \div 6 = 4$

---

ordered pair a pair of numbers, (x, y), that describes the location of a point in the coordinate plane, where the x-coordinate gives the point's horizontal distance from the origin, and the y-coordinate gives the point's vertical distance from the origin.

par ordenado par de números, (x, y), que describen la ubicación de un punto en el plano de coordenadas. La coordenada x indica la distancia horizontal del punto al origen, y la coordenada y indica la distancia vertical del punto al origen.

(x, y)

x-coordinate y-coordinate

---

origin the point (0, 0) in the coordinate plane where the x-axis and y-axis intersect.

origen el punto (0, 0) en el plano de coordenadas, donde se intersecan el eje x y el eje y.

English	Español	Example/Ejemplo
ounce (oz) a unit of weight in the customary system. A slice of bread weighs about 1 ounce. There are 16 ounces in 1 pound.	**onza (oz)** unidad de peso del sistema usual. Una rebanada de pan pesa aproximadamente 1 onza. 16 onzas equivalen a 1 libra.	16 ounces = 1 pound

Pp

English	Español	Example/Ejemplo
parallel lines lines that are always the same distance apart and never cross.	**rectas paralelas** rectas que siempre están a la misma distancia y nunca se cruzan.	
parallelogram a quadrilateral with opposite sides parallel and equal in length.	**paralelogramo** cuadrilátero que tiene lados opuestos paralelos e iguales en longitud.	
partial products the products you get in each step of the partial-products strategy. You use place value to find partial products.	**productos parciales** los productos que se obtienen en cada paso de la estrategia de productos parciales. Se usa el valor posicional para hallar productos parciales.	The partial products for 124×3 are 3×100 or 300, 3×20 or 60, and 3×4 or 12.
partial quotients The quotients you get in each step of the partial-quotients strategy. You use place value to find partial quotients.	**cocientes parciales** los cocientes que se obtienen en cada paso de la estrategia de cocientes parciales. Se usa el valor posicional para hallar cocientes parciales.	The partial quotients for $2{,}124 \div 4$ could be $2{,}000 \div 4$ or 500, $100 \div 4$ or 25, and $24 \div 4$ or 6.
partial sums the sums you get in each step of the partial-sums strategy. You use place value to find partial sums.	**sumas parciales** las sumas que se obtienen en cada paso de la estrategia de sumas parciales. Se usa el valor posicional para hallar sumas parciales.	The partial sums for $124 + 234$ are $100 + 200$ or 300, $20 + 30$ or 50, and $4 + 4$ or 8.
partial-products strategy a strategy used to multiply multi-digit numbers.	**estrategia de productos parciales** estrategia que se usa para multiplicar números de varios dígitos.	$$\begin{array}{r} 218 \\ \times\ \ 6 \\ \hline 48 \\ 60 \\ +\ 1{,}200 \\ \hline 1{,}308 \end{array}$$ (6 × 8 ones) (6 × 1 ten) (6 × 2 hundreds)

English	Español	Example/Ejemplo
partial-quotients strategy a strategy used to divide multi-digit numbers.	**estrategia de cocientes parciales** estrategia que se usa para dividir números de varios dígitos.	$$\begin{array}{r} 6 \\ 25 \\ 500 \\ 4)\overline{2,125} \\ -2,000 \\ \hline 125 \\ -100 \\ \hline 25 \\ -24 \\ \hline 1 \end{array}$$ The partial quotients are 500, 25, and 6. The quotient, 531, is the sum of the partial quotients. The remainder is 1.
partial-sums strategy a strategy used to add multi-digit numbers.	**estrategia de sumas parciales** estrategia que se usa para sumar números de varios dígitos.	$$\begin{array}{r} 312 \\ +235 \\ \hline \end{array}$$ Add the hundreds. 500 Add the tens. 40 Add the ones. + 7 $\overline{547}$
pattern a series of numbers or shapes that follow a rule to repeat or change. See also *terms of a pattern*.	**patrón** serie de números o figuras que siguen una regla para repetirse o cambiar. Ver también *términos de un patrón*.	
pentagon a polygon with exactly 5 sides and 5 angles.	**pentágono** polígono con que tiene exactamente 5 lados y 5 ángulos.	
perimeter the distance around a two-dimensional shape. The perimeter is equal to the sum of the lengths of the sides.	**perímetro** longitud del contorno de una figura bidimensional. El perímetro es igual al total de las longitudes de los lados.	60 yards 40 yards 40 yards 60 yards The perimeter of the soccer field is 200 yards. (60 yd + 40 yd + 60 yd + 40 yd)

English	Español	Example/Ejemplo
period a group of three places in a number, usually separated by commas. The first three periods are the ones period, the thousands period, and the millions period.	**período** grupo de tres valores posicionales de un número, generalmente separados por comas. Los primeros tres períodos son el período de las unidades, el período de los millares y el período de los millones.	321,987 987 is the first period.
perpendicular lines two lines that meet to form a right angle, or a 90° angle.	**rectas perpendiculars** dos rectas que se unen para formar un ángulo recto, o un ángulo de 90°.	
pint (pt) a unit of liquid volume in the customary system. There are 2 cups in 1 pint.	**pinta (pt)** unidad de volumen líquido del sistema usual. 1 pinta equivale a 2 tazas.	2 cups = 1 pint
place value the value of a digit based on its position in a number.	**valor posicional** valor de un dígito según su posición en un número.	The **2** in 3.52 is in the **hundredths** place and has a value of **2 hundredths** or **0.02**.
plane figure a two-dimensional figure, such as a circle, triangle, or rectangle.	**figura plana** figura bidimensional, como un círculo, triángulo o rectángulo.	
PM the time from noon until before midnight.	**p. m.** tiempo que transcurre desde el mediodía hasta la medianoche.	PM 5:10
point a single location in space.	**punto** ubicación única en el espacio.	*A*
polygon a two-dimensional closed figure made with three or more straight line segments that do not cross over each other.	**polígono** figura bidimensional cerrada formada que tiene tres o más segmentos de recta que no se cruzan.	Polygons / Not Polygons
pound (lb) a unit of weight in the customary system. There are 16 ounces in 1 pound.	**libra (lb)** unidad de peso del sistema usual. 1 libra equivale a 16 onzas.	16 ounces = 1 pound

English	Español	Example/Ejemplo
power of 10 a number that can be written as a product of tens.	**potencia de 10** número que puede escribirse como producto de decenas.	100 and 1,000 are powers of 10 because $100 = 10 \times 10$ and $1,000 = 10 \times 10 \times 10$.
prime number a whole number greater than 1 whose only factors are 1 and itself.	**número primo** número entero mayor que 1 cuyos únicos factores son 1 y él mismo.	2, 3, 5, 7, 11, 13, 17, 19 are prime numbers.
product the result of multiplication.	**producto** el resultado de la multiplicación.	$5 \times 3 = 15$
protractor a tool used to measure angles.	**transportador** herramienta que se usa para medir ángulos.	

Qq

quadrilateral a polygon with exactly 4 sides and 4 angles.	**cuadrilátero** polígono que tiene exactamente 4 lados y 4 ángulos.	
quart (qt) a unit of liquid volume in the customary system. There are 4 cups in 1 quart.	**cuarto (ct)** unidad de volumen líquido del sistema usual. 1 cuarto equivale a 4 tazas.	4 cups = 1 quart
quotient the result of division.	**cociente** el resultado de la división.	$15 \div 3 = 5$

Rr

ray a straight row of points that starts at one point and goes on forever in one direction.	**semirrecta** fila recta de puntos que comienza en un punto y continúa infinitamente en una dirección.	
rectangular prism a solid figure with 6 rectangular faces.	**prisma rectangular** figura sólida con seis caras rectangulares.	

English	Español	Example/Ejemplo
regroup to compose or decompose tens, hundreds, thousands, and so forth.	**reagrupar** componer o descomponer decenas, centenas, millares, etc.	10 tenths can be regrouped as 1 whole, or 1 tenth can be regrouped as 10 hundredths.
remainder the amount left over when one number does not divide another number a whole number of times.	**residuo** en la división, la cantidad que queda después de haber formado grupos iguales.	Remainder $17 \div 5 = 3 \text{ R } 2$
rhombus a quadrilateral with all sides the same length.	**rombo** cuadrilátero con todos los lados de la misma longitud.	
right angle an angle that looks like a square corner and measures 90°.	**ángulo recto** ángulo que parece la esquina de un cuadrado y mide 90°.	90°
right triangle a triangle that has one right angle.	**triángulo rectángulo** triángulo con un ángulo recto.	90°
round to find a number that is close in value to a given number by finding the nearest ten, hundred, or other place value.	**redondear** hallar un número que es cercano en valor al número dado hallando la decena, la centena o otro valor posicional más cercano.	48 rounded to the nearest ten is 50.
row a horizontal line of objects or numbers, such as in an array or table.	**fila** línea horizontal de objetos o números, tal como las que aparecen en una matriz o una tabla.	★ ★ ★ ★ ★ ★ ★ ★ ★ ★ ★ ★ ★ ★ ★
rule a procedure that is followed to go from one number or shape to the next in a pattern.	**regla** procedimiento que se sigue para ir de un número o una figura al número o la figura siguiente de un patrón.	17, 22, 27, 32, 37, 42 rule: add 5

English	Español	Example/Ejemplo

Ss

scale (on a graph) the value represented by the distance between one tick mark and the next on a number line.

escala (en una gráfica) el valor que representa la distancia entre una marca y la marca siguiente de una recta numérica.

Points Scored During the Game

Students: Alan, Cate, Gary, Mae

Number of Points Scored: 0, 2, 4, 6, 8

---

scalene triangle a triangle that has no sides the same length.

triángulo escaleno triángulo que no tiene lados de igual longitud.

---

scaling resizing a quantity by multiplying by a factor.

poner a escala cambiar de tamaño una cantidad multiplicándola por un factor.

	Words	Symbols
stretching	6 doubled is 12.	$2 \times 6 = 12$
shrinking	Half of 6 is 3.	$\frac{1}{2} \times 6 = 3$

---

second (s) a unit of time. There are 60 seconds in 1 minute.

segundo (s) unidad de tiempo. Sesenta segundos equivalen a 1 minuto.

60 seconds = 1 minute

---

side a line segment that forms part of a two-dimensional shape.

lado segmento de recta que forma parte de una figura bidimensional.

side

---

solid figure a three-dimensional figure.

figura sólida figura tridimensional.

A rectangular prism is a solid figure.

English	Español	Example/Ejemplo
square a quadrilateral with 4 square corners and 4 sides of equal length.	**cuadrado** cuadrilátero que tiene 4 esquinas cuadradas y 4 lados de igual longitud.	
square unit the area of a square with side lengths of 1 unit.	**unidad cuadrada** el área de un cuadrado que tiene lados de 1 unidad de longitud.	1 unit 1 unit 1 unit 1 unit
standard form the way a number is written with numerals.	**forma estándar** manera de escribir un número usando dígitos.	The standard form of *twelve* is 12.
subcategory a category within a larger category. It shares all the same attributes as the larger category.	**subcategoría** categoría que está dentro de otra categoría. Tiene las mismas propiedades que la categoría más amplia.	Parallelograms are a subcategory of quadrilaterals.
sum the result of addition.	**suma** el resultado de la suma.	$34 + 25 = \mathbf{59}$
symbol a character, such as a letter or question mark, that can be used to stand for an unknown number in an equation.	**símbolo** cualquier marca o dibujo, tal como una letra o un signo de interrogación, que puede usarse para representar un número desconocido en una ecuación.	$18 - \mathbf{?} = 9$

Tt

English	Español	Example/Ejemplo
tenths the parts formed when a whole is divided into 10 equal parts.	**décimos (fracciones)/ décimas (decimales)** partes que se forman cuando se divide un entero en 10 partes iguales.	
terms the numbers or shapes in a pattern.	**términos** los números o las figuras de un patrón.	3, 9, 12, 15, 18, 21, 24

English	Español	Example/Ejemplo
thousandths the parts formed when a whole is divided into 1,000 equal parts.	**milésimas** partes que se forman cuando se divide un entero en 1,000 partes iguales.	$1 \div 1,000 = \frac{1}{1,000}$, or 0.001
three-dimensional solid, or having length, width, and height. For example, a cube is three-dimensional.	**tridimensional** sólido, o que tiene longitud, ancho y altura. Por ejemplo, los cubos son tridimensionales.	
trapezoid (exclusive) a quadrilateral with exactly one pair of parallel sides.	**trapecio** cuadrilátero que tiene exactamente un par de lados paralelos.	
trapezoid (inclusive) a quadrilateral with at least one pair of parallel sides.	**trapecio** cuadrilátero que tiene al menos un par de lados paralelos.	
tree diagram a hierarchy diagram that connects categories and subcategories with lines to show how they are related.	**diagrama de árbol** diagrama jerárquico que conecta categorías y subcategorías por medio de líneas para mostrar cómo están relacionadas.	Triangles / Scalene / Isosceles / Equilateral
triangle a polygon with exactly 3 sides and 3 angles.	**triángulo** polígono que tiene exactamente 3 lados y 3 ángulos.	
two-dimensional flat, or having measurement in two directions, like length and width. For example, a rectangle is two-dimensional.	**bidimensional** plano, o que tiene medidas en dos direcciones, como la longitud y el ancho. Por ejemplo, un rectángulo es bidimensional.	

English	Español	Example/Ejemplo

Uu

unit cube a cube with side lengths of 1 unit. A unit cube is said to have 1 cubic unit of volume, and can be used to measure the volume of a solid figure.	**cubo de unidad** cubo cuyos lados miden 1 unidad. Un cubo de unidad tiene 1 unidad cúbica de volumen y puede usarse para medir el volumen de una figura sólida.	unit cube volume = 4 cubic units
unit fraction a fraction with a numerator of 1. Other fractions are built from unit fractions.	**fracción unitaria** fracción cuyo numerador es 1. Otras fracciones se construyen a partir de fracciones unitarias.	$\frac{1}{4}$
unit square a square with side lengths of 1 unit. A unit square is said to have 1 square unit of area, and can be used to measure the area of a plane figure.	**cuadrado de unidad** cuadrado cuyos lados miden 1 unidad. Un cuadrado de unidad tiene 1 unidad cuadrada de área y puede usarse para medir el área de una figura plana.	1 unit 1 unit unit square
unknown the value you need to find to solve a problem.	**desconocido** el valor que se debe hallar para resolver un problema.	$18 - ? = 9$

Vv

Venn diagram a diagram that uses overlapping ovals (or other shapes) to show how sets of numbers or objects are related.	**diagrama de Venn** dibujo que contiene óvalos u otras figuras que se superponen y muestra cómo se relacionan conjuntos de números u objetos.	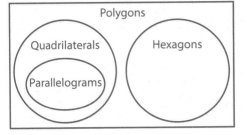
vertex the point where two rays, lines, or line segments meet to form an angle.	**vértice** punto donde dos semirrectas, rectas, o segmentos de recta se unen y forman un ángulo.	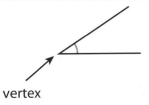

English	Español	Example/Ejemplo
volume the amount of space inside a solid figure. Volume is measured in cubic units such as cubic inches.	**volumen** cantidad de espacio que hay dentro de una figura sólida. El volumen se mide en unidades cúbicas como las pulgadas cúbicas.	Volume = 24 cubic units

Ww

weight the measurement that tells how heavy an object is. Units of weight include ounces and pounds.	**peso** medición que dice qué tan pesado es un objeto. Las onzas y las libras son unidades de peso.	**Weight** 1 pound = 16 ounces
word form the way a number is written with words or said aloud.	**en palabras** manera en que se escribe o se dice en voz alta un número usando palabras.	467,882 **four hundred sixty-seven thousand, eight hundred eighty-two**

Xx

x-axis the horizontal number line in the coordinate plane.	**eje x** recta numérica horizontal en el plano de coordenadas.	x-axis
x-coordinate the first number in an ordered pair. It tells the point's horizontal distance from the origin.	**coordenada x** el primer número de un par ordenado. Indica cuál es la distancia horizontal del punto al origen.	x-coordinate (4, 3) (0, 0)

English	Español	Example/Ejemplo

Yy

y-axis the vertical number line in the coordinate plane.

eje y recta numérica vertical en el plano de coordenadas.

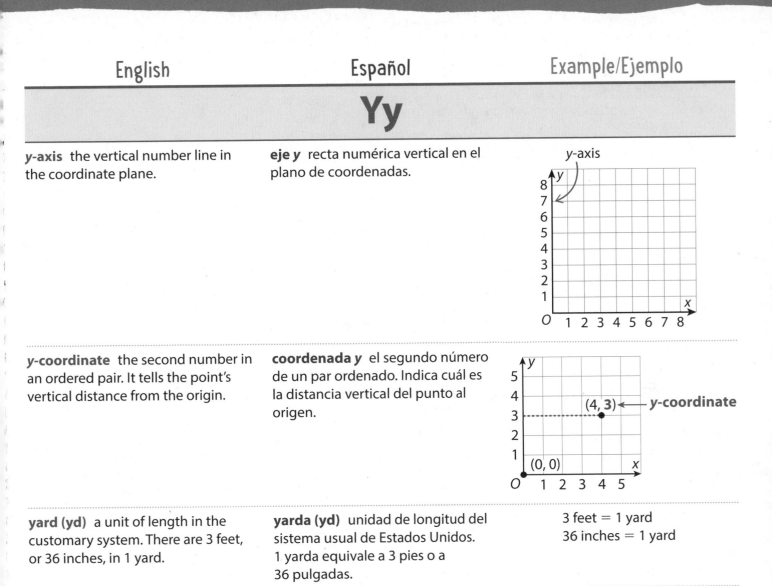

y-coordinate the second number in an ordered pair. It tells the point's vertical distance from the origin.

coordenada y el segundo número de un par ordenado. Indica cuál es la distancia vertical del punto al origen.

yard (yd) a unit of length in the customary system. There are 3 feet, or 36 inches, in 1 yard.

yarda (yd) unidad de longitud del sistema usual de Estados Unidos. 1 yarda equivale a 3 pies o a 36 pulgadas.

3 feet = 1 yard
36 inches = 1 yard

Acknowledgments

Common Core State Standards © 2010. National Governors Association Center for Best Practices and Council of Chief State School Officers. All rights reserved.

Photography Credits

United States coin images (unless otherwise indicated) from the United States Mint

Images used under license from **Shutterstock.com**.

iii freedomnaruk; **iv** graphicmaker, PrimaStockPhoto; **v** timquo; **vi** Danielle Balderas, Istimages; **vii** Aila Images, Cartarium, jeep5d; **1** Peter Turner Photography; **8** Quang Ho; **14** FabrikaSimf; **17** Issarawat Tattong; **20** Y Photo Studio; **22** Mega Pixel; **23** Picsfive; **32** c12; **36** Africa Studio, heraldmuc; **37–38** Tibet Saisema; **39** Nadiia Korol; **40** Garsya; **41** HeinzTeh; **42** Stephen Rees; **43** Kitch Bain, M. Unal Ozmen, Patty Chan; **44** Nik Merkulov; **46** Beth Swanson; **54** Gruffi, Inc., ORLIO; **58** ananaline; **59** Olga Popova; **60** Ievgenii Meyer; **62** Creativestockexchange; **64** Ivan Kurmyshov; **68** Qwasder1987; **72** PhotoStock10; **73** Mathier; **76** Cory Thoman, Studiovin; **77** Konstantin Faraktinov; **80** Aluna1, Nerthuz; **81** sumire8; **82** freedomnaruk, Natasha Pankina; **84** kibri_ho; **86** Dr Ajay Kumar Singh, Liskus, Roblan; **87** Nertuz; **88** Nerthuz, Topform; **91** Lucie Lang; **93** Trong Nguyen; **94** Nares Soumsomboon; **96** Sharon Day; **98** Photka; **100** Steve Collender; **101** Evgeny Karandaev, Natasha Pankina; **102** Kleber Cordeiro, Natasha Pankina; **103** Africa Studio; **104** vitec; **106** Bernatskaya Oxana, vitec; **108** Natasha Pankina, Worker; **110** Sanit Fuangnakhon; **111** Tatevosian Yana; **117** Bubutu; **130** Jiang Hongyan; **131** Capslock, rCarner; **132** Elnur, Rica Photography; **137** rCarner; **145** Ivonne Wierink; **148** Africa Studio, Stefano T; **149** Edward Hardam, Photogal; **150** Masterchief_Productions; **155** Bezikus, mhatzapa; **156** PrimaStockPhoto; **160** Jeffrey B. Banke; **163** GrashAlex; **166** Ajt, jingdi, Odua Images; **167** Garsya, Pavel L Photo and Video; **170** Artmim; **171** neotemlpars; **172** pio3; **174** Eric Isselee; **175** Quang Ho; **176** Eric Isselee; **177** Jojje; **180** Julian Rovagnati; **181** 6493866629; **182–183** Yellow Cat; **185** Somboon Bunproy; **188** Krasowit; **189** Pete Saloutos; **190** Mny-Jhee; **192** Maxpro; **193** Craig Barhorst, Stockagogo; **194** Jojoo64; **196** Goran Bogicevic; **197** Andrey_Popov; **198** irin-k; **199** AVprophoto; **200** Ruslan Semichev; **204** Eric Isselee, r.classen; **205** Sari Oneal; **206** Mike Truchon; **208** 3DMAVR; **209** Hue Ta; **210** Hong Vo; **212** AVprophoto; **214** fivespots; **218** inxti; **219** Maks Narodenko; **220** Y Photo Studio; **222** Moving Moment; **223** Vitaly Raduntsev; **226** 1989studio, jiangdi, LAURA_VN, MaraZe; **227** Art65395; **228** Anastasia Prisunko; **230** HomeStudio; **231** Holy Polygon; **232** Holy Polygon; **236** Africa Studio; **237** Eivaisla; **240** JeniFoto; **242** gresei; **244** Imfoto; **245** Your Design; **246** Baibaz; **247** MIGUEL GARCIA SAAVEDRA; **248** graphicmaker, pirtuss; **249** Kostsov; **250** Tish1; **252** Valzan; **253** Mariyana M; **255** Kiprej, kubais, Mariyana M; **256** Lunatictm; **258** artjazz, mhatzapa; **259** Nungning20; **260** 3DMAVR, serazetdinov; **266** Ayman alakhras, Mega Pixel, Natasha Pankina; **267** Perun; **269** paulista; **270** Sirtravelalot, Tapui, Valzan; **271** Elena Zajchikova, Wk1003mike; **272** Wk1003mike; **274** Grey_and; **275** Alisafarov; **276** Ryzhkov Photography; **278** art'n'lera, Tim Masters; **280** George3973, Marionhassold; **281** DenisNata; **282** DenisNata; **284** marilyn barbone; **286** JeniFoto; **288** Victor Moussa; **289** liskus, oksana2010; **290** Picsfive; **291** Crepesoles, Natasha Pankina; **292** Natasha Pankina, Susan Schmitz; **294–295** Grafikwork; **296** Alina Demidenko, Marssanya; **297** Tsuguliev; **298** Marssanya, Vincent noel;

299 Africa Studio, stock photofan1, Kao; **305** Alex Staroseltsev; **308** EtiAmmos, LifetimeStock; **309** akiyoko; **312** Wira SHK; **313** Julia_Lelija; **314** D7INAMI7S; **316** Kletr; **318** artnLera, jantima14; **319** Nattika; **321** blue67design, JRP Studio; **324** Winiki; **325** mhatzapa, rsooll; **329** AlenKadr; **330** cubolabo, timquo; **332** James Steidl; **334** symbiot; **335** ducu59us; **338** Carolyn Franks; **340** liskus, SeDmi; **345** Sarah2; **346** Andrey_Popov, Levent Konuk; **347** saruntorn chotchitima; **350** thodonal88; **351** Chayatorn Laorattanavech; **355** primiaou, Valentyna7; **357** Tiger Images; **358** Tiger Images; **360** Natasha Pankina, Sanit Fuangnakhon; **363** balabolka, cubolabo; **366** Keith Bell; **368** aarrows; **372** Africa Studio; **373** JeniFoto; **374** Hong Vo, Photka, Tommy Atthi; **375** LoopAll; **376** Africa Studio; **378** Bscmediallc, timquo; **379** vincent noel; **380** Binh Thanh Bui; **382** Madlen; **384** Eric Isselee; **386** Sapnocte; **387** Africa Studio; **389** Cherdchai charasri; **394** Quang Ho; **400** Gencho Petkov; **401** STILLFX; **402** Rose Carson; **403** Bilevich Olga; **406** urfin; **407** Perlav; **410** Ed Samuel; **413** Dmitry Polonskiy, Hdesislava, LukaKikina; **418** Tim UR; **424** Africa Studio, Quang Ho; **429** Andrey Lobachev, Birute Vijeikiene; **434** Dslaven; **435** Evikka, Mike Flippo; **436** COLOA Studio, Fablok, hitforsa; **437** Cunaplus unaplus; **438** Mayakova; **440** Maetisa; **441** Eivaisla; **442** Evikka; **443** Timquo; **444** Fotoearl; **447** KAMONRAT; **448** LanKS; **449** lenetstan; **450** Arthito; **451** Gino Santa Maria; **454** Lisovskaya Natalia; **455** Coprid; **456** Symbiot; **458** baibaz; **459** absolutimages, Natasha Pankina; **460** a_v_d; **462** tratong; **463** margouillat photo; **467** KucherAV; **468** Iriskana, Pixelbliss; **469** iamtui7; **470** 9comeback, Laurelie; **471** a_v_d, advent; **474–475** Trinset; **476** Africa Studio; **478** Mike Flippo; **479** Africa Studio; **480** The_Pixel; **481** MaraZe; **482** Erik D, Monticello; **484** Nataliia Pyzhova; **485** Happy monkey; **486** Diana Taliun, smilewithjul; **488** IB Photography; **489** FakeStocker; **490** Pixelbliss, Stockforlife; **491** Viktar Malyshchyts; **494** Christoforos Avramidis; **496** Motorolka, Rangizzz; **497** Motorolka; **498** Danny Smythe, Vinicius Tupinamba; **499** Madlen; **505** Ariya Phornpraphan; **508** Lano4ka, vesna cvorovic, zorina_larisa; **509** Africa Studio; **510** akepong srichaichana; **512** Roxana Bashyrova; **513** Bennian; **514** Istimages; **516** mkos83, Natasha Pankina; **518** Eric Isselee; **519** Danielle Balderas, Feng Yu; **520** M. Unal Ozmen; **527** Bjoern Wylezich; **529** Barry Blackburn, Tapui; **530** wk1003mike, Wonderful Future World; **531** M Kunz; **534** Alexandr Korolev, Natasha Pankina; **535** PrimaStockPhoto; **536** kudla, olnik_y; **538** mlorenz; **539** Voronina Svetlana; **540** Cipariss; **541** BERNATSKAYA OXANA, mhatzapa; **542** Bernatskaya Oxana, mhatzapa; **544** Vladimir Sazonov; **545** Eric Isselee, qingqing; **546** kanashi, mhatzapa; **547** Nikolai Tsvetokov; **548** Mmaxer; **549** Africa Studio; **551** Jiang Hongyan; **552** Hong Vo; **553** LuXpics; **554** Paket; **555** Hurst Photo; **556** Juburg; **557** Julie vanec; **558** Nik Merkulov; **560** Mrs_ya; **561** Nik Merkulov; **562** Valentyn Hontovyy; **566** artnLera, Elena Schweitzer; **568** Garsya, Natasha Pankina; **569** Hans Geel; **570** Kuznetsov Alexey; **572** Duplass, olnik_y; **578** Galina Petrova; **582** MaxFX; **586** T. Dallas; **590** Peter Hermes Furian; **604** Butsaya; **607** Diana Taliun; **608** Gts; **610** Gts;

Front Cover Credits

©Paul Bradbury/OJO Images/Getty Images

612 Kitch Bain; **614** Alexander Raths; **615** Natasha Pankina, Nearbirds; **621** Alexandru Nika; **625** M. Unal Ozmen; **626** Aila Images; **628** jeep5d; **629** Eric Isselee, Nantawat Chotsuwan; **634** MirasWonderland; **640** Milya; **646** Gjermund; **647** Cartarium; **669** Africa Studio, Nubenamo; **670** Joe Belanger; **672** M. Unal Ozmen; **674** Keith Homan; **677** Ifong; **680** Nuttapong; **681** Billion Photos; **682** Gresei; **684** Iriskana, Kitamin; **685** Cigdem; **686** Nata-Lia; **689** Africa Studio; **691** Ben Barnes; **692** Ben Barnes, liskus; **694** Ivan Anta; **696** JeniFoto; **701** marssanya, Mellutto; **704** Bedrin; **706** Swill Klitch; **A5** Showcake; **A13** Trinacria Photo

Student Handbook, appearing in Student Bookshelf and Teacher Guide only: HBi ArtMari, Rawpixel.com, Pixfiction, Disavorabuth; **HB1** Africa Studio, opicobello; **HB2** iadams; **HB3** Palabra; **HB5** Havepino; **HB6** Tatiana Popova; **HB8** Chiyacat; **HB9** Kyselova Inna, Markus Mainka; **HB10** ArtMari; **HB11** Disavorabuth; **HB12** ArtMari, Disavorabuth; **HB13–HB14** ArtMari; **HB16** Rawpixel.com